AMERICAN FRONTIERS

ALSO BY GREGORY H. NOBLES

Evolution and Revolution: American Society 1600–1820,
co-author James A. Henretta (1987)

*Divisions Throughout the Whole: Politics and Society in
Hampshire County, Massachusetts, 1740 to 1775* (1983)

AMERICAN FRONTIERS

CULTURAL ENCOUNTERS
AND CONTINENTAL CONQUEST

GREGORY H. NOBLES

HILL AND WANG

A DIVISION OF FARRAR, STRAUS AND GIROUX

NEW YORK

973
NOB

LIBRARY OF CONGRESS CATALOGING-IN-PUBLICATION DATA

Nobles, Gregory H.
    American frontiers : cultural encounters and continental conquest
    Gregory H. Nobles.
        p.   cm.
    Includes bibliographical references (p.   ) and index.
    1. America—Colonization.   2. United States—History—Colonial period, ca. 1600–
1775.   3. United States—Territorial expansion.   4. Culture diffusion—America—History.   5. Frontier and pioneer life—America.   6. Indians of North America—First contact with Europeans.   7. Indians of North America—Government relations.
    I. Title.
E101.N63   1997
973—dc20   96-9784
                                                                                       CIP

For Anne

CONTENTS

PREFACE

I n writing this book, I had to unlearn much of what I had
learned for years. I first heard about the frontier when I was in
first grade, but I wasn't in school at the time. I was in front of my
family's black-and-white TV, watching *Disneyland* one Sunday evening in 1954. That was the night Walt Disney, a true pioneer of
American popular culture, broadcast the first episode of *Davy
Crockett, King of the Wild Frontier*. I thought it was great. Fess
Parker, the actor who played Davy, was tall and good-looking, and
he spoke with a quiet conviction that inspired immediate confidence. Whenever he uttered Davy's motto—"Be sure you're right,
then go ahead"—he made it seem like the simplest, most sensible,
and most serious thing I had ever heard an adult say. But probably
the most memorable part of the show was the theme song, "The
Ballad of Davy Crockett." Played or sung as background music for
the screen action, it could be as light and jaunty as the canter of
Davy's horse or, in more serious moments, as slow and solemn as
a hymn. (By the spring of 1955, "The Ballad of Davy Crockett"
had become the No. 1 song not just in the United States but in
countries all over the world—some of which did not have television
yet.)

   A terrific show with a terrific song: I was hooked. So, apparently,
were my schoolmates at the Henry W. Longfellow School in Dallas and kids all across the country. We all begged our parents to
buy us Davy Crockett toys and clothing. I got a T-shirt and a
plastic version of Davy's rifle, Ol' Betsy. Other kids had lunch

boxes, cap pistols, and, above all, fake coonskin caps. We played Davy Crockett after school, and we watched each of the three *Davy Crockett* episodes for new Davy ideas. The big favorite for me and my fellow Texans was the third episode, "Davy Crockett at the Alamo," where he was "fightin' for liberty." Davy fought as hard as he could, right up to the end when he had to swing Ol' Betsy by the barrel because he was out of bullets. In fact, it took me a long time to accept what some historians tell us really happened —that he surrendered to the Mexicans and was executed.

Even when *Davy Crockett* had been relegated to reruns, a long string of TV Westerns filled the airwaves in the nineteen-fifties and sixties: *Gunsmoke, Maverick, Cheyenne, Sugarfoot, Wyatt Earp, Wagon Train, Wanted: Dead or Alive*—the list could go on for perhaps a page. So, too, could the movies available to us at Saturday matinees. We even had the opportunity to explore a fictionalized frontier in person. Six Flags Over Texas, a new theme park, opened between Dallas and Fort Worth, offering suburban kids a new way to spend their time (and their parents' money) in a high-energy interpretation of the past. If we had been paying attention to something other than the rides and the junk food, we might have reflected on those flags. We knew four of them pretty well: the U.S. flag and the Texas state flag, which everyone took for granted; the Confederate flag, which still had its strong adherents in the state; and the Mexican flag, which, in the context of the Alamo saga, represented the "bad guys" who had to be beaten so Texas could be—well, Texas. But the other two flags—the Spanish and the French—most of us more or less ignored, since their people never made their way into TV. The Indians, who *did* figure prominently both on TV and in our neighborhood fantasy play, had no flag, thus no formal recognition at all. But we went to theme parks for recreation and consumption, not for education and reflection, and we went on about the business of play without thinking much about the omission.

But, in a sense, theme parks and TV shows and movies are an important part of modern American education. They help purvey —and perpetuate—popular images and stories of the past. Often these stories are oversimplified and stereotypical, offering one-sided views that implicitly separate the world into "good guys" and "bad guys." Yet that simplicity is the source of their power: repeated over and over, the images and stories that permeate popular culture come together to form a more enduring American myth, what some historians call a "master narrative," which provides both an explanation for the past and a justification for the present. In the 1950s, for instance, Disney's Davy was "fightin' for liberty" in the context of the Cold War, and the "King of the Wild Frontier" became a not-so-subtle symbol for America's expansionist stance in the post-war world.

For the next two decades, in fact, it seemed that the frontier meant more to the purveyors of popular culture than to professional historians. As a high school student, I dutifully read Frederick Jackson Turner's classic 1893 essay, "The Significance of the Frontier in American History," but when I was in college and then graduate school in the late 1960s and early 1970s, the frontier was fairly unimportant in scholarly circles. The "new social history" was hot at the time, and like many other graduate students in early American history, I focused on a close analysis of New England communities. If anything, my own entry into frontier history was rather inadvertent: looking for a part of the landscape that had not yet been claimed and completely covered by earlier studies, I worked on the hill towns of western Massachusetts, on the "near frontier" of eighteenth-century New England.

The longer I did research on that region, however, the more I became interested in what other scholars were doing in other areas that were commonly defined as some form of "frontier." Like me, some were writing about backcountry communities in the East; indeed, by the late 1980s, these new studies had created a kind of academic Appalachian Trail that ranged from Maine to Georgia. Other early Americanists were publishing new histories, or ethnohistories, of Indian peoples, bringing Native American scholarship into the center of a field that had long focused primarily on Euro- (and especially Anglo-) Americans. At the same time, a similar upsurge of scholarship was taking place in the history of the West. During the 1980s, the so-called New Western Historians had begun to rejuvenate their field by rejecting the Turnerian tradition that had dominated historical studies of the West throughout most of the twentieth century. More than anyone else, they created a reinterpretation of Western history that not only changed the way we think about the nineteenth- and twentieth-century

West but challenged historians to reformulate their notions of the frontier in other eras and areas.

By the early 1990s, it had become increasingly clear that the history of the frontier was certainly not what it used to be. No longer the primary property of the entertainment industry and the last few students of the "Turner School," the frontier had re-emerged as a serious issue among historians. It struck me, though, that despite the recent outpouring of scholarship on various frontier regions, there was still no single-volume study to summarize and synthesize this remarkable new research, to connect the frontier histories of the East and West (not to mention points in between), and, above all, to put it all into a coherent, accessible narrative. That was the reason for writing this book.

Because the historiography of the frontier, like the frontier itself, has been hotly contested terrain, I think it is necessary to comment about a few of the words that figure prominently in this book. For one thing, the very definition, even use, of the term "frontier" has come into question. As I will explain in more detail in the Introduction, the traditional notion of the frontier as the outer boundary of European (and especially Anglo-American) settlement has been generally discarded as not only ethnocentric but imprecise, obscuring a more complex pattern of human contact. In recent years, historians have begun to use phrases like "cultural contact zone" or "inter-group contact situation." While not altogether graceful, such terms have the advantage of being neutral, emphasizing the various forms of interaction between peoples rather than simply reinforcing a one-sided story of European settlement. My own working definition of "frontier" is a region in which no culture, group, or government can claim effective control or hegemony over others. In that regard, contact often involves conflict, a sometimes multisided struggle with an undetermined outcome.

By the same token, it is now unwise, nearly impossible, to talk about "the frontier" as a set of places where a common process of contact, struggle, and settlement was repeated over and over. There were many frontier experiences among the European colonizers of North America, not just the English but also the Spanish and the French (those other two flags over Texas) and other, less prominent European players in the fierce and often brutal process of colonization; these "other" European experiences are now closer to the mainstream of colonial American history. More to the point, sophisticated studies of Native Americans have given new emphasis to the economic, diplomatic, and military concerns of Indian groups before, during, and after European colonization. As major players in the process of contact, Indians of course had their own frontier experiences. Given the many relationships among the many peoples, the title of this book uses the plural, "frontiers."

The other word in the title, "American," raises problems of its own. The most immediate has to do with place. The history of contact between Europeans and Native Americans encompasses the whole Western Hemisphere, Central and South America as well as North America; moreover, North America includes a vast expanse of territory, from the Caribbean to Alaska. Yet, in an effort to balance the intellectual perils of defining one's focus too narrowly and spreading oneself too broadly, I have confined my narrative primarily to the part of America that became the lower forty-eight United States. Although other American regions, especially Mexico and Canada, occasionally figure in the picture, I have left a fuller analysis of their respective frontier histories to others. I hope that the emphasis offered here will encourage readers to investigate those other histories from a comparative perspective.

The other problem with the term "American" has to do with people. Although it is common and quite often convenient to use "American" to refer only to citizens of the United States, I have tried not to do so. Everybody who settled in North America, no matter what the country or continent of origin, had a legitimate claim to be called an American. Since it is impossible, or at least intellectually meaningless, to assign the term to everyone, Euro-Americans and Native Americans alike, I have decided not to assign it outright to anyone.

On the other hand, when writing of Native Americans, I also use the term "Indian," which is undoubtedly the most enduring misnomer in American history. Unfortunately, many of the names native peoples called themselves cannot be traced, and other names cannot be trusted. Most native groups referred to themselves by terms that usually translated roughly as "The People." Calling

one's own people "The People" was an understandable bit of eth-
nocentrism, not only suggesting a central status in the universe,
but also distinguishing "us" from "them." But in many cases, the
original names people gave themselves have become lost in translation (or transliteration) as words passed from ear to ear and language to language. Many surviving names did not come from "The
People" themselves, in fact, but from their enemies, who made up
unflattering names for unfriendly neighbors. Such inter-group
name-calling was common throughout North America, and many
of the names stuck; in some cases, they are all we have.

There are other, more neutral-sounding terms available, like
"native inhabitants" or "indigenous peoples," and those will on
occasion appear in the text that follows. But like "cultural contact
zone" or "inter-group contact situation," those terms sometimes
seem awkwardly academic, clumsy as nouns and impossible as ad-
jectives. A phrase like "indigenous peoples in the inter-group contact situation" may be less culturally encumbered than "Indians on
the frontier," but the latter reads better. Most important, if understood correctly—that is, with an awareness of, and therefore a
reasonable defense against, the inherent cultural assumptions embedded in all language—words like "frontier" and "Indian" can
still serve as a useful form of shorthand for the more technical
terminology. I will use them as such, and that is how readers should
read them.

When I was in the midst of writing this book, I described the
project to a colleague at a historians' convention. As an expression
of scholarly sympathy, he said, "That's a real bear"—an appropriate, if unconscious, frontier metaphor, I thought. There were
times, in fact, when the extensive subject matter, not to mention
the massive amount of primary and secondary material, seemed
almost overpowering, too much to wrestle into a single book. In
the end, I have not tried to tame it all. I have tried, rather, to
emphasize and analyze what I take to be the most significant issues
in the history of the North American frontiers and to put them in
a chronological framework that encompasses more than four centuries. Clearly, there are events and issues that have to be discussed
briefly or omitted, and I can only direct the reader to the Biblio-

graphical Essay at the end to find specialized studies that offer opportunities for further exploration.

Although I have no intention of replacing Frederick Jackson Turner's "frontier thesis" with one of my own, I do develop an overarching argument that places the sometimes complex patterns of intercultural contact within a broader context of ongoing Euro-American conquest; moreover, I emphasize especially the role of imperial or national governments in promoting state-planned programs of expansion and settlement. There is, in short, an inescapable (albeit certainly not inevitable) outcome. Still, this book is not a comprehensive history, much less "the" history, of "the" frontier. Instead, it provides an interpretive synthesis, an overview with a point of view.

To the extent that I have succeeded, I must share the success with a number of friends and fellow historians who have helped along the way. Michael McGiffert first suggested I write an essay on the early American frontier, and then he patiently applied his remarkable editorial skills until the essay was ready for his journal, *The William and Mary Quarterly*. Other editors—David Thelen of *The Journal of American History*; Bruce Bowlus and William Grant of *The Hayes Historical Journal*; and Mary Kupiec Cayton, Elliott J. Gorn, and Peter W. Williams of the *Encyclopedia of American Social History*—also provided outlets for earlier essays that helped me develop some of the broader themes of this book. I am grateful not only to those editors but also to numerous referees, some of whom remain anonymous, all of whom have been acknowledged in print elsewhere.

I am likewise grateful for grants that supported research trips. The National Endowment for the Humanities, the American Antiquarian Society, and the Georgia Tech Foundation funded my work in its early stages; a few years later, the Council for the International Exchange of Scholars and the New Zealand–United States Educational Foundation gave me a Fulbright position at Massey University in New Zealand, where, thanks especially to the support of Jenny Gill and Barrie Macdonald, I was able to write and, above all, to try out some of my ideas in various seminar presentations and informal discussions. My colleagues and students at Massey provided a receptive and perceptive audience, bringing their Pacific perspective to bear on my rendering of American frontier history; so did other New Zealand scholars at Victoria University, the University of Canterbury, and Otago University.

Back in the United States, Michael Bellesiles, John Mack Faragher, Julie Roy Jeffrey, and Neal Salisbury deserve even greater thanks for reading parts of this book while it was in manuscript form. As he has on several occasions in the past, Alfred Young offered just the right advice at just the right time, reminding me to write my own book and not try to accommodate everyone's interests. Arthur Wang and Eric Foner have done as much as editors can do, reading every chapter carefully and critically.

The women who live with me—my wife, Anne Harper, and my daughters, Phoebe and Sarah—have also had to live with this book for several years, and I'm grateful for their patience. Sarah accompanied me to New Zealand, where she did plenty of reading while I wrote and always provided great background music for our road trips. In her frequent e-mail from New York, Phoebe kept me posted on American culture and, in doing so, made me realize that I can now only aspire to being the second-best writer in the family. Anne has plenty to do in politics and community life without reading my rough drafts (which I long ago realized is the best arrangement for our marriage, anyway), but I appreciate the many ways she helped me keep writing; she certainly deserves the dedication.

Despite all that assistance and support, I still take final responsibility for the book and for whatever weaknesses or flaws it may still contain. Beyond that, I can only echo the sentiments of that great bear-wrestler, Davy Crockett, who closed the preface to one of his books with these words:

> On the subject of my style, it is bad enough, in all conscience, to please critics, if that is what they are after. They are a sort of vermin, though, that I sha'n't even so much as to brush off. If they want to work on my book, just let them go ahead; and after they are done, they had better blot out all their criticisms, than to know what opinion I would express of *them*, and by what sort of a curious name I would call *them*, if I was standing near them, and looking over their shoulders.

Perhaps I should also offer my own scholarly corollary to Davy's more familiar dictum: Sometimes, even if you can't be sure you're right, you have to go ahead.

AMERICAN FRONTIERS

INTRODUCTION:
REOPENING THE FRONTIER

I n the spring of 1993, a young filmmaker told a reporter from *The New York Times* about all the trouble she was having finding any place to shoot a Western. "New Mexico is booked," she complained, "and almost all of Arizona and a lot of Montana. It's crazy. . . . There's a new Kevin Costner film that's booked practically all of New Mexico." The once wide-open spaces of the West now seemed closed to her, "booked" by other filmmakers who had got there first and left no room for her cameras to roam. Three years earlier, in fact, the object of her disaffection, Kevin Costner, had uttered a similar sentiment in the opening minutes of his hit movie *Dances with Wolves*. Costner's character in the film, Lieutenant John J. Dunbar, had behaved recklessly enough in a Civil War battle to be declared a hero, and for his exploits he was given his choice of duty assignments. Staring into the camera, Dunbar said slowly, "I've always wanted to see the frontier," and then added, "before it's gone." It is arguable, of course, whether or not a Civil War soldier in the 1860s might really have worried about getting to the frontier before it was gone, but a filmmaker in the 1990s no doubt knew that the line would resonate with modern audiences.

In different ways, one apparently spontaneous and the other quite consciously scripted, both filmmakers were expressing variations on a common theme about the fate of the American frontier: it is a part of the past that has been crowded out by the present.

Indeed, the popularity of their particular cinematic genre, the Western, depends largely on its portrayal of a place that no longer exists—or exists only as a memory most often tinged with regret over opportunities lost: what once was wild has now been tamed; what once was open has now been closed—even, apparently, to those who want to make more Westerns. The filmmakers might not have known, however, that the timing of their respective expressions about the end of frontier opportunity marked a centennial of sorts. By 1993, the idea had been around for at least a century.

——————•••——————

The still-common notion of the "closing" of the frontier stems largely from the work of Frederick Jackson Turner (1861–1932), perhaps the most prominent American historian of his era and even now a major figure in the pantheon of the profession. Turner was by no means the first historian to write about the frontier, but he was certainly the first to bring it to the forefront of historical scholarship.

On July 12, 1893, when he was a young professor at the University of Wisconsin, Turner delivered perhaps the most famous paper ever to be presented to an annual meeting of the American Historical Association, "The Significance of the Frontier in American History." At the time, however, Turner's paper failed to generate much immediate interest even among the small audience of his fellow historians. The AHA meeting was being held in Chicago that year in conjunction with the World's Columbian Exposition, a grand display of the cultural and technological wonders of the age. No doubt, many of Turner's fellow historians were, like their present-day counterparts at professional meetings, too busy exploring the exhibits and restaurants to bother attending an evening session featuring a paper by a young colleague. But after the AHA meeting was over, Turner circulated his paper among prominent scholars—including Theodore Roosevelt and Woodrow Wilson, two future presidents of the AHA as well as of the United States —and it was published in the *Proceedings* of the State Historical Society of Wisconsin. The essay gradually gained attention, and by the early decades of the twentieth century it had established

Turner's reputation as a formidable figure in the historical profession.

Turner's essay is a familiar staple to scholars, but for the purposes of this book, it merits a brief summary. "The Significance of the Frontier" began by pointing to the significance of a seemingly bland bureaucratic statement. The Superintendent of the Census had observed that, as of 1890, there were scarcely any substantial unsettled areas in the United States, and for that reason, he declared, the discussion of the American frontier "can not . . . any longer have a place in the census reports." To Turner, those words were momentous:

> This brief official statement marks the closing of a great historic movement. Up to our own day American history has been in large degree the history of the colonization of the Great West. The existence of an area of free land, its continuous recession, and the advance of American settlement westward, explain American development.

Thus, Turner found in the frontier "a factor in American history of the highest significance," the critical variable that could not only help define the character of the nation but make it truly distinctive.

It was Turner's emphasis on the distinctiveness of American history as much as his focus on the frontier that made his essay such a significant departure from the norms of contemporary scholarship. At the time Turner wrote his essay, the historical profession in the United States was still in its infancy; when Turner presented his paper to the American Historical Association, the organization was only in its tenth year and had just 631 members. Many historians from the United States still did their graduate work in European universities, and even those who got their Ph.D.s in this country worked under mentors who had been trained, or certainly strongly influenced, by European historians. (Turner's own mentors—William Allen at the University of Wisconsin, where Turner received his B.A. and M.A. degrees, and Herbert Baxter Adams at Johns Hopkins University, where he earned his doctorate—were both products of German graduate education.)

Among these German-trained historians, the dominant line of analysis used to explain the history of the United States was the "germ theory," the notion that American institutions had evolved from European, specifically Teutonic, origins. Deep in the forests of medieval Germany, so the theory went, the ancestors of the Anglo-Saxons developed forms of social and political organization that influenced the development of England and, by extension, the American colonies. In an era of increasing immigration—especially of "undesirable" aliens from southern and eastern Europe and Asia—this sort of historical explanation had a certain appeal to those Americans who could trace their own roots back beyond the colonial era to England and northern Europe: what was truly American was, at its root, truly Anglo-Saxon. But in that sense, of course, nothing was truly American.

To Turner, the frontier was. Like the germ-theorists, Turner had a fascination with forests as the source of social evolution, but what he saw in the forests of the American frontier was an environment where European antecedents could not survive. "Complex society is precipitated by the wilderness into a kind of primitive organization based on the family," Turner explained, and the settler's reversion to primitivism allows for the growth of a wholly new form of life:

> Little by little he transforms the wilderness, but the outcome is not the old Europe, not simply the development of Germanic germs. . . . The fact is, that here is a new product that is American. . . . Thus the advance of the frontier has meant a steady movement away from the influence of Europe, a steady growth of independence on American lines. And to study this advance . . . is to study the really American part of our history.

In short, the frontier became the breeding ground of a culture unique to the North American continent, an antidote to the European germ.

Even Turner's definition of the frontier differed from the earlier European and American norms. In Europe, the term "frontier" referred to the border zone between two nations. In North America, Turner explained, the frontier was not a fixed boundary but a moving line, "the outer edge of the wave—the meeting point between savagery and civilization." More to the point, there was no single line, but a succession of frontiers that followed upon each other:

Stand at Cumberland Gap and watch the procession of civilization, marching single file—the buffalo following the trail to the salt springs, the Indian, the fur-trader and hunter, the cattle-raiser, the pioneer farmer—and the frontier has passed by. Stand at South Pass in the Rockies a century later and see the same procession with wider intervals between. The unequal rate of advance compels us to distinguish the frontier into the trader's frontier, the rancher's frontier, or the miner's frontier, and the farmer's frontier.

The frontier was not simply a place; it was a recurring process that moved (or, to use Turner's more energetic terms, "leaped" or "skipped") across the continent in stages, leaving newly born societies to develop in its wake.

But most important of all, Turner argued, this process of frontier settlement promoted freedom, opportunity, and democracy. The very people he identified as the agents of frontier advance—the fur traders, farmers, and so forth—were ordinary people, not members of the European or even American upper classes. The farther these common folk pushed westward, the farther away they got from elite influence. The frontier opened to them "a gate of escape from the bondage of the past" and encouraged the growth of "freshness, and confidence, and scorn of older society, impatience of its restraints and its ideas." On the frontier, common people were free to fashion new social and political relationships that reflected their desires for personal independence and local self-government.

Those relationships not only affected life in frontier settlements, they ultimately shaped the very nature of the nation. Continued westward expansion and the settlement of successive frontier regions gradually made the customs of frontier regions the national norm: "The growth of nationalism and the evolution of American political institutions were dependent on the advance of the frontier. . . . [T]he people of the United States have taken their tone from the incessant expansion which has not only been open but has even been forced upon them." With those last words, Turner suggested that the frontier's effect on the creation of an American national character was not just natural but seemingly inevitable.

In general, Turner's 1893 essay brought remarkably innovative insights to the study of American history. In the minds of many people, it was Turner who finally put the "American" in American history, who told the story in a way that emphasized the exceptionalism, even uniqueness, of the national experience. The freshness of the frontier provided an upbeat, positive perspective on the past that soon attracted a loyal following among historians. To be sure, Turner took the self-effacing stance that his essay made "no attempt to treat the subject exhaustively; its aim is simply to call attention to the frontier as a fertile field for investigation . . . [that] can be isolated and studied as a factor in American history of the highest importance."

And that is certainly what he and his disciples did. Turner was not a prolific writer by scholarly standards—it can be argued that "The Significance of the Frontier in American History" was the most significant piece he ever published—but he was by all accounts a superb teacher, a supportive promoter of his students and their work. As one of Turner's students, Avery Craven, observed, "Frederick Jackson Turner wrote less and influenced his own generation more than any other important historian." Teaching first at Wisconsin and then at Harvard, Turner inspired his students with his scholarly curiosity and his warm personality, especially, according to Craven, "the rich quality of his voice, the kindly twinkle of his eye, the genuine modesty in regard to achievements, the keen humor of lasting quality." Carl Becker, one of Turner's Harvard graduate students who himself became one of the most famous figures in the profession, noted that, as a teacher, Turner spoke "with the manner of one who utters moral truths." Turner's students took those "truths" and spread the gospel of the "frontier thesis" throughout major universities across the country. For almost three decades after the publication of his original essay, Turner had an ever-expanding circle of supporters. By the time of his death in 1932, the "Turner School" of historians had secured a prominent place in the profession, and an able body of followers helped maintain the Turnerian legacy throughout the first half of the twentieth century.

Every thesis, of course, eventually has an antithesis, and so did Turner's—many times over. Despite the many positive responses to Turner's work in the early part of the century, historians have raised scholarly challenges, ranging from mild revision to outright (and often outraged) rejection. In some cases, Turner's critics have picked on petty particulars he never pretended to defend; others have created an oversimplified caricature of his argument that shows little appreciation for the tentativeness, much less the subtlety, of his argument. Still, insightful critics have found substantial flaws in both the internal logic and the overall approach of his argument, and their work has steadily undermined the Turnerian foundations of frontier history.

In Turner's own time, the first major critique of his thesis challenged the emphasis on the frontier as the critical force in American history. Most historians were willing to concede to Turner that westward movement to the frontier was "a factor in American history of the highest importance," but not all were able to accept his notion that "American history has been in large degree the history of the colonization of the Great West." Other factors—urbanization, immigration, and industrialization, to name the most significant—were equally important, if not more so.

By the 1920s, for instance, Charles A. Beard had put forth an alternative analysis of American history in two classic works, *An Economic Interpretation of the Constitution of the United States* (1913) and *The Rise of American Civilization* (1927), the latter written with his wife, Mary R. Beard. Both works stressed the primacy of economic interests as the motivating forces behind historical action. Thus, in the nineteenth century, so the Beardian argument went, the critical issue in American history was not the movement to the West, but the conflict in the East—or, more specifically, the growing tension between the emerging system of industrial capitalism in the North and the entrenched system of plantation slavery in the South. The coming of the Civil War (or the "Second American Revolution," to use the Beards' term) was the culmination of a clash of interests that had existed for years. Charles Beard was not altogether unsympathetic to Turner's work—he considered it refreshing, especially compared to the narrow and often turgid work of other historians—but he considered Turner's emphasis on the Western frontier inadequate to explain the ongoing development of an industrializing nation.

Other historians of Turner's generation pointed out that westward migration was not the only significant form of human movement in the United States in the nineteenth century: continued waves of immigrants from Europe and other parts of the world made a major contribution not just to the nation's population but to its very character. Turner's emphasis on American exceptionalism overlooked or obscured the continuing significance of international influence on American culture. Moreover, scholars also noted that migration within the United States did not always move in one direction, toward open land in the West: people moved from farm to city and, in many cases, from west to east. Thus, the factories of Eastern cities were as much a part of the American experience as the farms of the Western frontier. Turner's picture of the independent frontiersman suggested an engaging, even comforting image, but it was hardly the portrait of the quintessential American.

By the middle of the twentieth century, the Turner thesis was still widely regarded as an impressive monument to an important academic achievement, but a monument that was beginning to crumble at its foundation. In 1946, a scholar writing in *The American Historical Review* observed that "none of our university departments of history is complete without a frontier specialist, and no one . . . would essay a history of the United States, whether for the profession, or the schools, without paying homage to the Turner hypothesis." Turner's emphasis on the significance of the frontier, he continued, had been "productive not only of caviar for seminars but of common fare for journalists and radio commentators." (He could easily have included novelists, filmmakers, and other creators of popular culture.) Within a few years, however, many history departments did indeed begin to consider themselves quite complete without a frontier specialist; if they still served the Turner thesis as an intellectual appetizer to undergraduates and first-year graduate students, they no longer included it as a main course. In the post-war era other issues—especially American foreign policy and domestic issues such as race, ethnicity, and social conflict—rose to the top of the academic agenda, and the history of the frontier had become associated primarily with the history of the American West, which in most major universities was often considered an antiquarian backwater. Despite the efforts of a few remaining disciples, most notably Ray Allen Billington, to keep the Turnerian emphasis on frontier history alive, the Turner thesis was becoming, if not a ruin, then certainly a relic of an earlier age. In general, it seemed as if the field of frontier scholarship were coming to a close.

Yet academic agendas have a curious way of changing, and by the 1980s the frontier was on its way back to a respectable place in scholarly circles. A number of younger historians—some of whom first watched Walt Disney's frontier on television as children but later came of age politically and intellectually when John Kennedy's "New Frontier" policies led the United States deeper into war in Vietnam—began to rethink the significance of the frontier. To be sure, the frontier, and especially the West, had become encumbered with ahistorical myths, but it was still, as Turner had noted, "a fertile field for investigation." All the issues that engaged "mainstream" historians—war and peace, political and social conflict, race, class, and, more recently, gender—were manifest in frontier regions. Yet, in order to revive the frontier as a field of serious study, they felt they had to free themselves, as historian Susan Armitage has put it, from "the dead hand of Frederick Jackson Turner." In a sense, recent scholars of frontier regions, especially the New Western Historians, have resurrected the Turner thesis only to make sure it is buried again.

Above all, the new scholarship has challenged Turner's notion of the frontier and the perspective from which he viewed it. Most historians would now agree (and the Turnerian die-hards, perhaps, reluctantly admit) that Turner's notion of the term "frontier" was an ethnocentric, or Eurocentric, concept that had meaning only from the perspective of the colonizing culture. His description of the frontier as "the outer edge of the wave—the meeting point between savagery and civilization" made clear his preconceptions, even prejudices. It was European "civilization" that met Indian "savagery" at the farthest point of European penetration in the New World wilderness. The land beyond was uncharted, uncontrolled, and therefore threatening.

But for the New World natives—the people the Europeans called Indians—there was no such notion of a frontier. To them the land was not a howling wilderness, but home. By the same token, they were not savages, but civilized people. They had well-established territories, stable social systems, and extensive trade networks. Like Europeans, they often made war on their enemies, but they never set out to annihilate other tribes. It was only with the arrival—or, as some scholars now describe it, the invasion—of Europeans that Native Americans faced a threat to their very existence. The advance of the newcomers, with their diseases and their desires for land, ultimately forced natives into long-term retreat. Indeed, when seen from the perspective of Native Americans, the westward movement of Euro-Americans was hardly the positive process Turner described. Rather than freedom, opportunity, and democracy, it brought displacement, destruction, and death.

If nothing else, the record of Indian–European relations in North America has rendered terms like "savagery" and "civilization" essentially meaningless, or certainly made it impossible to apply either term exclusively to one culture or the other. One might well revise Turner's definition to describe the frontier as the meeting point where otherwise civilized people often exhibited savage behavior. A better approach is to define "frontier" in terms that are less loaded in favor of Euro-American culture. In recent years, post-Turnerian scholars have begun to use terms like "contact zone," "zone of interpenetration," or "middle ground," thus suggesting an area of interaction between two or more cultures in which neither culture is assumed to have an altogether superior position. The recognition of this interaction helps us redefine the frontier not just as a place, or even as a frequently repeated, one-dimensional process of contact, settlement, and development. It involves, rather, a much more complex process of mutual exchange in which neither culture, Native American or Euro-American, could remain unchanged.

Above all, the point is not to reduce the history of the frontier to a morality play about cultural monoliths, the "civilized" Europeans and the "savage" Indians (or, as some might just as easily argue, vice versa). Neither side was that simple. Euro-Americans fought among themselves for control of the continent, and they often enlisted Indian allies to help them defeat fellow Europeans. Equally important, there was considerable conflict even within individual European cultural groups. Anglo-Americans, for instance, were divided by gender, class, religion, and a host of other factors, and those differences became the source of recurring intracultural struggles over the course of several centuries.

By the same token, the natives the Europeans lumped together as Indians were in reality a remarkably diverse people encompassing many different cultural and tribal groups. They had different belief systems, different ways of life, and different relationships with Europeans. Like Europeans, they could be honorable allies or vicious enemies, equally capable of creating beauty and committing atrocity. And, like Europeans, they deserve respect both for the integrity of their own cultures and for their contributions to the broader synthesis we now call "American" culture. In fact, the first step to understanding the significance of the frontier in American history is to appreciate how many different sorts of Americans there were on the frontier—not just Native Americans and Euro-Americans, but also African-Americans, Mexican-Americans, and Asian-Americans—and how each group contributed to the making of frontier history.

Finally, no matter what the ethnic group, Turner's picture of the frontier still overlooked women. The "Turner School" allowed no room for women's studies in the curriculum. Neither, for that matter, did Turner's early critics. For years the debate about the history and the nature of the frontier was carried on largely by men and about men. In 1944, Nancy Wilson Ross, an anthropologist, published a comprehensive account of white women on the frontier, *Westward the Women*, but her work stood virtually alone for over two decades. Beginning in the early 1970s, with the increasing scholarly interest in the history of women, new studies began to ask important questions about the opportunities for equality open to white women on the frontier. There was no single answer, in fact, because there was no single type of frontier woman: a farm wife on the Great Plains, for instance, lived a different life from a prostitute in a Rocky Mountain mining camp. More to the point, both of them lived different lives from the men around them. As several studies of migrant families have shown, wives often went west with much less enthusiasm than did their husbands, and even their perception of the land itself suggested a distinct perspective on their new environment. No doubt, prostitutes and their clients likewise had different outlooks on their respective prospects in frontier society. More recently, studies of women of non-European ethnic and cultural backgrounds have added greatly to the multicultural mosaic that defines frontier history.

Now, just over a century after the publication of Turner's essay, the point is clear: Turner was an insightful, innovative historian, but his notion of the frontier was seriously flawed. Some of the standard terms once taken almost for granted—not just "frontier," but "expansion," "settlement," "progress," and even "freedom"—

now seem somewhat loaded, skewed to the particular perspective of Euro- or Anglo-Americans. The history of the frontier is not a clear-cut account of westward migration by white people. As Peggy Pascoe has noted, historians are now rethinking the notion of the frontier as a place of "interactions among the various cultural groups who lived in or passed through the area . . . a cultural crossroads rather than a geographic freeway to the West." It is a story of continuing encounter that can be told from many perspectives, from the standpoint of native inhabitants as well as Euro-American invaders, immigrants as well as emigrants, women as well as men, even land and animals as well as people. Clearly, no one would dare write about "How the West was One."

Is it still meaningful, though, to write about "How the West was Won"? That depends, again, on one's point of view, especially about the implications of the term "won." To portray the history of the frontier, as Turner did, as a near-inevitable national victory for the Euro-American people of the United States clearly runs counter to recent research that provides multiple perspectives on the past; writing in such triumphal terms narrows our awareness of the true complexity of historical developments. Yet, by the same token, the more recent emphasis on cultural diversity and the intercultural exchange inherent in contact relationships can likewise divert our attention from one important, virtually inescapable outcome—the conquest of the continent by Euro-American powers, culminating in the military, economic, and political control exerted by the United States at the end of the nineteenth century. The task is to account for that outcome without making it seem like the massive westward march of a monolithic people, much less their Manifest Destiny.

One way to approach the problem of telling the story in accurate and somewhat more dispassionate terms is to borrow a phrase from Turner—not "the closing of the frontier," but "the colonization of the Great West." In many respects, "colonization" helps put the process of conquest in its proper historical context as a phenomenon that operates on several levels. In the study of the early era of European exploration and settlement of North America, we commonly understand colonization to be a state-sponsored process of expansion and appropriation, or at least the extension of national military and economic power. By the same token, colonization also involved the migration of thousands of ordinary people—trappers, traders, farmers, and other common folk—who usually settled a new territory for their own reasons. Yet the point is that the notion of colonization reminds us that the massive population movements to America were fundamentally political, not merely demographic, processes.

We can usefully extend the concept of colonization to encompass the expansion of the United States in the nineteenth century —after the period commonly called the "colonial era" had come to an end. That is, after the American Revolution, the former colonial subjects continued to be colonizers, seeking to assert control over the continent and over the other peoples who lived on it. In that sense, westward expansion cannot be seen primarily as a process carried out, as Turner suggested, by restless citizens seeking to gain greater opportunities or perhaps to escape the restraints of government. Rather, it was a process that depended on the participation, even the active promotion, of the national government. To be sure, the relationship between settlers and the state was often a troubled, even tumultuous one, and the desires of independent-minded people often clashed with the designs of government officials for "orderly" settlement. Still, whatever the underlying uneasiness, common people and policymakers ultimately became allies in a process of conquest. By the end of the nineteenth century, that process was essentially complete. The frontier may not have been completely "closed," but it had certainly become subject to the authority of the United States.

But that notion of frontier history as a process of colonization and conquest raises another difficult problem of definition: when does the process stop, or, put differently, when does the history of the frontier come to an end? For Turner, of course, the end came in 1890, when the Superintendent of the Census assessed the spread of white settlement and declared the American frontier "closed." Other historians would now argue (as I do in this book) that 1890 makes sense as a stopping place for other reasons—most dramatically, with the death of Sitting Bull and the defeat of Sioux resistance in the Ghost Dance movement. But, in reality, there is no end to the story. As Patricia Limerick has recently argued, it is impossible to bring the process to such a definite conclusion. Many of the issues that formed the history of the frontier up to 1890—new towns and territories, land sales and settlement, gold rushes and oil booms, and, above all, the ongoing struggles between Indians and whites, speculators and settlers, ranchers and farmers, bureaucrats and taxpayers—have by no means been resolved or put to rest. Over a century after the official closing of the frontier, people are still struggling over many of those issues, from Maine to California, and even farther west, to Alaska and Hawaii.

And that, ultimately, is the most important point. As both a phenomenon in American life and a field of study in American history, the frontier has not stayed closed. Turner's particular notion of the frontier may now be discredited, but the broader subject he brought to the center of scholarly attention is not. Questions of cultural contact, territorial conquest, settlement patterns, and social relations are at the heart of historical study. The frontier—this important, albeit imprecise, zone of initial interaction between cultures—represents an excellent setting in which to examine them. Perhaps equally important, there are some great stories to tell in the process. The whole cast of characters—explorers, adventurers, soldiers, settlers, prostitutes, preachers, cowboys, and, always, Indians—makes for great drama. They are certainly more exciting, if not more significant, than some of the other figures—the Puritan ministers, Jacksonian political hacks, or Cold War diplomats—who also populate the pages of history books. Even the scenery of the frontier—the dark forests of the East and, farther west, the stark plains, deserts, and mountain ranges—is both rugged and romantic, always an inspiring image to novelists, artists, and filmmakers, not to mention academics locked away in university libraries.

For a variety of reasons, then, the frontier now stands as a central focus of historical research. The goal of post-Turnerian historians is still to make the history of the frontier comprehensive and coherent, but also to make it more complex and inclusive—and therefore closer to the reality of human experience. That, at least, is the goal of this book.

ONE

Nicolo Joannis Vischeri, "Novi Belgii/Novaeque Angliae," 1659, portion. *Courtesy American Antiquarian Society*

THE CONTACT OF CULTURES
ON THE FIRST FRONTIERS

The sleeping Pequots had no warning when the attackers snuck into their village, and they had no chance once the shooting started. In the early hours of May 26, 1637, Captain John Mason of Connecticut had quietly deployed his troops—some ninety Englishmen from Connecticut and Massachusetts and several hundred Narragansett and Mohegan Indians—around a Pequot settlement on the banks of the Mystic River. Still undetected in the pre-dawn darkness, Mason and his men crept up to the Pequot wigwams and poked their guns inside. In the outburst of gunfire, some Pequots managed to rouse themselves and resist, but many more died within a few feet of their beds. So chaotic was the dimly lit firefight that the attacking Englishmen also shot some of their own Indian allies.

Rather than risk more of his men in the crossfire, Captain Mason ordered them to withdraw from the village; first, however, they set fire to the straw mats that covered the Pequot wigwams. Once outside the burning village, Mason formed his men into two concentric circles—Englishmen on the inner ring and their Indian allies, whom Mason did not completely trust, on the outer—and waited for the inhabitants to flee. Those Pequots who did not die in the flames of the village soon died at the hands of the Englishmen. As Plymouth Governor William Bradford later reported, "some [were] hewed to pieces, others run through with their rapiers, so that they were quickly dispatched and very few escaped."

In all, some three hundred to seven hundred Pequots died that morning, and only a handful made their escape through the English line. (By comparison, their attackers lost only two killed and around forty wounded, many of the casualties coming as the result of what soldiers of a later generation would call "friendly fire.") The Narragansetts in the outer ring were shocked at the killing, protesting that "it is too furious, and slays too many men." But the Englishmen took satisfaction in the slaughter. "It was a fearful sight to see [the Pequots] thus frying in the fire . . . and horrible was the stink and scent thereof," wrote Bradford, "but the victory seemed a sweet sacrifice, and [the Englishmen] gave the praise thereof to God, who had wrought so wonderfully for them, thus to enclose their enemy in their hands and given them so speedy a victory over so proud and insulting an enemy." In fact, most of the Pequots in the village were not "proud and insulting" warriors, but women, children, and older men. The main force of Pequot warriors was encamped in a second village about five miles away. Captain Mason had chosen his target well. With or without God's help, he could hardly have failed to achieve a speedy victory.

As soon as the Pequot warriors in the second village became aware of the attack, they rushed to the scene of the massacre. Too late for rescue, they pursued Mason's men back to their ships, which lay in anchor on the Mystic River, waiting to evacuate the English. But the timely arrival of more ships with reinforcements of forty Massachusetts militiamen saved the English force. Faced with the superior numbers and firepower, the Pequots retreated.

Over the course of the next several weeks, they tried to evade the English and Narragansett pursuit. Some made their way to other tribes, where they found refuge. Others were not so fortunate. The Pequot leader, Sassacus, and forty of his men escaped as far as the territory of the Mohawks on the Hudson River, where they offered the Mohawks a sizable gift of wampum (strings of tiny shells highly valued as symbols of prestige and power among northeastern Indians) in exchange for safe haven. Unfortunately for Sassacus and his men, the Narragansetts had already been there, and they, too, had given the Mohawks a similarly large gift of wampum to turn them against the Pequots. After taking the wampum from the Pequots, the Mohawks executed Sassacus, sending his scalp and hands back to the English as proof of his death. Captain Mason crowed, "Thus did the Lord scatter his Enemies with his strong Arm! The Pequots now became a Prey to all Indians. Happy were they that could bring in their Heads to the English." Many captured Pequots were spared execution only to be given to Indian groups allied with the English or put into prison; others were sold into slavery and lived out their lives far away from home, working alongside enslaved Africans on the brutal sugar plantations of the West Indies. Thus, within the space of a few hours, or at most a few weeks, the Pequot tribe was dispersed and nearly destroyed; a year later, in 1638, the Treaty of Hartford declared the tribe dissolved.

The sudden devastation of the Pequots had its roots in complex relationships that reached back for decades. Long before the English began to settle the land they would call New England, the Pequots had emerged as one of the most powerful peoples in the region. Although the extent of their own territory was sizable— they inhabited the eastern end of Long Island and the watershed of the Pequot (now Thames) River in what is now southeastern Connecticut, a total of around two thousand square miles—their influence reached much farther beyond their territorial bounds. Through warfare and trade, they had established dominance over smaller, weaker groups in the Connecticut River Valley, who paid them an annual tribute of goods and services in exchange for protection. Through marriage and kin ties, the Pequots had also established an alliance with the other dominant group in the region, the Narragansetts to the east. No alliance between proud and powerful peoples is perfect, however, and these two major tribes of southern New England often struggled against each other for control of trade and tribute. In general, even before Europeans entered the region, the Pequots and their Narragansett neighbors lived according to a delicate diplomatic arrangement that usually maintained a workable peace but never put completely to rest their competing ambitions and underlying antagonisms.

The arrival of Europeans only increased Pequot problems. European diseases spread quickly among the Pequot people, and a population that had been around thirteen thousand in the pre-contact era fell to around three thousand by 1630. Moreover, contact with Europeans created not just a demographic crisis but diplomatic concerns as well. The first Europeans to settle in the

Pequot sphere of influence were not the English but the Dutch, who followed the fur trade into the region in the 1620s. They established commercial ties with both the Pequots and the Narragansetts to supply beaver and other pelts valued by wealthy Europeans for decorative apparel. Beginning in 1632, the Dutch West India Company purchased from the Pequots and one of their tributary tribes two small tracts of land on the Connecticut River, and they built a trading post called the House of Hope, near the site of present-day Hartford. Given the various competing interests in the region, however, there could be little hope for lasting friendly relations. When some Pequots attacked and killed a small band of Indians, probably Narragansetts or their allies, who came to trade with the Dutch, both the Dutch and the Narragansetts were outraged, and they armed themselves for retaliation. Feeling threatened both militarily and commercially, the Pequots turned to the English as allies. In November 1634 they entered into a treaty with the Puritan authorities of Massachusetts Bay, inviting them to trade and urging them to help restore peace with the Narragansetts.

The treaty worked only for a short time. Within a year, the Anglo–Pequot relationship soured as increasing numbers of Puritan colonists began moving into Pequot territory to settle on the Connecticut River. The English were attracted to the region partly because of their antipathy toward the Dutch, whom they hated to see gaining an advantage in the lucrative fur trade. But English settlement in the Connecticut Valley also stemmed from two fundamental factors of the early Puritan experience in Massachusetts Bay: land hunger and religious controversy. Ever since the founding of the colony in 1630, the rapid growth of the Puritan population led Massachusetts leaders to look for new places to plant families and farms; the fertile bottomlands of the Connecticut Valley seemed ideal. Then, in 1634, a group of newly arrived Puritans led by the Reverend Thomas Hooker began to challenge the orthodoxy and authority of the colony's leadership. Rather than stay in the Boston area to cause trouble for the authorities, the dissident Puritans moved almost a hundred miles away to the Connecticut Valley in 1635.

There they caused trouble for the Pequots. The settlement of three new English towns on the Connecticut River—Wethersfield, Windsor, and Hartford—and a garrison at the mouth of the river,

Fort Saybrook, created uneasiness among the Pequots, whose power base no longer seemed secure. Indeed, the Pequots were already feeling pressure from the Puritans about the death of one John Stone, a freebooting English ship captain who had been killed by members of a Pequot tributary tribe in 1634. To be sure, the English had no real reason to grieve Stone's loss—he had been condemned in Plymouth Colony and banished from Massachusetts Bay just before his death—but they used his death as an excuse to demand tribute and other concessions from the Pequots. Eventually, in 1636, the magistrates of Massachusetts Bay organized a military expedition, ostensibly to seek out the Indian killers of Stone and another Englishman, John Oldham, killed by Narragansetts on Block Island. At that point, the Pequots and the Narragansetts might well have joined together against a common foe, but skillful English diplomacy kept them apart. But now the presence of Puritan settlers in Pequot country activated other diplomatic arrangements. The English inhabitants of Wethersfield violated the terms of their purchase agreement by driving local Sequin Indians out of the town's boundaries, and the Sequins turned to the Pequots for help. The Pequots obliged by surprising a group of settlers working in the fields, killing nine and taking two captive.

This fresh shedding of English blood helped leaders in Massachusetts Bay and Connecticut smooth over their earlier antagonisms long enough to turn their full attention to suppressing the Pequots. And so, a month later, in the early morning hours of May 26, it was in that spirit of cooperation that Captain Mason's combined Connecticut and Massachusetts force, supported by their Narragansett and Mohegan allies, fell upon the sleeping Pequot village.

The patterns of diplomacy, trade, and warfare that surrounded the destruction of Pequot power may seem complex, but therein lies an important point: Indians and Europeans seldom engaged in a simple, two-sided relationship. Above all, it is important to understand at the outset that neither "Indian" nor "European" has meaning as a monolithic, cohesive culture with a sense of unity and a single-minded strategy. In the story of the Pequot War, "European" meant both the Dutch and the English, two peoples who shared similar cultural roots but who also showed intense hostility toward each other in their rivalry for New World wealth. Equally important, as the tension between the Reverend Hooker and the Puritan leadership suggests, even colonists who came from the same country, spoke the same language, and professed the same religion could be disharmonious and downright hostile toward one another. On the Indian side, the divisions were even more numerous. The Pequots and the Narragansetts competed as much as they cooperated, and both tribes depended on their dominance over smaller Indian groups in the region—the Nipmuks, Massachusetts, Mohegans, Sequins, Western Niantics, and Eastern Niantics. And finally, whether defined by culture, kinship, confederation, or diplomatic necessity, no alliance endured forever. No less than Europeans, Indians were capable of pursuing self-interested and well-crafted policies to protect their territory and trade; accordingly, they sought to forge political and commercial alliances that would be most favorable to their particular needs.

Such inter- and intra-cultural relationships complicate the sometimes oversimplified picture of Europeans versus Indians, but they also give it the depth and richness of detail that make it truly meaningful. The real significance of the North American frontier lies not only in the single-minded conquest eventually achieved by one people over others but also in the complex roles played by all the peoples that took part in the struggle.

———•—•———

The Pequots, like the Puritans who attacked them, settled in New England as the result of migration. To be sure, the Pequots' trip was shorter—probably from the Hudson Valley of New York to the southeastern section of Connecticut—and it was earlier—at least a century before the arrival of Europeans. In that regard, it was a late part of a centuries-long population movement that provides an alternative approach to the history of the frontier.

The first pioneers to settle North America did not move east to west; they moved north to south and west to east. Their migration began around twenty to forty thousand years ago, when glaciers still covered much of the continent. (In this first and longest era of early American history, precise dating is always difficult and usually debatable.) Across the treeless, frozen land bridge of the Bering Strait linking Siberia and Alaska came a steady stream of Asiatic people searching for new food sources in a frigid environment. Gradually, over the course of thousands of years, they spread as far south as the tip of South America and as far northeast as the Atlantic coast of Canada. Along the way they broke up into many groups that developed distinct languages and cultures. Scholars now estimate that there were upward of two thousand languages and dialects spoken among North American Indians. In the eastern half of North America alone, for instance, there were four basic language groups—Iroquoian, Algonquian, Siouian, and Muskogean—that gave birth to dozens of different tongues, most of them mutually unintelligible. In that regard, many of the native inhabitants of North America were as "foreign" to each other as they were to Europeans.

Yet amid the remarkable cultural and linguistic diversity lies evidence of equally remarkable contact and exchange among native peoples. In excavations of ancient village sites, archaeologists have found foods and minerals that were not indigenous to the immediate region. Native peoples in the Southeast, for instance, planted gourds and corn that originally came from Central America, and they used copper mined in the Great Lakes region. Going in the other direction, marine shells from the Atlantic coast wound up far inland in the Midwest. In general, this widespread dispersal of goods indicates the existence of extensive long-distance trade among native peoples before Europeans arrived in the Americas. Individual groups might have traded only with their nearest neighbors, but those neighbors in turn traded with people farther away, and so the network stretched for hundreds and even thousands of miles. Moreover, in addition to trade goods, Indians exchanged information on agriculture, handicraft, and religious ritual.

Historical and archaeological research can scarcely scratch the surface of early Indian life, but it has uncovered several notable examples of highly developed North American societies before the European era. These early Indian societies underscore the importance of inter-group contact among Indian people long before their contact with Europeans. In the desert Southwest, for instance, the hunter-gatherers who occupied the region around four thousand or five thousand years ago began to have contact with people from Mesoamerica (what is now central and southern Mexico), who introduced them to maize and squash. Over the course of several millennia, these desert-dwelling people increasingly shifted from hunting to horticulture as their main means of sustenance. By the sixth century A.D.—a thousand years before the Spanish would enter the area—they had developed sophisticated farming techniques and irrigation systems, which were crucial in the harsh, arid environment. They also began to build permanent villages, some of which had elaborate multifamily apartments (what the Spanish would later call "pueblos") that housed hundreds of people. The Anasazi people, who flourished from the tenth through the thirteenth centuries, had a collection of villages in Chaco Canyon (in northwestern New Mexico) that held a population numbering between six thousand and fifteen thousand. Moreover, an extensive system of wide, straight roads reached out from the canyon for miles, offering access to trade and religious ceremonies in the canyon. By the time the Spanish arrived, the Anasazi, Hohokam, and Mogollon cultures of the Southwest had declined, probably because of drought, but their Hopi, Pima–Papago, and Zuni descendants still inhabited hundreds of pueblo communities throughout a vast region.

To the east, in the valleys of the Mississippi and Ohio rivers, the remains of hundreds of huge mounds memorialize other cultures that flourished long before European arrival. In the first century B.C., for instance, the Hopewell culture held sway over the whole region of what is now Ohio and Illinois. (The term "Hopewell" is not an Indian word, of course. It first came into use at the 1893 Columbian Exposition in Chicago, where Frederick Jackson Turner delivered his famous address on "The Significance of the Frontier." Another scholar at the event, archaeologist Warren K. Moorehead, displayed artifacts he had dug from ancient mounds on the Ohio farm of Captain M. C. Hopewell, and the label stuck.) The Hopewell burial mounds—earth sculptures that were themselves significant works of art and engineering—contained a remarkable array of stonework and other artifacts testifying to the trade and talents of the Hopewell people. Their culture flourished for about five centuries, then faded between the fourth and fifth centuries A.D. for a combination of reasons—climatic changes, a decline in trade, warfare—that historians still seek to explain more fully.

Several centuries later, beginning perhaps as early as the eighth century A.D., there arose an equally impressive Indian society in the Mississippi Valley. Influenced by Mesoamerican as well as Hopewell cultures, the Mississippian culture used maize production and trade to support a number of sizable towns of several hundred to several thousand inhabitants. The largest center of the Mississippian culture, the palisaded city known as Cahokia, near the site of present-day St. Louis, had around twenty thousand inhabitants in its metropolitan area at its peak (ca. A.D. 900–1250), and it was the nexus of trade throughout a wide region. Like the Hopewell civilization, the Mississippian culture declined long before the arrival of Europeans, again for probably much the same reasons. But these early Indian cultures had a definite influence on the native peoples that populated the eastern woodlands of North America—the area of the most extensive and sustained interaction with Europeans in the early period of contact.

The Indians of the eastern woodlands were no newcomers. Around twelve thousand to fifteen thousand years ago, when the earth experienced a warming spell and the glaciers began to recede, North American natives began to move into the region between the Appalachian Mountains and the Atlantic. As the environment changed, so did they. The early migrants followed the big game of the Pleistocene era—mammoths, mastodons, bison, and caribou— that fed on lichen and other forms of post-glacial vegetation. Hunting with stone-tipped spears, these early Americans were almost too successful for their own good: the mammoths and mastodons became extinct between eleven thousand and nine thousand years ago, partly because of climatic changes but also because of overhunting. Beginning at about the same time and continuing for several thousand years more, the warming earth brought forth a succession of new trees—first spruce, then pine, then oak and hemlock—that form the forests of the region today. The emergence of new trees and other forms of plant life gave native peoples an alternative to following the dwindling herds. Bands began to settle in a particular area and to feed themselves by hunting, fishing, and gathering wild plants. In time, perhaps three thousand or four thousand years ago, plant gathering turned to primitive farming, and most (but not all) Indian groups in the eastern part of North America added agriculture to their other sources of subsistence.

There was no single "Indian way of life," of course, but despite the significant differences among Indian peoples, the historical record reveals important points of cultural connection and comparison. One of the most striking is religion. It is admittedly dangerous to generalize about the belief systems of hundreds of groups in a period of thousands of years, but some fundamental elements do seem to recur in all parts of the continent. Most important was the relationship of native people to the earth and to the living things of the earth. Unlike the Judeo-Christian narrative in the Book of Genesis, in which God created human beings to "have dominion over the fish of the sea, and over the fowl of the air, and over every living thing that moveth upon the earth," Indian creation stories reminded people that they were part of nature, that they had a reciprocal relationship with their environment.

Among the Pueblo people in the Southwest, for instance, the origin of human life began when two women were born in the underworld. There, as historian Ramón Gutiérrez recounts the story, "Tsichtinako (Thought Woman) nursed the sisters, taught them language, and gave them each a basket that their father Uchtsiti had sent them containing the seeds and fetishes of all the plants and animals that were to exist in the world." One of the pine seeds they planted grew into a tall tree that broke through the earth's surface, and the women emerged into the sunlight. Once on the earth, Gutiérrez continues, "Thought Woman taught the sisters how to give life to the animal fetishes in their baskets so that the animals would give them life in return." From their baskets they also scattered the pebbles that would grow into mountains and the seeds that would grow into a variety of plant life. Similar stories existed among the Creek people of the Southeast, who told of people first coming out of the earth, and among the Iroquois people of the Northeast, who told of a woman falling from the sky and planting seeds in the mud on the back of a sea turtle. In these and other creation stories, the emphasis on seed-bearing women as first beings underscored the connection between human life and plant life, making it clear that people were deeply embedded in the natural world, not superior to it. As a result, Indian religions tended to see all earthly objects—not just plants and animals, but stones, soil, and water as well—as living things, all of which had a spiritual relationship to human beings. Thus deer hunters, both in the Southwest and in the Northeast, prayed to the animals before the hunt and gave them thanks afterward for providing for their needs. As Calvin Martin explains, both human beings and animals were assumed to understand their respective roles in the hunt, and Indians had "a sense of cautious reverence for a conscious fellow-member of the same eco-system who, in the view of the Indian, allowed itself to be taken for food and clothing."

In the eyes of most European Christians, the Indians' reverence for the many manifestations of spirituality in the world seemed nothing more than polytheistic paganism. No matter how bitterly Protestant and Catholic clergymen disagreed on the tenets of the One True Faith, they stood united in their scorn for native religious beliefs. The English Puritan missionary Thomas Mayhew said that the Indians he first encountered on Martha's Vineyard in the 1640s were "mighty zealous in their worship of false gods . . . of things in heaven, and earth, and sea . . . [of] "men-gods, women-gods, and children-gods." But in addition to those "false gods"— or, more to the point, because of them—Mayhew noted ominously that "the Devil also had his kingdom among them." Like hundreds of other priests, ministers, and missionaries of the Christian faith, Mayhew took it as his task not just to describe the Indians' religion but to condemn it as devil worship.

Therein lies a more general point: most contemporary observations of native ways of life must carry a cultural disclaimer. Much of what historians know (or think we know) about early Indians comes from the pens of Europeans. Indians had, for the most part, an oral culture; they passed information and tradition down by word of mouth, not in books, pamphlets, letters, diaries, and other documents. Some of that oral history has been preserved and transmitted over the generations, and historians are now beginning to turn to native voices for a more complete understanding of the past. Still, it is largely the written record left by Europeans that has been preserved in the archives where historians work.

In fact, European explorers, soldiers, mapmakers, and other early travelers in North America were often especially imaginative writers who told remarkable tales of the land and its first inhabitants. Some of those accounts were quite fanciful, even fraudulent, full of distortions and downright lies. Some were haughty and hostile, written from the standpoint of superiority to "savages." Still others, however, were surprisingly sympathetic, trying to convey an accurate account of what Indian people said and did. Sometimes European observers were so impressed with Indian life that they had to bend over backward to find something critical to say. For instance, the naturalist William Bartram, who traveled among the Creek people of the Southeast in the late eighteenth century, wrote very favorably of his Indian hosts—so much so, he feared, that "some of my countrymen who may read these accounts of the Indians . . . will charge me with partiality or prejudice in their favour." For the sake of balance, or perhaps just for the sake of his own credibility among his fellow Euro-Americans, Bartram took pains to add that he would also "endeavour to exhibit their vices, immoralities, and imperfections." Bartram knew, as other writers knew, that his readers would not believe (or accept) an altogether positive picture.

Yet, no matter how arrogant or appreciative, European observers were, almost by definition, culturally biased: they perceived native peoples through the prism of their own experience, and they almost always portrayed Indian practices with a point of reference to European custom. It is necessary, then, to read their accounts with caution and even skepticism, to read between the lines and look beyond the preconceptions and prejudices, and, as much as possible, to read back into the pre-contact past to perceive Indian life from the perspective of the Indians themselves. As a case in point, we can attempt to apply such a reading to the early European observations of the native peoples of the eastern woodlands.

Even before coming to North America, some Europeans had developed a preconceived vision of the land and its people—or, more to the point, the way Indian people lived on the land. As Robert Cushman, an early Puritan promoter of migration to America, explained to his fellow inhabitants of England:

> This then is a sufficient reason to prove our going thither to live lawful: their land is spacious and void, and they are but few and do but run

over the grass, as do the foxes and wild beasts. They are not industrious, neither have [they] art, science, skill or faculty to use either the land or the commodities of it; but all spoils, rots, and is marred for want of manuring, gathering, ordering, etc. . . . so it is lawful now to take a land which none useth and make use of it.

In a sense, Cushman and other European writers identified Indians with the environment, but not in the way Indian people understood their reciprocal relationship with nature. Rather, because Indians lived lightly on the land, without "ordering" it, they seemed as transient as animals, having no more claim to permanence, much less possession, than the "foxes and wild beasts" that roamed the forests. Thus the land across the Atlantic seemed empty and un- used, just waiting to be inhabited and improved by European settlers.

But much of what made the land seem so "spacious and void" was indeed the result of Indian land use. Nothing struck European newcomers more immediately, for instance, than the Indian prac- tice of burning woodlands. The Italian-born mariner Giovanni da Verrazano, who explored the coast of North America for France in 1524, claimed that he could smell the "sweet fragrance" of wood smoke while still miles offshore, and closer inspection of the coast revealed the effect of the forest fires. Instead of finding the dense, dark forests of their imagination, Verrazano and other early Eu- ropean explorers came upon surprisingly open spaces. They soon learned that the park-like appearance of the landscape resulted from the long-standing native practice of setting controlled fires, usually twice a year, in the spring and fall.

This system of slash-and-burn (which is still practiced in parts of the world today) had a number of benefits. First, it got rid of the tangle of underbrush that harbored insect pests like ticks, lice, mosquitoes, and fleas. Second, it attracted other forms of plant and animal life more beneficial to human use. The burned-over forest floor sprouted new growths of grasses, shrubs, and small saplings, and the low vegetation provided food for deer, wild turkeys, and other small game. Third, the open space between trees made it easier for Indians to hunt game and, equally important, to avoid being hunted themselves by human enemies lying in ambush. All this Europeans could perceive easily enough. What many of them failed to understand, however, was that seasonal burning provided a fourth, and perhaps most important, result: it replenished the soil with nitrogen and other nutrients, making the land more productive. Ash, not fish, was the Indian farmer's main fertilizer.

Europeans often failed to comprehend or appreciate the practices common to Indian agriculture, because they were so different from their own. Yet, by the time of European contact, native peoples of the eastern woodlands had developed a successful system of agriculture, growing a diversity of crops such as corn, squash, pumpkins, beans, melons, and tobacco. In fact, the diversity was sometimes evident in a single plot of planted ground. Indians often planted several crops—corn, beans, and squash, for instance—together on one mound, where the stalks and leaves intertwined in what at first appeared a tangle of vegetation. But the root systems reinforced each other, making the plants less susceptible to damage from wind and rain. The profusion of leaves above ground also helped control soil erosion and weeds. The cultivation of beans, which began several hundred years before Europeans arrived, was an especially useful addition to Indian agriculture. Beans not only returned nitrogen to the soil but they enhanced the nutritive value of other foods. As modern nutritionists now point out, the proteins and amino acids in beans and corn interact when the two foods are eaten together, and this protein complementarity results in more total protein than would be produced if the beans and corn were eaten separately. In general, Indians who engaged in farming along with hunting, fishing, and gathering enjoyed much greater health and well-being than those who did not.

Yet Indian agriculturists did not live a life of abundance. They ate when they had food, and they went hungry when they did not, sometimes several days at a time. Their ability to do without a steady diet and other basic necessities impressed Europeans—but not always in a positive manner. European observers often remarked on the Indians' apparent inability to ration their resources and usually concluded with a critical judgment that Indians were therefore wasteful, unable to make a decent living out of the New World's obvious natural bounty. John Lawson, the surveyor-general of North Carolina in the early part of the eighteenth century, observed that the natives of the South Atlantic region "are not possess'd with that Care and Thoughtfulness, how to provide for the Necessaries of Life, as the Europeans are." To some extent, that apparently carefree nature appealed to Lawson, who noted that Indians "never walk backward and forward as we do, nor contemplate the Affairs of Loss and Gain, the things which daily perplex us." But it also led him to conclude that they were "no Inventors of Arts or Trades worthy of mention," and were thus little above the beasts, and hardly the equal of Europeans. At best, the Indian seemed improvident, and to Europeans, that was dangerously close to indolent.

One factor that contributed further to this European perception of Indian indolence was the sexual division of labor. In European eyes, Indian men seemed to enjoy a life of comparative leisure; when they were not fighting, they spent most of their time hunting or fishing or taking life easy. Their wives provided virtually everything they needed. William Wood, the English author of the widely read *New England Prospect* (1634), spent several pages describing the work of Indian women in the coastal region of Massachusetts, whose "employments be many." Women were responsible for building (and, when necessary, moving) the multifamily roundhouses. They made a variety of goods and utensils—woven mats, baskets, clothing, and shoes—and generally took care of the "ordinary household drudgerie." Outside the house, women assisted men in fishing and hunting by gathering lobsters for bait and by serving as their "Porters to lugge home their Venison." Above all, women were farmers. Admiring the Indian women's cornfield, Wood observed that "they exceede our *English* husbandmen, keeping it so cleare with their Clamme shell-hooes, as if it were a garden rather than a corne-field, not suffering a choaking weede to advance his audacious head above their infant corn."

There were other sorts of infants to tend, of course, yet Wood noted that women's work went on, with little time to pause for pregnancy or childbirth: "A bigge bellie hinders no business, nor a childebirth takes much time, but the young Infant being greased and sooted, wrapt in a Beaver skin, bound to his good behaviour with his feet up to his bumme, upon a board two foote long and one foot broade, his face exposed to all nipping weather; this little *Pappouse* travells about with his bare footed mother to paddle in the Icie Clammbankes after three or four dayes."

Wood was by no means alone in his emphasis on the "drudgerie" and hard work that befell Indian women. European observers frequently commented on the apparently unequal burdens they bore. Philip Georg Friedrich von Reck, one of the Protestant emigrants from Salzburg who settled in Georgia in 1736, described women of the Creek nation as being treated "not much better than slaves." At home, he said, a Creek woman had to wait upon her husband and do all the household work; on the hunt she had to "haul all the baggage and household goods, yet meanwhile her husband carries only his gun, mirror, shot pouch, and sometimes a bottle of brandy." On the other hand, von Reck also suggested that the women "do all this so willingly that it seems rather their kind intention than a burden on them." It is of course difficult, if not impossible, for a European man to know the true feelings of an Indian woman. Indian women—like other women in other times and places—carried a great deal of baggage, both physical and cultural; indeed, the latter may have been the heavier. But if they resented the traditional sexual division of labor in their society, they were not likely to tell someone like von Reck.

The issue of work and gender roles is a matter in which European observations must be read with due caution for cultural bias. After all, Europeans were themselves hardly in the vanguard of gender equality. Their apparent sympathy and concern for the burdens of Indian women often provided only a thin cover for a cultural stereotype of Indian men as idle and lazy. Hunting and fishing were forms of recreation among Europeans, and they failed to calculate the contribution of this form of food providing to the overall survival strategy of the group. Moreover, the lines of division were not always as rigid as Europeans might have thought. Men sometimes took responsibility for clearing fields for cultivation, and they were usually in charge of growing tobacco, which was an important part of Indian rituals. That is not to say that Indian society was any more enlightened or egalitarian in its gender relations than European; by modern standards, the two might even seem strikingly similar in their sexual division of labor. But the European *perception* of laboring women and lazy men would lead them to make the misguided and ultimately dangerous assumption that because Indian men did not work as European men did, they had no real claim to the land.

Indians did have a very strong sense of their claim on the land. The basic social unit among most eastern Indians was the village, a band of up to several hundred people who occupied a well-defined territory. The bounds of the village were determined not by a surveyor's map but by the physical landscape—a range of mountains or hills, a large pond, the watershed of a river. Moreover, the village was not a fixed site of permanent houses and palisades. The people of the village-band shifted from site to site within their territory, moving their houses closer to the coast or river in fishing season, for instance, or perhaps to recently cleared land when old fields had become infertile. In that sense, Indians were neither permanently rooted nor perpetually rootless. They used different parts of their territory as need and season dictated. As Francis Jennings has aptly put it, "The Indian did not wander; he commuted."

Traditions of mobility and family had a profound effect on the Indians' understanding of ownership. Within the village, people owned their personal belongings—clothing, weapons, implements, and so forth—but no single person or household owned the land as private property: an individual household might cultivate a particular parcel of land in a given year, but the land was not theirs exclusively, nor was it theirs forever. Neither was what they produced from the land. People in the village were tied together by extensive kinship networks, and the interrelationships among family groups encouraged cooperative labor and shared resources. No household could accumulate goods at the expense or to the exclusion of others.

If anybody had a claim on wealth or ownership, it was the village leader, called the sachem or, in northern New England, the sagamore. As William Cronon explains, "a sachem 'owned' territory in a manner somewhat analogous to the way a European monarch 'owned' an entire European nation: less as personal real estate than as a symbolic possession of a whole people." The sachem had the authority to assign plots of land to households, and he (or, in some cases, she) received a portion of the crop as a form of tribute. But that authority was by no means absolute; whether gained through inheritance or useful service, it had to be maintained through consent. As von Reck noted in his observations of the Creek people, "the king is not distinguished from his subjects. . . . He rules merely through good advice, which they nevertheless follow exactly." Thomas Nairne, who lived among the Chickasaws in the

Mississippi region in the early years of the eighteenth century, pointed out that if an Indian leader did not fulfill his role well, then "the people don't regard him as king, for it seems they're of the whiggish opinion that the Duties of kings and people are reciprocall, that if he failes in his they've sufficient cause to neglect their's." Suitably impressed, Nairne concluded that "Plato nor no other writter of Politicks even of the most republican principles, could ever contrive a Government where the equallity of mankind is more Justly observed than here among the savages." At a time when Europeans had not yet accepted the revolutionary notion that government rests on the consent of the governed, Indians seemed to offer a radical (and, to some, perhaps refreshing) alternative to the divine right of kings.

In addition to directing the internal affairs of the village, sachems also conducted foreign policy. Like their European counterparts, they used trade, diplomacy, and war to promote the interests of their people. But they used those foreign-policy tools quite differently. Trade, for instance, was not a means to control commodities, monopolize markets, or accumulate profits through aggressive economic expansion. Rather, it was a way for one group to exchange something it had in abundance for another group's surplus—say, shellfish for furs. In that manner, both groups could increase their access to a wider variety of foods and goods. Moreover, trade was not just an exercise in exchange; it was an expression of friendship. It often took the form of elaborate gift-giving, a ceremonial sealing of diplomatic relations between two groups in which goods added to the weight of words.

When economic diplomacy failed, there was always war. Wars were frequent among Indian groups, but they were never final. That is, the object of war was not to devastate or destroy one's enemies, only to defeat them. Even victory had its limits. European observers often pointed out, with some surprise, that Indians seldom made war to take territory. To be sure, they fought to defend their land, but, more important, they fought to defend their honor. As John Lawson put it, "The Indians ground their Wars on Enmity, not Interest, as the Europeans usually do." Another eighteenth-century explorer of the North American interior, Jonathan Carver, explained the Indian rationale for war in more detail:

The extension of empire is seldom a motive with these people to invade, and to commit depredations on the territories of those who happen to dwell near them. To secure the rights of hunting within particular limits, to maintain the liberty of passing through their accustomed tracks, and to guard those lands which they consider from a long tenure as their own, against any infringement, are the general causes of those dissensions that so often break out between the Indian nations, and are carried on with so much animosity. . . . But interest is not either the most frequent or most powerful incentive to their making war on each other. The passion of revenge, which is the most distinguishing characteristic of these people, is the most general motive. Injuries are felt by them with exquisite sensibility, and vengeance pursued with unremitted ardour.

The "unremitted ardour" of honor could lead to brutal warfare, but not to total warfare. Warriors did not destroy whole villages and crops, nor did they slaughter women, children, and the aged. Even in fighting other warriors, Indians sought not so much to kill as to capture. Among some Indian groups of the eastern woodlands, warfare was a form of mourning, a means of grieving the loss of loved ones killed by the enemy. The spirit of the dead could not rest, they believed, until enemy warriors had been killed or taken captive.

Capture often meant torture. After being brought back to the village of the victors, several captives were usually selected for slow death by burning, beating, stoning, or stabbing. Hours later, when the victim finally died, the villagers sometimes drank his blood and ate his heart to take on his strength and courage. Europeans—who were no amateurs at torture—expressed shock and disgust at such treatment of prisoners, calling the Indians "barbarians" and "cannibals." But Indians, even the victims themselves, took torture for granted as part of the mourning process, or at least as the predictable price of defeat. Young men were taught from an early age never to show weakness in the face of torture, but to sing of their own courage and to mock the efforts of their tormentors.

Moreover, torture was not the only, or even the most common, fate awaiting prisoners. In many cases, the vanquished captives— men, women, and children—were distributed among the households of the victors to serve as replacements for lost kin. Once adopted, they were immediately accepted as members of the family and of the village as a whole. The point is not that Indians practiced a "humane" form of warfare—that is a contradiction in terms—but rather that they engaged in a limited conflict that had reasonably well defined rules and goals.

Through trade or warfare, or often a combination of the two, some Indian groups established dominance over others. Dominance did not imply utter subjugation, but subordination within a reciprocal relationship. One group's recognition of its subordinate status to another was usually expressed symbolically in the form of tribute, a gift of food or handicrafts. In more practical terms, the tributary group agreed to provide territorial access and military assistance to the dominant group, for which it received an assurance of peace and protection in return. Prominent and personally powerful sachems expanded their network of influence far beyond their immediate neighborhoods, forming a far-flung confederacy, or tribe, of tributary groups. For instance, immediately preceding large-scale European settlement in New England, the Pequot sachem Tatobem (the predecessor of Sassacus) managed to unite several Pequot bands under his authority, and the Pequot confederacy in turn gained dominance over other Algonquian-speaking tribes in the area. Similarly, in the Chesapeake region the sachem Powhatan used military conquest, marriage, and inheritance to organize a number of Algonquian tribes into an extensive confederacy under his control. By the time the first English settlers arrived to establish Jamestown in 1607, the Powhatan confederacy reached dozens of miles deep into the interior and was by far the most powerful political force in the region.

But the Pequots, Powhatans, and all other Algonquian-speaking tribes along the east coast were eventually overshadowed by a still greater confederacy to the west. The Iroquois Five Nations—from east to west, the Mohawks, Oneidas, Onondagas, Cayugas, and Senecas—formed the largest and most powerful Indian alliance in eastern North America. According to tradition, the alliance was formed sometime between 1400 and 1600 by the legendary Mohawk sachem, Hiawatha. During a period of grief-stricken isolation in the woods, Hiawatha had a vision of a supernatural figure, Deganawidah, who directed him to bring the Iroquoian people together into a protective confederacy. Like a Mohawk Messiah, Hiawatha traveled among the Iroquois people preaching peace and unity, and eventually he organized the Great League of Peace. No longer would the Iroquois tribes make war on each other, but they would submit their inter-tribal grievances to a council of chiefs drawn from all five tribes. With their connections reinforced by matrilineal kinship links—by female family ties—the Iroquois formed a loose alliance that stretched from the Adirondack region of New York westward past the Finger Lakes and on into the Great Lakes region of Pennsylvania and Ohio.

Making peace with each other did not mean that the Iroquois would be equally friendly toward other tribes. Indeed, the Iroquois gained the reputation of being ferocious fighters, the scourge of other tribes both on the east coast and in the Midwest. They were not invincible, of course, and sometimes their military power was exaggerated by Indians and Europeans alike. Still, Iroquois incursions into the territory of their traditional Algonquian-speaking enemies forced tribes all along the east coast to keep constant watch on their western flanks. For many of those tribes, in fact, Europeans seemed the lesser of the two evils.

Agriculture, trade, diplomacy, and warfare—all the activities so familiar in European history—were common parts of Indian history long before Europeans arrived on the scene. Unfortunately, much of that history can never be fully known. The important point is that Indians did have patterns of existence that were distinct from, but still not altogether dissimilar to, those of Europeans. Despite what European detractors would say, Indians were not savages living squalid, vagrant, and violent lives in an empty wilderness. And despite what some of their defenders would later say, neither were Indians saints living in harmony with the environment and each other in an idyllic state of nature. They were, like all people elsewhere, too complex and contradictory to lend themselves easily to broad cultural generalizations. The only thing one can say with certainty is that once Indians began to interact with Europeans, their way of life would never be the same.

From the moment Christopher Columbus set foot on the sands of the tiny island he named San Salvador on October 12, 1492, he began taking the measure of the native population. The Taino people who greeted him and his men on the beach were "all as naked as their mothers bore them," which gave Columbus a good opportunity to observe that they were "very well-built people, with handsome bodies and very fine faces." Their skin was the color of "sunburned peasants, not at all black, as would be expected." (Columbus, like many other Europeans of his era, assumed that the closer people lived to the Equator, the darker they would be because of their exposure to the sun.) Although the natives painted their bodies and faces, they did not strike Columbus as fierce-looking people. Indeed, they appeared "friendly and well-dispositioned," bearing no arms but small and seemingly innocuous spears tipped with fish teeth. When Columbus showed one of them his own sword, "through ignorance he grabbed it and cut himself." That was the only blood shed that day.

Almost immediately, the newcomers and the natives struck up a lively trade, with the Europeans exchanging glass beads, bells, and red caps for "parrots, balls of cotton thread, spears, and many other things." But Columbus's final calculation of that first encounter had less to do with the value of the natives' goods than with the value of the natives themselves: "They ought to make good and skilled servants, for they repeat very quickly whatever we say to them. I think they can easily be made Christians, for they seem to have no religion. . . . With 50 men you could subject everyone and make them do what you wished."

Columbus may not have been the first European to set foot in the Western Hemisphere, but his arrival there was the first step in a sustained process of permanent European settlement. The Columbian voyages set off a surge of exploration and expansion that eventually overwhelmed the native inhabitants of this "New World." Moreover, Columbus's initial evaluation of those natives was indicative of the enduring attitudes Europeans brought to intercultural relations. In this brief encounter (or any time thereafter), it apparently never occurred to Columbus that the people he called Indians could be his equals. Naked and painted, they looked like savages. Friendly and generous, they looked like good trading partners. Unthreatening and uneducated, they looked like possible servants. They might even make good Christians since, as Columbus somehow assumed, they had no religion. But it was clear to Columbus—and to the other early European explorers who followed him—that the only suitable status for native peoples would be subjection to their European superiors.

Although Columbus bragged that he could subdue the natives with fifty men, it was millions of germs that overpowered the indigenous population. Almost from the first moment of contact, even before Europeans began to settle the Western Hemisphere in large numbers, European diseases made a silent, invisible entry into the continent and swept across the land, killing a huge proportion of the unprotected population. Throughout the early period of European contact, the most immediate and certainly the most significant change in the native way of life was the dramatic increase in death.

Over the course of centuries, native peoples had been relatively safe from disease. The cold killed germs carried by the initial emigrants who made the long trek from Siberia across the icy land bridge to North America. Spreading over an otherwise uninhabited continent, their descendants developed natural antibodies to help them resist disease. An Indian in the Yucatán peninsula reflected on conditions in the pre-contact era:

> There was then no sickness; they had no aching bones; they had then no high fever; they had then no smallpox; they had then no burning chest; they had then no abdominal pain; they had then no consumption; they had then no headache. At that time the course of humanity was orderly.

No one really knows how many Indians inhabited North America before the arrival of Europeans. Population estimates for the area north of Mexico range from a low of around a million upward as high as fifteen million, although a range of five million to ten million would probably be more reasonable.

But the comparatively sudden exposure to new microorganisms brought to their land by European fishermen and explorers left them physically defenseless. Everywhere Indians came into contact with Europeans—from the Caribbean islands to the Atlantic coastal region to the lower Great Plains to the desert Southwest —the population plummeted, sometimes by as much as ninety percent. Soon after landing on an island off the coast of Texas in 1528, the Spanish explorer Cabeza de Vaca observed that "half the natives died from a disease of the bowels and blamed us." Similarly, when the English explorer Thomas Harriot led his party through

Indian villages in the coastal regions of Carolina in the 1580s, he reported that "within a few dayes after our departure from every such towne, the people began to die very fast, and many in short space. . . . The disease was also so strange, that they neither knew what it was." In fact, many Indians died from European diseases without ever actually seeing a European face. Trade and communication spread deadly microbes from village to village, infecting men, women, and children with smallpox, measles, and other strains of European illness.

If the native villagers had no idea what disease they had, they quickly saw what it did. The Puritan writer William Bradford reported that after an outbreak of smallpox in the upper part of the Connecticut River Valley in 1634, Indians there "died most miserably."

> For usually they that have of this disease have them in abundance, and for want of bedding and linen and other helps, they fall into a lamentable condition as they lie on their hard mats, the pox breaking and mattering and running one into another, their skin cleaving by reason thereof to the mats they lie on. When they turn, a whole side will flay off at once as it were, and they will be all of a gore blood, most fearful to behold. And then, being very sore, what with cold and other distempers, they die like rotten sheep.

Bradford, of course, was no great friend of the Indian, as his later comments on the massacre of the Pequots would make clear. But his description of the agonizing deaths of smallpox victims captured at least a measure of the misery that afflicted native peoples in the aftermath of European contact. A similar description could have applied almost anywhere in the contact zones of America.

Disease-borne death not only caused personal grief and suffering; it also undermined the foundations of native culture. Elderly people were especially vulnerable to disease, and when they died, much of their knowledge of crafts and customs died with them. Native leaders also fell victim. As Bradford observed in his account of the 1634 smallpox epidemic:

> The chief Sachem him self now died, & almost all his friends & kindred. But by the marvelous goodness & providence of God not one of the

English was so much as sick, or in the least measure tainted with the disease.

The inability of Indian sachems and shamans to prevent the spread of disease or to heal its victims (including themselves) created doubt and demoralization among their people—especially when they saw that Europeans were not similarly afflicted. The leading historian of these disastrous diseases, Alfred W. Crosby, has noted that "some Indians . . . turned on the whites whom they blamed for the epidemics, but most were obliged by their circumstances to direct their fear and rage against themselves." In general, those Indians who somehow survived the scourge of European diseases lived through not only a demographic crisis but a crisis of confidence as well.

At the same time, these epidemics sometimes served to increase the confidence of the Europeans. Noting the disease-borne devastation of northeastern Indian people, John Winthrop wrote that by "sweeping away great multitudes of the natives . . . God hath hereby cleared our title to the place." The grim legalism of Winthrop's analysis of the demographic disaster only underscored what many European newcomers already understood in the first stages of staking their claims to North America, from New England to New Spain: the thinning of the Indian population made it much easier to plant new settlements in the New World soil.

What Europeans had begun unwittingly with germs, they carried on aggressively with guns. In the early era of contact, firearms gave Europeans a technological superiority that offset their numerical inferiority to the native population. Columbus well understood the advantages of arms. In December 1492, after running aground on the island of Hispaniola, he responded to the inhabitants' hospitality by staging a demonstration of European firepower: his men shot off a small cannon and a musket, and "the King was spellbound when he saw the effect of their force and what they penetrated. When the people heard the shots, they fell to their knees." Thus Columbus introduced modern weaponry to the people of the Caribbean. In the centuries that would follow, guns would intimidate thousands of Indians and kill many thousands more.

But the European explorers who followed Columbus did not cross the ocean just to shed Indian blood. Their goal was not extermination of the native population but appropriation of natural resources. It was by no means coincidental that European exploration and colonization of the New World came in a time of great economic expansion. Beginning in the fifteenth century, Mediterranean traders sought to push beyond the known boundaries of their world, searching for sea routes to Asia. With the support of newly consolidated monarchies and newly organized mercantile companies, Spanish and Portuguese explorers took the lead in finding new lands, where merchants in turn might find new products and new markets. No matter what early European settlers might say about setting sail on behalf of God and country, their anticipation of New World wealth cannot be overstated: it underlay all European efforts at conquest, colonization, and even religious conversion.

The famous Spanish *conquistadores* who followed Columbus to the New World in the sixteenth century—Hernán Cortés, Francisco Pizarro, Juan Ponce de León, Hernando de Soto, and Francisco Vásquez de Coronado—carved a deadly path as they moved into the American interior. They carried with them as justification the Requerimiento, a royal document drafted in 1514 that called for Indians to accept Catholicism and the Spanish crown or accept the consequences. *Conquistadores* would have this order read to the Indians before battle and then commence the attack with the assurance (in their own minds, at least) that they had offered an alternative to war. Cortés's conquest of the Aztec empire in Mexico (1519–21) and Pizarro's long march through Central America to subjugate the Incas in Peru (1531–33) were the most significant victories of the Spanish invaders. Making an impressive display of their horses and firearms—and, equally important, taking advantage of internal hostilities among the native population—Cortés and Pizarro overthrew the most powerful political forces in America.

Their search for wealth turned out to be little more than armed extortion. After subduing the indigenous peoples in Mexico and South America, they forced thousands of Indians down into the silver mines. They also established large landholdings, called *encomiendas*, where Indian laborers worked at growing crops and raising stock. Technically, the native peoples thus employed for the benefit of Spain were not slaves: they were "voluntary" workers who provided labor and paid tribute in exchange for the patronage, protection, and religion of the Spanish *encomendero*. In practical terms, they were often little better off than slaves.

The Spanish *conquistadores* who first ventured into North America never quite achieved the same degree of military success, but they did probe remarkably deep into the continent and frequently made violent contact with native people. Ponce de León explored Florida in 1512–13 and again in 1521, allegedly looking for the fabled "fountain of youth" but actually searching for gold and slaves. Not surprisingly, he encountered stiff native resistance, and his second expedition ended when he died from wounds received in a battle with Indians. A similar fate befell de Soto's 1539–42 expedition, which moved northward through Florida to the Savannah River and then to the southern Appalachians. Finding nothing but hostile Creek Indians, de Soto marched his men back southwest to the Gulf of Mexico and then westward toward the Mississippi River. Along the way, they faced more resistance from the Choctaws and Chickasaws. They eventually crossed the Mississippi and went as far west as eastern Oklahoma and then returned to the Mississippi, where de Soto contracted a fever and died in 1542. The remnants of his expedition rafted back to Mexico the following year. While de Soto was wandering through the Southeast, Coronado led a huge expedition of several hundred soldiers and over a thousand Indian baggage carriers northward from Mexico into the Southwest. In their search for the fabled Seven Cities of Cibola and the golden kingdom of Quivera, Coronado's men explored vast expanses of the region, from present-day New Mexico to Colorado and onto the Great Plains, bullying and brutalizing native peoples wherever they went. The Spaniards ultimately came up empty-handed, however, and Coronado returned to Mexico in 1542, impoverished by his expedition.

The early Spanish explorers of North America did not get the wealth they wanted, nor did they always get out alive. Native resistance took its toll on the *conquistador* campaigns, and Ponce de León and de Soto were only two of the most prominent victims. But the Spaniards did establish extensive claims from Florida to California, and they laid the groundwork for the military and missionary settlements that would follow in the seventeenth century. Moreover, the *conquistadores'* initial armed approach against the New World natives—truly the arrogance of power—set the precedent for bloodshed that stained the wider range of relationships between Europeans and Indians.

At least one Spaniard spoke out against this pattern of aggression and exploitation. Bartolomeo de Las Casas, a Dominican friar who had himself formerly been an *encomendero* in Cuba, criticized the cruelty visited upon the natives and even questioned the right of the Spanish to continue their conquest of the New World. Indians, argued Las Casas, were rational beings who had no knowledge of Christianity and, the Requerimiento notwithstanding, no obligation to accept it at gunpoint. Like any Catholic priest, Las Casas hoped to convert the natives to his own faith, but he did not feel that his fellow Spaniards were justified in converting Indian land to their own use.

Las Casas was prominent and persistent enough to make the Spanish rulers consider the moral implications of their actions, but another priest, Juan Ginés de Sepúlveda, offered unapologetic support for Spanish domination. Unlike Las Casas, Sepúlveda had never set foot in the New World, but his lack of familiarity with the native people did not stop him from offering a hostile analysis of their culture. In Sepúlveda's eyes, Indians were sinful savages who could be saved from their own wickedness only by coercive conversion. Force was not only justified but necessary to bring them the benefits of the Christian faith and Spanish culture: "How can we doubt that these people—so uncivilized, so barbaric, contaminated with so many impieties and obscenities—have been most justly conquered by such an excellent, pious, and most just king?"

The Spanish king of whom Sepúlveda wrote, Charles I (the Holy Roman Emperor Charles V), tried to occupy the middle ground between Las Casas and Sepúlveda. He would not renounce Spain's claims to the New World, but neither could he countenance the naked exploitation and near-enslavement of its people. In 1542–43 he issued the New Laws that prohibited the creation of new *encomiendas*, imposed greater regulation on already established *encomiendas*, and forbade Indian slavery. In 1550, Charles ordered all further conquest stopped, pending a royal investigation; in the meantime, the word "conquest" was to be replaced by inoffensive official euphemisms, "pacification" and "settlement." But as had been the case with all previous attempts to impose greater royal control of *conquistadores* and *encomenderos*, the new legislation was occasionally resisted and generally ignored. The breadth of the ocean and the depth of desire led Spaniards in the New World to continue their conquest without much regret or regulation.

Spanish priests became very effective agents of pacification. Although the Jesuits established several short-lived missions in Florida in the late sixteenth century, it was the Franciscans who played the dominant role in promoting the Christian religion throughout the Spanish colonies. Motivated by a spirit of self-denial and sacrifice, the followers of Saint Francis willingly accepted (and some even sought) martyrdom in the name of their faith. The Franciscan priests were far from passive victims, however. They proved very active in devising ways to undercut the Indians' religious culture. They substituted Christian symbols for Indian ones—the cross for prayer sticks, for instance—and appropriated native sacred space for the construction of churches. They also engaged in a sort of theological theater to impress the people, having Spanish soldiers kiss their feet to show the reverence that was due them, or staging ceremonial dramas designed to demonstrate the mysteries, but also the superiority, of the Christian faith. Perhaps most important, the Franciscans used these allegorical entertainments to insert themselves between Indian children and their parents, presenting themselves as alternative authority figures who appeared to have more power than Indian adults. "Whatever the text of these didactic plays and dances," Ramón Gutiérrez explains, "the subtext ensconced in the generational casting (Indian children playing angels or Christians, the Indian adults playing devils, infidels, or enemies) was the defeat of Indian culture and the subordination of adults to Christianized youths." In general, the friars' goal was to replace the Indians' original identity with a new, Hispanicized and Christianized one. The missionaries could never have succeeded without the help of the military, of course, but the religious zeal of the Franciscans played as crucial a role as the armed might of the *conquistadores* in establishing a long-lasting Spanish presence across the southern frontiers of North America.

The other major European groups who settled principally in the northern and eastern parts of the continent—the English, French, and Dutch—likewise pursued various interrelated approaches in dealing with the native peoples. There was always armed force, of course. The most effective leader of the first permanent English settlement at Jamestown, Virginia, Captain John Smith, was an admirer of Cortés, and in 1609 he adopted a *conquistador*-like stance in demanding food from Powhatan, the leader of a powerful Indian confederacy in the Chesapeake region. "You promised to freight my ship," Smith blustered, "and so you shall, or I mean to load her with your dead carcasses." In 1622, when the Indians in the region retaliated against continuing English encroachment by launching devastating attacks on English settlements, another Virginia official reacted by declaring that the English would henceforth pursue "a perpetual war, without peace or truce." In the northern English settlements in New England, as we have seen in the case of the war against the Pequots, Puritan settlers could be just as relentless in their efforts to reduce Indian power. So could the French and the Dutch. Nowhere in North America could colonization have proceeded, much less succeeded, without resort to arms.

But as the experience of the Spanish indicated, religious faith could be as powerful as armed force. Among the French, Jesuits assumed the main missionary role played by the Franciscans in the Spanish conquest. Yet, while the Franciscans drew inspiration from the spiritual value of self-sacrifice and martyrdom, the Jesuits relied more on the impressive power of intellect. "Man for man," James Axtell has written, "the Jesuits were the best and most rigorously trained minds in Europe," and they used that training to good advantage in North America. By displaying their intellectual abilities before Indian people—reading the written word, healing the sick, predicting eclipses and other such natural phenomena—they undermined the influence of native religious leaders. Like the Franciscans, they were especially intent on inserting themselves into the existing familial and social relations of Indian people; above all, they worked at gaining influence among the young, training them to renounce the traditional beliefs of their parents as sinful and to accept the new ways of the Europeans. Never numerous but always intense, "these unarmed missionaries became some of the most powerful agents of colonialism and change in native America," Axtell concludes. "To an extent unimaginable before Columbus, blackrobed foreigners now decided for many natives what to eat, how to live, when to work, whom to obey, and even their fate after death."

Protestant missionaries, by comparison, seldom achieved the success of their Catholic counterparts, at least in the first century of contact. To be sure, the sponsors of the first permanent English settlements in North America claimed that religious conversion was much more important than profit. As the charter of the Massachusetts Bay Company put it in 1629, one of the primary goals of the colony was "to win and excite the Natives of the Country to the Knowledge and Obedience of the only true God and Saviour of Mankind, and the Christian faith." When the English actually settled Massachusetts Bay, however, their desire for land soon overshadowed their commitment to conversion. Puritan ministers quite easily justified having "devil-driven" Indians forced off the land. One notable exception—and perhaps the exception that proves the rule—was the Reverend Roger Williams, who dared to challenge his countrymen's "depraved appetite after the great vanities, and . . . great portions of land, land in this wilderness." When Williams raised even more disturbing ideas during the early 1630s—including, among other things, the notion that the native people of New England, not the King of England, had the more legitimate claim to the land—the Puritan authorities eventually charged him with heresy and sedition. He was banished from Massachusetts Bay in 1636—on the eve of the Puritan campaign against the Pequots.

In the wake of the Pequot War, another Puritan minister, the Reverend John Eliot, became the main figure in a sustained missionary movement in Massachusetts that was intended, as the government of the colony put it, to get the Indians "to live in an orderly way among us." Beginning in 1651, this "Apostle to the Indians" led in establishing fourteen "Praying Towns," where he hoped to get Indians to convert to Christianity and live according to English norms. Yet even though this Anglicizing effort succeeded in bringing in over a thousand Indians—most of them, it should be noted, from the Nipmuk and Massachuset tribes, who had already had their population, power, and property greatly reduced as a result of contact with the English—no more than ten percent of the Praying Town Indians actually converted to Christianity. In general, Puritan missionaries had neither the ceremonial attractions nor the flexible strategies that French and Spanish missionaries used to make Catholicism appear accommodating to Indian beliefs. When it came to religious conversion, Puritans paid a price for their rigid convictions.

But when it came to trade, questions of the spirit quickly gave way to calculations of profit among all European groups. Beginning with Columbus, the Europeans who established early contact in North America frequently commented on the Indians' surprising desire to trade, even on what seemed to the Europeans to be unfavorable terms. In his early encounters with the Micmac people of the northern Atlantic coastal region, the French explorer Jacques Cartier found the Indians quite eager to trade, holding up their furs on sticks so that the Frenchmen on board ship could see their wares. When they finally got down to business, the Micmacs kept up a lively trade "till they had nothing but their naked bodies, for they gave us [all] whatsoever they had." Although the French, English, and Dutch hoped to emulate the Spanish by getting gold, silver, and other precious commodities, they had to settle for more prosaic products. Still, Indians offered them a variety of desirable trade goods: baskets and other handmade items; exotic plants, like ginseng and snakeroot; and animal products, especially deerskins and furs. Indeed, in the first century of contact, nothing was more important or more profitable than furs, especially beaver pelts. European clothiers turned beaver fur into warm hats and coats, and beaver became the rage among fashion-conscious consumers in seventeenth-century high society.

In part, the Indians' eagerness and apparent generosity in trade stemmed from their traditional notions of exchange, in which gifts helped reinforce patterns of friendship and reciprocity. But Indians also developed consumer desires, and they were willing to pay a good price to get what the Europeans had to offer. After all, local furs were comparatively easy for them to get, and therefore easy to let go. Imported foreign goods—glass beads, mirrors, colored cloth, metal pots, hatchets, knives, guns, and liquor—were much harder to come by, and Indians took advantage of the opportunity to trade.

That did not mean, however, that Europeans always took advantage of them. As Indians became increasingly involved in trade with Europeans, they developed a sense of how to bargain. John Lederer, an explorer who traveled extensively in the western parts of Virginia and the Carolinas in the 1670s, warned his fellow Europeans that they could not take their Indian customers for granted:

> In dealing with the Indians, you must be positive and at a word: for if they perswade you to fall any thing in your price, they will spend time in higgling for further abatements, and seldom conclude any Bargain. Sometimes you may with Brandy or Strong liquor dispose them to an humour of giving you ten times the value of your commodity; and at other times they are so hide-bound, that they will not offer you half the Market-price, especially if they be aware that you have a designe to circumvent them with drink.

Moreover, many European traders learned that Indians could be, as James Merrell has put it, "discriminating shoppers." Colored cloth that might be attractive to one group might not appeal to another, and beads of the wrong size and color would generate very little interest. Only when the trader brought the right goods to the right group would both sides come away from the deal feeling they had got a good bargain.

What the Indians did not bargain for, however, was the effect this trade would ultimately have on their culture. In some respects, European trade goods revolutionized the Indians' ways of life. Guns, for instance, increased the Indians' killing power in hunting and war and became a kind of status symbol. As one Englishman in seventeenth-century Virginia observed, "[T]hey think themselves undrest and not fit to walk abroad, unless they have their gun on their shoulder, and their shot-bag by their side." Metal tools and cooking utensils were also important acquisitions as labor-saving devices that made it easier to clear fields, raise crops, and cook food; once an Indian had used a metal ax, he had little desire to go back to a stone one.

But just as there were obvious advantages to the new trade goods and technology, so there were disadvantages, albeit less immediately apparent. In general, the more Indians came to rely on European goods, the less they relied on their own. Again, guns are a good case in point. Indians could make minor repairs to wooden stocks or replace ramrods, but they could not cast more complex metal parts or make gunpowder. Even so-called consumer durables—knives, tools, cooking utensils, and so forth—created another sort of need; when Indians could trade for such items, they gave up making them. Handicraft skills did not suddenly collapse, but they declined over time, further increasing the gap between Indian products and European imports.

The expansion of trade with Europeans likewise widened the gap between Indian groups. Warfare had been common long before the arrival of Europeans, but competing attempts to expand and control regional trade only exacerbated existing tensions. The fur trade was the most common cause of conflict. As we have seen, the Pequots became brokers for the fur trade in the Connecticut Valley by asserting their dominance over other Indians in the region. Their success in doing business with both the Dutch and the English increased their wealth and prestige for a while, but it also increased the enmity of the neighboring Narragansetts. That rift proved to be a formidable—and for the Pequot sachem Sassacus, a fatal—factor in the Pequots' near-destruction in 1637.

In order to maintain their purchasing power in furs and skins, Indians had to expand the scope of the hunt. In some regions, they overhunted beaver and deer almost to the point of local extinction. As they went farther afield to find more animals, fur hunters inevitably encroached on each other's territory, and that often led to bloodshed. In the early part of the seventeenth century, for instance, the Mohawks and other tribes in the Iroquois League raided Algonquian groups that traded with the French along the Saint Lawrence River. The Mohawks also began to intercept pelts on their way to the French, trading them instead to the Dutch who had established a trading post at Fort Orange on the Hudson River. These attacks gained them both trade goods and captives, who were adopted into the Iroquois groups to help replenish a disease-stricken population. (According to Daniel Richter, smallpox epidemics in 1633 and 1640–41 had cut the population of the Five Nations by more than half, and the Mohawks had lost perhaps three-quarters of their numbers.)

In the middle decades of the seventeenth century, these raids escalated into a long-lasting series of Beaver Wars. Armed with guns provided by their Dutch trading partners, the Mohawks led

Iroquois attacks against the Hurons to their north and west and the Susquehannocks to their south. Trading the plunder taken from their victims to increase their arsenal of firearms, the Iroquois turned their superior weaponry against the Hurons in a decisive expedition in 1649. (The Hurons, too, had suffered devastating losses from diseases brought into their midst by French missionaries.) The Iroquois campaign virtually destroyed the Huron confederacy as an effective force and certainly disrupted the Hurons' trade relationship with the French.

But in the long run, as Richter points out, the Iroquois' attempt at commercial conquest only pulled them into a destructive downward spiral: "The benefits of war . . . came at a tremendous social cost: a seemingly endless cycle of death from disease, wars to find new captives to replace the losses, pillaging furs to trade for guns, new wars, and more deaths in battle transformed the Great League of Peace into a Great League for War." Once their traditional enemies also gained access to European guns, the Iroquois no longer had the firepower to overwhelm their opponents. Moreover, once their Dutch trading partners were defeated by the English in 1664, they no longer had a strong European ally to provide arms and supplies. By 1666, the Iroquois had been seriously damaged if not defeated, and they had to accept a peace treaty with the French. The real winners of the Beaver Wars were neither the Iroquois nor their Indian enemies, but the French and their European enemies, the English.

Even "winners," however, could enjoy little long-lasting satisfaction and security. In the interaction between Indians and Europeans, the balance between war and peace was never steady, but always subject to shifts in interest and alliance. Both Indians and Europeans played the game of diplomacy with considerable shrewdness and skill, making and breaking treaties as they thought best suited their immediate economic and military needs. Indeed, Europeans entered into an economic and political context that had already been made complex by long-standing networks of trade and continuing struggles for power. The European newcomers, themselves divided by competing New World interests, only added another dimension to the diversity.

Yet that proved to be the critical, ultimately decisive dimension. Europeans did not come to North America just to explore, convert, and trade, of course; they came to stay. From their first footholds they extended their reach into the interior and planted permanent settlements. As they did so, the eastern half of North America became a patchwork of power bases, with European enclaves interspersed among traditional tribal territories. How fast these European enclaves grew and how far they reached became the central factor in defining the early history of the American frontiers.

TWO

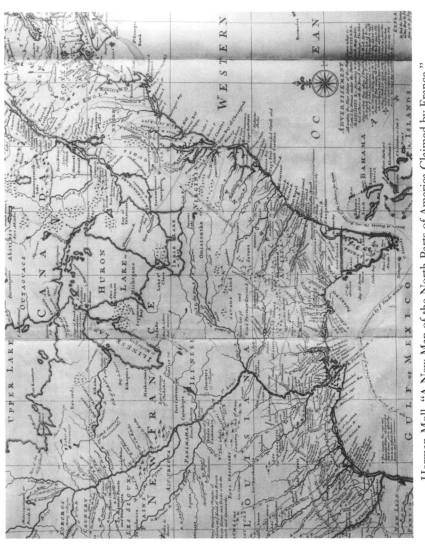

Herman Moll, "A New Map of the North Parts of America Claimed by France," 1720, portion. *Courtesy American Antiquarian Society*

THE STRUGGLE OF EMPIRES
TO CONTROL THE FRONTIERS

S ir Robert Mountgomery never set foot in North America,
but he had great plans for developing the frontier. In 1717,
the Scottish baronet petitioned the Lords Proprietors of South
Carolina for a sizable grant of land between the Savannah and
Altamaha rivers, territory that would eventually become Georgia.
He wanted to create a new British colony that would be a
profitable imperial outpost on the southeastern frontier. He
already had an impressive name for it: the Margravate of Azilia.
The idea of Azilia was attractive to the South Carolina Proprietors, who wanted to create a buffer zone to protect their
colony from attack by the Spanish and Indians to their south.
The idea was equally attractive to Mountgomery, who wanted
to set himself up as the colony's Margrave, the governor for
life.

To encourage support for his plan, Mountgomery published a
prospectus for developing this "Most Delightful Country of the
Universe." He promised that English settlers would find rich
resources—valuable minerals, tall trees, abundant fruits, grains,
fish, and fowl—and lovely landscapes "so fine, and so diversified;
that the Sight is entirely charm'd with them." What English settlers would not find in abundance, Mountgomery promised, were
native settlers: "Nor is this tempting Country yet inhabited, except
in those Parts in the Possession of the *English*, unless by here and
there a Tribe of wandering *Indians*, wild and ignorant, all artless,

and uncultivated, as the Soil, which fosters them." Thus, this American paradise seemed ripe to be plucked.

On one level, Mountgomery's claims were standard promotional stuff, the kind of verdant verbiage one could find in almost any sales pitch for New World settlement. What makes his proposal especially interesting and important, however, is its clearly articulated prescription for future frontier growth. Mountgomery's plans called for developing a series of large, fortified squares, twenty miles on each side and enclosed by a high wall. At the very center of each square would sit a governor's house, which would be surrounded by a gridwork of streets, then open space bordered by trees, then a larger grid pattern of 116 estates, and finally, "four great Parks" that enclosed cow pastures and deer parks. Here nature would be both improved and subdued.

These squares within squares defined not just a regular spatial pattern but a regimented social pattern as well. It was important to Mountgomery that plan precede people. Common settlers, he observed, could not be trusted to arrange themselves advantageously, because of the "Folly of fixing at random, and destroying their Interest by Indulging their Humour." It was necessary to "dispose them regularly," to impose order over them, so as to promote, even protect, their true interests—not to mention those of the Margrave himself. Eventually, Mountgomery projected, "the Families they leave will prove a constant Seminary of sober Servants, of both Sexes, for the Gentry of the Colony; whereby they will be under no necessity to use the Dangerous Help of *Blackamoors*, or *Indians*." Thus the Margravate of Azilia would be a productive province where regularity, regimentation, and reproduction would combine to create a hard-working, self-perpetuating, single-race class of workers to serve the needs of their superiors. To a member of the aristocracy like Mountgomery, such a social system must have seemed Utopia indeed.

Unfortunately for Mountgomery, his Margravate of Azilia never materialized. The original grant from the South Carolina Proprietors gave him three years to put his plan into action, and he failed to raise either the necessary sums or settlers in that time. By 1720, his last-ditch efforts to secure support proved unsuccessful, and the whole venture died a quiet death. In the end, Mountgomery's elaborate plan amounted to little more than a pamphlet and a place name on some eighteenth-century maps, or, in the twentieth century, a footnote to British settlement and city planning.

Though never realized, this fanciful design offers several revealing insights into the assumptions underlying European, and especially Anglo-American, plans for settling the North American frontier in the eighteenth century. Above all, it points to the economic and military importance of the frontier in the expanding imperial struggles for control of the continent. Mountgomery might have greatly (and consciously) misrepresented the limited presence of "wandering Indians" in the region, but neither he nor his South Carolina supporters could ignore the threat of Indian or European competition. His plan for a fortified, walled bastion was a larger, more elaborate version of the fortresses and trading posts the European powers constructed to anchor their territorial claims. Moreover, this militarized zone would also be a pacified zone, where straight lines laid over an abundant landscape defined well-designed areas of human habitation. The lines that enclosed the land symbolized control not only of plants and animals but of people themselves. In the eyes of Mountgomery and other promoters of North American development, the frontier was hardly intended to be an open space of unfettered freedom for the pioneer farmer or trapper. It was envisioned as an ordered environment in which productive settlers accepted the authority of their superiors and supported the economic strategy of their sponsoring nation.

History seldom unfolds so neatly, of course. Throughout the eighteenth century, most a priori plans for frontier order were torn apart by people actually living on the land. Frontier regions remained the scene of continuing struggles for control—struggles between Indians and Europeans, between European imperial powers, even between European powers and their own settlers. By the end of the century, the largest group of Euro-Americans, Mountgomery's fellow subjects of the British crown, would rise up against imperial control and claim the right to determine future growth for themselves. Yet even in the new American nation, the United States, the future would be much like the past: those who attempted to impose a predetermined order on the frontier would find that their plans invariably ran up against the people who lived there.

———•———

The fact that the Margravate of Azilia ever made its way onto a few maps of North America provides in itself a useful lesson about the methods Europeans used to establish their claims to the continent. The lines and lettering that defined the colony gave it, albeit briefly, a more real presence on paper than it ever achieved on the land itself. Maps carry a certain authority, an assumption about the validity of scientific information conveyed in pictorial form. In the era of European exploration, maps were as much art as science, panoramic pictures of the Earth drawn from above, a perspective impossible in the pre-flight era. They often represented the world not as it really was but as the mapmaker (or, more to the point, the mapmaker's sponsor) wanted it to be. Thus maps became important instruments of imperial policy.

Yet, as documents of the struggle for control of the North American continent, the maps of the early European cartographers reveal just how fluid and fragile their assertions of authority could be. In many cases, mapping actually *preceded* exploration and certainly exceeded knowledge gained from direct observation. Much of what mapmakers claimed to know about the New World was based on incomplete information or vivid imagination. Well into the eighteenth century, for instance, some mapmakers depicted California as an island, a huge and wholly separate land mass set off from the rest of the continent. Much of the interior remained undefined, labeled simply "unknown" or "uninhabited." Even in the best of cases, actual surveys were expensive, and mapmakers had to rely on second-hand information from Indians and other inhabitants, not all of whom were friendly or forthcoming. In times of war, such informants often found it even more in their own interest to spread outright disinformation. Misleading mapmakers in such a way was an understandable strategy, but it resulted in many flawed drawings of the continent.

Yet, whatever they lacked in topographical detail, early European maps made up in political design. To a large degree, in fact, their main purpose was not to describe the land but to claim it. In the course of imperial competition for the North American continent, mapmakers often laid claim to much more territory than military leaders could ever hope to hold. Such claims did not go unchallenged, of course, and, well into the eighteenth century, European mapmakers fought battles on paper that seemed almost as significant as those their military counterparts waged on land and sea. English mapmakers put their mark on most of eastern North America, extending their claims as far west as the Mississippi and designating the coastal waters of the Atlantic as the "Sea of Carolina," the "Sea of Virginia," and the "Sea of New England." Not to be outdone, French mapmakers showed their country to be in control of most of the North American interior, limiting the English to the regions east of the Appalachian Mountains; in some cases they even took a piece out of the British possessions in the Carolinas. Then an English mapmaker, whose 1750 map "greatly improved" upon the French map from which it was copied, issued a stern warning to the French: because of recent Indian treaties, his map declared, "the Subjects of His Brittanic Majesty . . . [have] a right of possession from Lake Erie to the Chikasas at the River Missasipi; whereas in many of those Parts the French have no other Title than that of Intrusion and Force." This right had to be recognized, the cartographer continued, and the French mapmakers "are therefore advised to put their Louisiana farther West."

Mapmakers used maps not only to change or challenge the claims of competing European powers but also to diminish, even deny, the presence of Indian peoples on the land. Where Sir Robert Mountgomery used words to dismiss the significance of "wandering Indians," mapmakers often accomplished the same task with a variety of verbal and nonverbal elements—borderlines, place names, landmark symbols, lettering, and decorative material. The size and placement of the printed word, for instance, could create a symbolic image of the implied relationships between people and places: native people could be moved westward, out of the way of white settlement; their names could also be rendered in smaller print and visually relegated to an inferior and presumably less threatening status. (To understand the importance of this imagery, consider the effect if the situation were reversed—that is, if the names of Indian groups were printed in large letters and the names of European colonies in small: the power of the Europeans would no longer seem quite so imposing, nor would the prospects for settlement seem so encouraging.)

The implied meanings of European maps becomes clearer when one considers contemporary maps made by Indian peoples. As the Anglo-American cartographer Lewis Evans observed, Indians "do not generally bound their Countries with Lines." Yet his fellow explorer, Jonathan Carver, admitted that although Indians were, in his mind, "totally unskilled in geography . . . they draw on their birch-bark very exact charts or maps of the countries with which they are acquainted." Like Europeans, Indians drew maps to show relationships between people and space. The surviving maps of native peoples often reveal an ethnocentric view of a relatively limited, self-contained world. The mapmaker's group stood at the center of the map, usually symbolized by a circle and surrounded by other circles representing other groups. In this regard, as Gregory Waselkov has noted, Indian maps, like European maps, "are indeed political documents, graphic depictions of the balance of power." Yet, by drawing lines linking the circles, Indian mapmakers emphasized connection between peoples rather than control of the land.

By contrast, their European counterparts simply drew straight boundary lines and painted over huge swaths of land that ran westward almost to infinity, far beyond any reasonable reach. These straight-line designs represent the supreme assertion of cartographic control, the assumption that the straightness of the line could supersede the actual irregularity of the land—not to mention the people living on it. Throughout the era of colonization, maps were not so much records of actual exploration as outlines of anticipated appropriation. Long before Euro-Americans established dominance over the North American landscape or its native peoples, their maps gave them a vision—or perhaps a visualization— of future control. By drawing lines across the continent and imposing themselves in print, they literally mapped out a New World order.

It is one thing to claim control of land pictured on a map, of course, but quite another to establish control of the land itself; during the European colonization, the first process required ink, but the second required blood. The struggle for control of North America embroiled European governments and their American colonists in a series of wide-scale wars for almost a century—the War of the League of Augsburg or, as it was known in the English colonies, King William's War (1688–97); the War of the Spanish Succession, or Queen Anne's War (1702–13); the War of the Quadruple Alliance (1719–21); the War of Jenkins' Ear (1739–42); the War of the Austrian Succession, or King George's War (1740–48); and the Seven Years' War (1756–63). The fact that these wars acquired different names on different sides of the Atlantic underscores the two-front nature of the conflict, with fighting in both Europe and America. On the American continent, in fact, they were usually two-*frontier* wars, with separate theaters in the North and South. Throughout the long period of colonial conflict, the frontier was both the battleground and the prize.

It was an especially important prize to the English. From the beginning, English expansionists had looked longingly at North America as the solution to their country's social ills. As early as 1582, Richard Hakluyt had written about the benefits of sending "our superfluous population into those temperate and fertile parts of America which . . . are yet unpossessed by any Christians." Similarly, Robert Cushman made much the same argument forty years later, in 1622: pointing to the ill effects of human failure in what he described as an overcrowded and increasingly competitive society, Cushman implored English people not to "oppress, straiten, and afflict one another" but move to a "spacious land" in America where all could find new opportunity. In general, for a combination of demographic, economic, and religious motives, the English had followed a much more intensive approach to settlement than their European rivals. In addition to the soldiers, clergymen, and traders who were commonly in the vanguard of colonization, a comparatively large number of common people—men, women, and children, farmers, servants, and slaves—came to carve hundreds of towns, villages, and plantations out of the American wilderness. The combination of a high rate of reproduction and recurring immigration from Britain, other parts of northern Europe, and Africa created a sharp and steady rise in population; by 1750, the British colonies contained over 1.2 million people. By comparison, the Spanish and French colonies in North America numbered fewer than a hundred thousand European inhabitants, combined. Moreover, the English appetite for land to subdivide and settle as farms only increased with the growing number of mouths to feed. It was small wonder, then, that the British became especially aggressive expansionists in the first half of the eighteenth century.

Thus the course of conflict among the European powers led to the gradual extension of British influence over the eastern third of the continent. But expansion would not provide a permanent prize. Most of Great Britain's gains were undone by Anglo-American colonists in the American War for Independence (1775–83). The birth of the United States as an independent republic created a new competitor for control of the trans-Appalachian interior. Still, by the end of the eighteenth century, Britain, France, and Spain remained important forces on the American frontier, posing a challenge, sometimes a serious threat, to the claims of the new nation.

The complexities of Euro-American war and diplomacy were further exacerbated by the equally complex interests of Indian peoples, who also competed, both with Euro-Americans and with each other, for influence, territory, and trade. Indians played a critical role in each of the major European wars in North America, whether as active combatants or as interested neutrals; in some European-initiated campaigns, Indians made up well over half the fighting force. Indeed, given the small number of European soldiers or armed settlers on the North American frontier, European officials found it impossible to pursue their imperial policies over such a vast expanse of territory without Indian allies. One of the great ironies of American history is that Euro-Americans could not have taken control of the continent without Indian help.

That is not to say, however, that Indians became mere cannon fodder in these frontier conflicts. They entered into alliances with Europeans to pursue their own goals, especially to gain an advantage over their own Indian enemies. Moreover, Indians initiated hostilities, sometimes just when war-weary Europeans thought they had resolved their imperial conflicts. Two such Indian uprisings, the Yamassee War (1715–17) and Pontiac's Rebellion (1763–64), made the European powers painfully aware that treaties negotiated by ambassadors around a conference table could not guarantee peace on the American frontier. The United States would learn that lesson soon after gaining its independence—and would keep learning it for more than a century.

Yet in the more immediate context of the eighteenth century, when the ultimate outcome of the contest for the continent was still uncertain, Europeans and Indians interacted with each other in ever-changing patterns of diplomacy that defied simple assumptions of military or cultural superiority. In a sense, by confronting each other as significant actors, whether adversaries or allies, they also had to confront each other as equals.

The conflict the English colonists called Queen Anne's War provides a good illustration of the interplay of European and Indian interests. Unlike King William's War, which took place primarily on the northern frontier, Queen Anne's War was the first of the major two-front, two-frontier wars that marked the eighteenth century. It also directed greater attention to the trans-Appalachian territory, drawing Europeans deeper into the Indians' interior, thus creating new opportunities for intercultural contact —and for intercultural conflict as well.

The stage had been set in the South long before the war itself erupted. During the seventeenth century, Spanish Franciscans carried Christianity to the native peoples of Florida, and by the 1670s they had established a string of over thirty churches in four mission provinces—Guale, Timucua, Apalachee, and Apalachicola—that ran northward a hundred miles up the Atlantic coast from Saint Augustine and westward over 250 miles across the Florida panhandle. Although the Franciscans numbered only around forty, they claimed to have converted thousands of native people to the Catholic faith. To be sure, this missionary effort created resistance and occasional rebellion among the native peoples of Florida, but the result was still impressive: a handful of missionaries, working without much military support, had succeeded in establishing a seemingly permanent Spanish presence in Florida.

But beginning in 1670, with the creation of the Carolina colony, the English quickly became an important European presence in the Southeast, challenging the Spanish for influence over the Indians in the region. From their coastal enclave at Charles Town, aggressive Carolina traders ranged deep into the interior, where they developed relations with native peoples as far west as the Mississippi. As one trader later observed, "the English trade for Cloth always atracts and maintains the obedience and friendship of the Indians," who delivered tens of thousands of deerskins to be shipped back to England.

They also delivered hundreds, perhaps thousands, of other Indians to be shipped as slaves to the West Indies. The seemingly insatiable English demand for slave labor on Caribbean sugar plantations made slave-catching expeditions an important and profitable enterprise for both Indian captors and Carolina traders. This cruel commerce created strong, if sometimes short-lived, Anglo-Indian alliances. As Theda Perdue, a historian of Indians in the Southeast, has observed, "slaves became the objects of warfare rather than merely by-products." English-inspired Indian slave raids against Spanish mission settlements were instrumental in forcing the Spanish and their Indian allies to give up several outposts and adopt a defensive footing in Florida.

The other serious European competition to English expansion in the Southeast came from the French, who had settled in the region even later than the English. The French explorer Robert de La Salle claimed the lower Mississippi region for France in 1682, but it would be almost two decades before the French actually settled there in any numbers. In 1699, another explorer, Pierre Le Moyne d'Iberville, established a temporary base at Biloxi Bay, near the mouth of the Mississippi River; three years later he founded a more permanent settlement about fifty miles east along the Gulf of Mexico (where Mobile, Alabama, is today) and made it the capital of the new colony of Louisiana, named in honor of his king, Louis XIV. But Iberville knew that Carolina traders had already made contact with Indians in the interior, especially the powerful Chickasaws, and it would be only a matter of time before the English sought to break France's fragile hold on the region.

Realizing he could do little militarily, Iberville turned to diplomacy. First, he made an alliance with the Choctaws, who sought French assistance in their long-standing struggles against the Chickasaws. Then, in a remarkable display of persuasion, he brought Choctaw and Chickasaw leaders together and convinced them to put aside their mutual hostility (at least for a while), eject the English traders, and trade instead with the French. By extending the treaty to include the other main Indian group in the region, the Creeks, Iberville thus secured the safety of his infant settlement.

But stopping English expansion would not be enough for the French. Iberville's relations with the Indians were part of a much more elaborate strategy to uproot the English from Carolina and eventually drive them all the way up the Atlantic coast, even as far as New York. With that in mind, Iberville devised an attack on Charles Town in which a combined force of French, Spanish, and Indian allies would assault the English settlement from land and sea. The outbreak of war in Europe in 1702 provided a convenient context for this dramatic venture.

The attack, though long in planning, fell far short in execution. Iberville's expedition was not ready to make an assault until August 1706, and by that time the military leaders of South Carolina had fortified Charles Town and organized a defensive force of English settlers, African slaves, and Indian allies. The Franco-Spanish force foundered on the beaches, leaving behind more than two hundred captured troops, and the small French fleet was driven away. Over the next three years, rumors of new attacks circulated throughout Carolina, forcing the English to shore up both their defenses and their Indian alliances. In the end, however, the rumors proved to be no more than that.

In the meantime, the English were making their own moves. For several years before the outbreak of war, in fact, Carolina slave-dealers and their Creek Indian allies had already been making regular incursions into Florida, preying on the Apalachee Indians and destroying Spanish missions. Now the larger war legitimized larger efforts. In the summer of 1702, with the formal declaration of war still a rumor in the colonies, the governor of South Carolina, James Moore, assembled an expedition to attack the Spanish stronghold at Saint Augustine. Moore argued that the capture of Saint Augustine would not only undermine Spanish power to the south but also provide a staging area for attacks against the French in Louisiana. Some of Moore's critics in Carolina were skeptical of the venture, suggesting that it was little more than another lucrative slave raid (which he certainly intended it to be).

Moore's first attempt to overthrow the Spanish garrison at Saint Augustine ended in failure, but two years later, in 1704, he again led an expedition to Florida against the Apalachees, this time with much greater success. Having been shorn of his governorship in the wake of his 1702 defeat, he had only lukewarm support and no financial assistance from the Carolina assembly, which urged him to "endeavour to gain [by] all peaceable means if possible the Appalaches to our interest." But, without financial support, Moore had little patience for "peaceable means." He would have to finance his campaign by taking slaves and plunder. Leading a combined force of fifty Englishmen and a thousand allied Indians, he made devastating attacks against Apalachee settlements and Spanish missions, overwhelming some and forcing others to surrender. Some mission-based Apalachees even supported Moore in his effort: long disaffected by Spanish attitudes and now attracted by English guns and trade goods, they joined the attacks against the Franciscan missions. As David J. Weber points out, "Although Spaniards saw Englishmen as the sole cause of the destruction of the Florida missions, their demise should also be recognized as a massive rebellion by Indian neophytes."

In less than two years, James Moore captured several hundred Apalachees to be sold as slaves in the Charles Town market, and he forced over a thousand more to resettle on the southern border of South Carolina, where they could serve as a buffer against Spanish and French incursions. (So complete was Moore's conquest of the Apalachees, in fact, that it found its way onto an official map: the Apalachee area was later labeled "Wholly laid waste being destroyed by the Carolinians, 1706.") All this, Moore reported with satisfaction, "I have done with the loss of 4 whites and 15 Indians, and without one Penny charge to the Publick." Moore's expedition, combining the interests of empire and enterprise, was as effective as it was economical: the destruction of the Franciscan missions undermined Spain's influence in Florida, making it less likely that the Spanish could call on Indian allies in a fight against the English. In turn, the reduced threat to Carolina's southern frontier encouraged Carolina officials to become more aggressive in their efforts to extend their influence westward.

One of the most active promoters of westward expansion was Thomas Nairne, who had a brief yet colorful career on the Carolina frontier. Nairne owned a large plantation on Saint Helena, one of the coastal islands south of Charles Town, but the settled life of a planter was not enough for Nairne. He also made a name for himself as an Indian fighter as a member of Moore's expedition against the Apalachees, and he had gained the reputation of being one of the most knowledgeable men in the colony on Indian relations. After being appointed Indian agent for South Carolina in

1707, he journeyed into Indian territory as far west as the Mississippi, mapping the region and writing about the people he encountered. (The journal of his travels remains a remarkably useful account, with perceptive comparisons between Indian and English cultures.) His contact with Indians first paid off in 1708, when he negotiated a treaty with the Choctaws, who had earlier concluded an alliance with Nairne's equally colorful French counterpart, Iberville. Back in South Carolina, however, Nairne received little acclaim for his achievement: soon after his return to Charles Town, he was jailed, allegedly for treason, by Governor Nathaniel Johnson, with whom Nairne had feuded for several years.

Yet, even while locked up in the Charles Town jail, Nairne devised a grand design for the future of the frontier, which he sent to the Secretary of State in London; indeed, the leading historian of the Southern frontier, Verner W. Crane, has called Nairne a "visionary" among eighteenth-century Euro-American imperialists. Nairne first called attention to the strategic importance of the South Carolina frontier, which even the South Carolina Proprietors had not fully appreciated. By strengthening the southern border, England could create a strong bastion against Spanish and French encroachment into the northern English colonies—against just the kind of expansionist policy Iberville had in mind.

But Nairne was by no means talking of taking only a defensive posture. He also called for pushing England's claims westward, taking in the land in Florida recently inhabited by the Apalachees, the French outpost at Mobile, and the watershed of the Tennessee River as far as the Mississippi, perhaps even beyond. From the Mississippi it would be only one more step to reach for the Spanish mines farther west. The idea, as he explained to the government officials, was to pursue a policy so that "the English American Empire may not be unreasonably Crampt up." Nairne's reach exceeded England's grasp, at least in the immediate context of imperial warfare. Still, his vision of an expanding empire predicted the path of English policy throughout most of the eighteenth century.

In the northern theater of Queen Anne's War, in Canada and New England, the prospect of English expansion seemed much less likely. At the outset, the French had exercised greater finesse in establishing delicate diplomatic relationships with the dominant

Indian groups of the region, especially the Abenakis and Iroquois, long-standing enemies whose mutual hostility had festered seemingly forever. The Abenakis were lured away from a loose alliance with the English by the new governor-general of New France, the Marquis de Vaudreuil, an experienced soldier who had spent time in Canada and knew the ways of frontier warfare. Vaudreuil also counted on the help of French Mohawks, people of the Five Nations who had migrated north into Canada in the 1660s and had settled in Jesuit mission villages. On the other hand, the vast majority of the Iroquois, those who inhabited the traditional Five Nations territory in New York, essentially sat out the war and resisted the attempts of the English to recruit them as allies. Unlike the skillful Vaudreuil, the new governor of New York, Edward Hyde, Viscount Cornbury, lacked the proper appreciation for the customs of Indian diplomacy; soon after taking office in 1702, he offended the Iroquois with his clumsy, often insulting actions. But even if Cornbury had not been so incompetent in his diplomatic dealings, the Iroquois probably would have stayed out of the fray anyway. The long series of Beaver Wars—especially the most recent one, which became embedded in the European conflict the English called King William's War—had seriously depleted the Five Nations' fighting power: between 1689 and 1698, the number of warriors had fallen by perhaps a fifth. Now faced with the outbreak of another European war following so close on the heels of the last one, the weakened Iroquois were inclined to let others fight while they watched from the sidelines and rebuilt their strength. Thus, with the Abenakis as active allies and most of the Iroquois as cautious spectators, the French were able to threaten English settlements all across the northern frontier of New England.

The most devastating and dramatic event in the early part of the war came on February 29, 1704, with the celebrated sack of Deerfield, Massachusetts, a small, isolated English outpost of just under three hundred inhabitants on the upper Connecticut River—the "most Utmost Frontere Town in the County of West Hampshire," as it was described by the Massachusetts General Court. In the hours before dawn, an attacking force of between two hundred and three hundred men—around fifty French soldiers and *courers de bois* and the rest a variety of Indian allies—crept unseen across the snow to the palisades of the village. According to legend, the sentry on duty in Deerfield was either asleep or distracted, but whatever the case, he never saw the attacking party or sounded the alarm— until it was too late. Taking advantage of snow drifted high against the palisade, a group of Indians scrambled over the walls and opened the gates for the rest. Within minutes the attackers ran throughout the northern end of the town, breaking into houses and killing people who had scarcely awakened from sleep. Some of the stunned English settlers managed to get to their firearms and fight back, and for almost three hours the battle raged from house to house.

The flames from the burning village glowed in the pre-dawn sky, alerting the English inhabitants of towns thirty miles to the south. Reinforcements rushed to Deerfield, but by the time they arrived, around nine o'clock in the morning, most of the town had been laid waste. Forty-nine residents and five of the twenty soldiers garrisoned there had been killed, 109 had been taken prisoner, and seventeen out of forty-one houses had been burned. As the French and Indian force withdrew from the town with its string of captives, the English reinforcements flew to attack the stragglers in the rear, but they ran too far, fell into an ambush, and had to retreat.

The attackers had gained an almost total victory. Their point had not been to take and occupy the town, but to take captives and spread terror among the English settlers living on the northern frontier of New England. With this surprise attack in the dead of winter, a time when large forces were not generally expected to move on the offensive, the French served notice that they could strike suddenly, anytime and anywhere. They also showed the English (and perhaps the Iroquois as well) that their alliances with the Abenakis and other Indians were not mere paper arrangements. They had now been sealed in blood.

The Indians involved in the attack also had their own points to make. Indeed, as Evan Haefeli and Kevin Sweeney have demonstrated in a detailed analysis of the Deerfield attack, the very diversity of the Indian allies—Western Abenakis, including Cowassucks, Norwottucks, Pocumtucks, Pennacooks, Sokokis, and others; French Mohawks; and Hurons—suggests an almost equal diversity of motives: to take captives, to take revenge, to make good on alliances, or some combination of these and other considerations. In short, the French and the Indians played respective but related parts in an effective combined attack. As Richard Melvoin, a very even-handed historian of the sack of Deerfield, has observed, "[T]he raid made sense—at least from the French and Indian points of view."

But, in the long run, the attack on Deerfield also worked against the French and the Indians. It united and energized the English, shocking them into the realization that they had to do something in response. In the aftermath of the attack, some New England ministers, true to the ever-present Puritan emphasis on guilt, bemoaned the "awful and dreadful dispensation of Gods hand at Deerfield." The Massachusetts General Court likewise declared a day of fasting and prayer, urging the people to look inward for the sources of the divine displeasure that had surely brought on the disaster at Deerfield. But the government also called upon them to turn outward against their mortal enemies, the French and the Indians. French settlers and peaceful Indians who lived in the midst of English inhabitants immediately became the subject of close surveillance; any suspicion of intrigue with the French and Indian forces on the frontier could result in quick incarceration and even death. The governments of Massachusetts and Connecticut set aside their bickering and began cooperating in a renewed program of military preparedness, fortifying frontier towns and recruiting several hundred volunteers to patrol the northern frontier from Deerfield in western Massachusetts to Wells in the Maine territory. To encourage the volunteers, Massachusetts more than doubled its bounty on Indian scalps.

In addition to bolstering their defenses, the New England colonies began to take the offensive. Soon after the Deerfield debacle, Connecticut's Governor Fitz-John Winthrop suggested that Connecticut, Massachusetts, and New York undertake a joint expedition against Canada. Over the course of the next few years, in 1707 and again in 1709, New England troops attempted to take Port Royal (in French Acadia, or what is now Nova Scotia), but both attacks ended in failure and frustration. Finally, in 1710, the English colonists gained their prize. While British ships patrolled the waters off the coast, the New England troops besieged and, within a week, took Port Royal.

Their success in Canada had an important impact on the European struggle for control of North America. In 1713, when the

Anglo-American forces were in the process of staging yet another attack on Canada, the warring parties in Europe finally agreed to stop fighting. The Treaty of Utrecht, though concerned primarily with the redistribution of power and possessions in Europe, also changed the face of the American frontier—at least on paper. Not only did the French grant the British a sizable part of their Canadian claims—the Hudson's Bay territory, Newfoundland, and Nova Scotia—but they also gave them the right to claim sovereignty over the Iroquois and other Indians farther west in the interior. This apparent French concession to British military superiority meant, if nothing else, that New Englanders along the northern frontier, including the edgy inhabitants of Deerfield, could now breathe easier, hopeful that they could live for a while in peace and security. Moreover, the terms of the treaty brought into sharper focus the expansionist vision of men like Thomas Nairne, who were already taking aim at the trans-Appalachian West. Even though the British had neither the human nor the military resources to exert control over the vast territories they had acquired, they could dream of future conquest.

The dreams of the British, however, ran up against the reality of the Indians. No matter what the Treaty of Utrecht said about settling the struggle among Europeans, Indian peoples—who had not been party to the peace talks—had their own foreign policies to pursue and wars to fight.

That became evident even before the end of Queen Anne's War, in 1711, when the Tuscarora Indians rose up against the increasing European encroachment on their territory in what is now western North Carolina. The Tuscarora War was a comparatively short but brutal struggle, with gruesome atrocities committed by both sides. To combat the Tuscaroras, the governors of South Carolina and North Carolina cooperated in enlisting colonial militiamen and Yamassee, Cherokee, Creek, and Catawba allies, and this combined force smashed the Tuscaroras in a decisive battle in March 1713. Those Tuscaroras not killed or captured to be sold as slaves eventually withdrew from the Carolinas, migrating northward to join their kinspeople in the Iroquois Five Nations.

But the English settlers in South Carolina had little time to savor the victory in either Queen Anne's War or the Tuscarora War before they were faced with yet another conflict, this time against the Yamassee Indians. Since the beginning of the eighteenth century, the Yamassees had served South Carolinians as a useful buffer on the southern boundary, where they were both trading partners and military allies; they had even joined the Carolinians in their campaign against the Tuscaroras. But they had essentially the same grievances against English encroachment as the Tuscaroras had. Moreover, they especially resented the ill treatment they received from Carolina traders, who were widely accused of theft, rape, and even murder. By early 1715, the Yamassees had had enough, and in April they launched attacks against exposed settlements. (One of their first victims was their former neighbor Thomas Nairne, the Carolina Indian agent and architect of British expansion. They captured him on the first day of the war and then took their time over the next few days burning him, very slowly, at the stake.) For almost a year, the Yamassees, Creeks, and smaller Indian groups in the region posed a serious threat to South Carolina's security, coming dangerously close to Charles Town. But again, military cooperation between the Carolinas and, equally important, the recruitment of the Cherokees as allies stopped the Yamassee advance. Like the Tuscaroras, the Yamassees and Creeks were eventually driven out of South Carolina to seek refuge farther south.

The Tuscarora and Yamassee wars thus resulted in the removal of sizable Indian groups from the Carolinas. But the British success in war still did not open the way to easy expansion. Other powerful Indian groups remained an imposing presence on both the southern and the northern frontiers. Indeed, the many multisided conflicts served as a reminder that Indian peoples had their own territory and interests to protect, and they could make European expansion problematic if not impossible. That point would be reinforced repeatedly throughout the eighteenth century.

No case better illustrates the prominence of Indians in eighteenth-century warfare and diplomacy than that of the Iroquois confederacy (which, after the northward migration of the Tuscaroras, would expand from the Five Nations to become the Six Nations in the early 1720s). Not only were they a potent military force to counter the power of the Abenakis in the East, but they also stood as the main middlemen in the fur trade with Indians farther west, in the Ohio and upper Mississippi valleys. In the South, Iroquois carried on a seemingly endless yet generally successful series of conflicts against the Catawbas and Cherokees, which gave them an opportunity to gain both military glory and diplomatic leverage. Thus the Iroquois loomed as an unavoidable presence in the eastern part of the continent, and therefore an obvious object of European maneuvers.

The English had gained a significant advantage over their French adversaries in the late seventeenth century by forging a diplomatic arrangement known as the Covenant Chain. First established in 1677 by New York's Governor Sir Edmund Andros and reinforced in subsequent meetings over the course of many years, the Covenant Chain was essentially a non-aggression pact in which the Iroquois and some of their tributary allies—the Delawares, Shawnees, and Susquehannocks (or Conestogas, as they came to be called)—agreed to keep the peace with the English colonies. By making that arrangement, Andros relieved the pressure not only on his own colony of New York but also on all the English colonies from New England to Virginia, making it possible for the English to concentrate more of their military planning on the French. By the same token, peace with the English colonies meant that the Iroquois could likewise resist the economic and military power of the French, who were closely allied with the Hurons and other Iroquois competitors in the western fur trade. Moreover, the Anglo-Iroquois alliance gave the Iroquois freer range in carrying on intermittent warfare with their enemies both in the West and in the South.

To be sure, the Covenant Chain was not an all-encompassing alliance: the Iroquois confederacy still included groups that were friendly toward the French, not to mention others that preferred to remain neutral. More to the point, even though the Covenant Chain tilted the majority of the Iroquois people toward the English, it did not represent an ironclad commitment. In 1701, for instance, just on the eve of Queen Anne's War, the Iroquois were so weary and depleted from their own struggles in the long series of Beaver Wars that they chose a course of neutrality in the emerging European conflict, signing treaties with both the English and the French. Toward the end of Queen Anne's War, the English were able to coax the Iroquois out of their neutral stance and enlisted over four hundred warriors in the expeditions against Canada. But when the Anglo-American effort ended in failure, the Iroquois understood even better the value of neutrality. As Richard Aquila, a historian of the eighteenth-century Iroquois, explains, "The Five Nations filed away memories of those feeble military ventures. . . . The failure of the English expeditions of 1709 and 1711 convinced many Indians that the English, regardless of their promises or boasts, were not likely to conquer New France." The Covenant Chain notwithstanding, even the anglophile factions of the Iroquois continued to be cautious about taking up arms for the English.

Yet, while the Iroquois became disillusioned with English pretensions to power, they also had to consider the limits of their own power. Historians have recently argued that past perceptions of the Iroquois, both by European policymakers and by subsequent students of frontier affairs, greatly exaggerated the unity and authority of the Iroquois confederacy. The Iroquois confederacy was by no means a monolithic state with effective control over all its constituent parts. Confederacy policy was not codified in writing but was reinforced through the repeated renewal of face-to-face relationships among the leaders of many groups spread over a vast territory. Sometimes local groups made their own military or diplomatic moves, and other Iroquois leaders were powerless to stop them.

In some cases, in fact, the actions of one faction of the Six Nations worked to the detriment of another. In the early 1720s, for instance, both French and British officials began bargaining to build fortified blockhouses in Iroquois land to solidify their respective roles in the fur trade. The Onondagas, feeling uneasy with the construction of an English fortification in their territory at Oswego, agreed to allow the French to build a blockhouse at Niagara—which was not in their territory but in that of the Senecas. The Senecas were unhappy with the Onondagas' action, but they could do little to change it: when they sought to enlist other Indian allies to attack Niagara and other French outposts, almost everyone refused, or quietly failed to respond.

At the same time, a group of Iroquois leaders, mostly Cayugas and Onondagas, had begun to engage in dealings with English officials in Pennsylvania that ultimately resulted in the displacement of some of the Six Nations' southern allies. In order to gain assurances that the Pennsylvania government would not promote settlement in the northern part of the province, close to the Six Nations' homelands, the Iroquois delegation offered to sell Pennsylvania land in the Susquehanna region—an area occupied by the Delawares, Shawnees, and Conestogas, all of whom were part of the Covenant Chain. Pennsylvania officials were greatly interested in accelerating Euro-American settlement there for a variety of public and private reasons. By supporting new settlers in the Susquehanna region (mostly recent Scots-Irish and German immigrants), the Pennsylvania government would not only increase its claim to Indian land but could also strengthen its stance against its southern neighbor, Maryland, which had long disputed the border between the two colonies. Moreover, several Pennsylvania leaders—most notably Governor James Logan and Thomas and John Penn, the sons of the colony's founder, William Penn—also stood to make substantial personal profits in land sales.

The mutual diplomatic desires of the Iroquois and colonial leaders had a dramatic impact on the Indians whose homelands were in the Susquehanna region. In 1735, Governor Logan and the Penn brothers produced a dubious-looking copy of an allegedly lost 1686 deed, which said that the Delawares had agreed to cede a large swath of land in southeastern Pennsylvania—as wide a band as a man could walk in a day and a half. Despite the Delawares' complaints of fraud, the Pennsylvania officials went ahead and staged the walk in 1737 (using very swift walkers on a previously blazed trail), and the "Walking Purchase" provided the justification for depriving the Delawares of most of their lands.

Rather than support the Delawares and their other allies in the area, the Iroquois acted almost as agents for the English (and were paid handsomely for their efforts). In 1742, the Onondaga leader Canasatego berated those Delawares who had not already given up their lands and removed westward to the Ohio country:

Cousins . . . You ought to be taken by the Hair of the Head and shaked severely till you recover your Senses and become Sober; you don't know what Ground you stand on nor what you are doing. . . . We charge You to remove instantly. We don't give you the liberty to think about it.

You are Women; take the Advice of a Wise Man and remove immediately.

In general, the Iroquois role in helping dispossess the Indians of
the Susquehanna region was, as Daniel Richter has observed, "certainly one of the less admirable moments in the Six Nations' history." Nonetheless, Richter argues, it enabled them, once again,
to play the role of intercultural power broker—even when their
actual power was somewhat limited.

In a sense, the Iroquois almost always had frontier problems of
their own, certainly as great as those of the Europeans. Throughout the first half of the eighteenth century, they were trying both
to extend their influence over other Indian groups in the West and
South and to defend their own territory from the increasing intru-
sions of the French and the British. To do so, they had to develop
a delicate yet at times somewhat desperate sort of diplomacy that
combined all available approaches—aggression, neutrality, rap-
prochement, retreat—and courted all available allies, whether Indian or European. The Iroquois were always looking for allies, and
then always trying to use one alliance to enhance another: Europeans were impressed because the Iroquois seemed to have so
much influence over tributary tribes; other Indians were impressed
because the Iroquois seemed to have so much influence with Europeans. Perhaps the continuing significance of the Iroquois in
frontier affairs is a reasonable measure of their success. Richard
Aquila has argued that Iroquois diplomacy—what he calls their
"Restoration Policy"—enabled them to maintain internal unity
and shore up their strength against European encroachments. Yet
Francis Jennings offers a somewhat more skeptical view of Iroquois
diplomacy. "It was a juggling act that can only be admired for the
performers' virtuosity," he concludes, "but it was not the same
thing as independent power."

Taking a broader view, of course, one can say that everyone had
to be a juggler, and no one possessed independent power. All the
major players in the eighteenth-century frontiers—the Spanish,
French, and British, the Iroquois, Cherokees, Creeks, and numerous other Indian groups—had to be adept at keeping several dip-

lomatic balls in the air at once. Moreover, hardly anyone stayed in the same spot, but kept jockeying for bigger and better space on the stage. The resulting scene was a confoundingly complex pattern of multisided, cross-cultural alliances that rose and fell, turned and shifted with sometimes surprising speed. And in the midst of all the juggling and jockeying, there was almost always fighting. One war's wounds had scarcely healed before the next war inflicted new ones, and even peace treaties brought precious little peace.

The Spanish had reason to feel especially beset by the other European players in the imperial competition. When the War of the Quadruple Alliance broke out in Europe in 1719, France began to encroach on the holdings of its former ally. Acting before most Spanish officials in North America even knew that war had been declared, the French took the Spanish fort at Pensacola, Florida, and captured a Spanish mission in east Texas. Even more menacingly, they were reported to have their sights set on the Spanish garrison at Santa Fe. The Spanish sought to meet the French threat to New Mexico by sending an expeditionary force of forty-five Spaniards and sixty Pueblo Indians to the Great Plains, several hundred miles away in what is now Nebraska but what was then Pawnee territory. Unfortunately for this far-ranging force, the Pawnees were allied with the French and, more important, were opposed to having unwelcome outsiders in their neighborhood; they attacked the Spanish–Pueblo interlopers, killing half of them and sending the rest fleeing back to New Mexico.

Spain also had to deal with the British, who always had one eye turned toward the ill-defined borderland between South Carolina and Florida. (That, of course, had been the focus of Sir Robert Mountgomery's designs for the Margravate of Azilia in 1717.) In 1733, James Oglethorpe accomplished what Mountgomery had proposed—the establishment of an English enclave in the disputed area below South Carolina. In Oglethorpe's original design for this new colony called Georgia, paupers and other unfortunates from the prisons of England would be given a chance to serve both themselves and their nation by settling the southern frontier: working small farms as free men, they would also be defending British lands from Spanish invasion.

In practice, Oglethorpe and his fellow Georgians adopted a much less defensive posture. Branching out from the original town of Savannah, they established two forts to the south, one of them only fifty miles from Saint Augustine. When a new round of warfare between Britain and Spain started in 1739—first the War of Jenkins' Ear (1739–42) and then, overlapping it, the War of the Austrian Succession (1740–48)—Oglethorpe went on the offensive in earnest. Supported by Creek, Cherokee, and Chickasaw allies, he captured several Spanish forts north of Saint Augustine. (The last of these, Fort Mose, a settlement of runaway slaves who had escaped South Carolina with the encouragement of Spanish officials, lay just two miles from Saint Augustine.) Although Oglethorpe was never able to capture Saint Augustine, he did succeed in keeping the Spanish from moving northward. From that point on, the contest for territory on the Southern frontier became essentially a stalemate.

There was anything but a stalemate between the British and the French on the Northern frontier, however. The imperial struggles of the middle of the eighteenth century—King George's War and the Seven Years' War—created an increasing focus on the trans-Appalachian territory bounded by the Great Lakes, the Ohio River, and the Mississippi River. In turn, the growing competition between the European powers created important shifts in attitude and alliance among the Indian groups who lived there. For the remainder of the eighteenth century, that region would be at the center of frontier contention.

The French held much the stronger hand at the outset of the mid-century struggle. For decades, the fur trade had given them extensive ties with the many Indian peoples throughout the region—the Huron–Petuns, Mingos, Miamis, Wyandots, Ottawas, and others. By contrast, the British were comparative newcomers to the region, and not very numerous at that. Following the Shawnees and Delawares in their forced migration westward from Pennsylvania, Anglo-American traders had begun to penetrate the market in the Ohio country, but by the 1740s they were still minor players, little more than an annoying presence to the French. Moreover, even though their main Indian allies, the Iroquois, had long claimed dominance over tributary tribes in the region, the British could not count on them for much military support.

Yet the French played their hand foolishly, refusing to ante up as much as they should have. In the 1740s, in an effort to cut the costs of doing business with the Indians, the French began to curtail the supply of gifts and goods used for exchange in the fur trade. As furs began to fetch less, Indians began, understandably, to feel unhappy. They increasingly saw the French as two-faced allies who would ask them to go into battle on behalf of the French king yet expect them to accept less for the pelts they brought to French traders. This growing disenchantment with the French did not result in a wholesale shift of allegiance toward the British during King George's War; in fact, as Richard White notes, Indians increasingly came to "regard the British and the French as a single Christian threat." But in that sense, at least, the British had gained (or the French had fallen to) an equal footing in frontier relations.

Accordingly, both the French and the British started to strengthen their respective positions. In 1749, to reassert their presence south of Canada after their defeat in King George's War, the French sent Captain Pierre-Joseph Céloron de Blainville on a roundabout route from Canada through western New York and Pennsylvania into the Ohio country and back up across Lake Erie. At various points along the way, Céloron buried lead plates in the ground, supposedly to make clear to everyone the extent of French authority. Within a few years, the French decided that wooden stockades were much more visible and convincing than lead plates, and they began building new frontier forts in the Ohio country.

The British had the same idea. During the 1740s, Pennsylvania traders had begun establishing outposts in the region, and the provincial assembly supported their work to help bolster Pennsylvania's western claims. Virginia also claimed the Ohio territory; its colonial charter granted it land as far west as the Great Lakes. In the aftermath of King George's War, land- (and profit-) hungry Virginians began to look longingly at the Northwest, where they hoped to organize settlement and sell property; in 1749 the British government chartered two land companies, the Ohio Company and the Loyal Company, whose members included men from some of the colony's leading families. In 1753, to protect the interests of these elite Virginians against the rapidly fortifying French, Lieutenant Governor Robert Dinwiddie sent a young militia officer, George Washington, into the Ohio country to investigate French intentions. When Washington returned and reported that the French seemed intent on staying, Dinwiddie ordered that Virginia build a fort of its own at the point where the Allegheny and Monongahela rivers converged to form the Ohio River (modern-day Pittsburgh).

It was a fine site for a fort, but unfortunately, the French thought so, too. Soon after the Virginians began construction, a French force of around a thousand men captured the work party, destroyed their fort, and began building a fort of their own, to be named in honor of the French governor of Canada and the Ohio country, the Marquis de Duquesne. Once again, George Washington arrived on the scene—too late to protect his fellow Virginians but not too late, he hoped, to dislodge the French. With a comparatively small force—fewer than five hundred men—under his command, he built his own outpost nearby, the aptly named Fort Necessity. Before Washington could attack the French at Fort Duquesne, however, they attacked him at Fort Necessity, on July 3, 1754, and forced him to surrender. The French officer in command, Captain Coulon de Villiers, graciously allowed Washington and his surviving men to go back to Virginia. After all, their nations were at peace.

But not for long. The flurry of fort-building in the Ohio country soon drew Britain and France back into war—this one the last great imperial war fought in North America, the final major frontier struggle among the European powers. It began in July 1755, when a combined force of British regulars and Virginia militiamen commanded by the British General Edward Braddock marched again on Fort Duquesne, only to fall, foolishly, into a catastrophic ambush at the hands of the French and their Indian allies. (General Braddock was killed in the battle, along with two-thirds of his troops. Young Washington, now on his third mission to Pennsylvania in the space of two years, had to lead his second retreat to Virginia.) The colonial conflict soon escalated to become a global struggle among the powers of Europe, the Seven Years' War (1756–63). In this case, however, the North American front was no longer a mere sideshow in a larger European conflict. It was the main theater of the fighting, and both the British and the French committed thousands of regular troops to the fight.

In the early years of the conflict, the fighting focused on various French garrisons. In July 1758, the British–American army made successive (and near-suicidal) assaults on the French stronghold at the southern end of Lake Champlain, Fort Ticonderoga, only to retreat with heavy casualties. Then, just a few weeks after the debacle at Ticonderoga, British fortunes changed for the better. Fort Louisbourg, the strategic French garrison on Cape Breton Island that had been taken by Anglo-American troops in 1746 and then given back by the treatymakers at the end of King George's War, fell to the British in late July. In August, so did Fort Frontenac, the critical French outpost at the point where Lake Ontario empties into the Saint Lawrence River. Three months later, in the face of an advancing Anglo-American force, the French blew up and abandoned Fort Duquesne. The second half of 1758 proved to be a turning point for the British, setting the stage for a large-scale invasion of Canada. The celebrated victory of the British General James Wolfe over the French General Louis Joseph, Marquis de Montcalm, at Quebec in September 1759 gave the British one of the keys to control of the Saint Lawrence, and the capture of Montreal a year later gave them another.

At that point, the European war for American empire was all but over. According to the Treaty of Paris in 1763, the French surrendered all of Canada and their North American possessions east of the Mississippi River, with the exception of New Orleans. The Spanish, who had entered the war late on the side of France, gave up Florida. The British had achieved a stunning triumph in the long struggle for control of the continent.

As always, however, European claims to control extended only as far as the nearest Indians. Indeed, the British had recognized their vulnerability in Indian affairs at the outset of the war, even before the shooting had started in earnest. In June 1754, colonial delegates met with Iroquois leaders in Albany, New York, to try to gain Iroquois support for the impending imperial conflict. The Iroquois were not impressed with the Anglo-American appeal, however, especially since colonial land agents were continually encroaching on Indian land. They eventually offered a few vague statements of friendship and accepted thirty wagonloads of gifts in return, but they left Albany without giving the British any assurances. Throughout the early stages of the war, only the Mohawks provided significant military support for the Anglo-Americans; the westernmost of the Six Nations, the Senecas, joined with the Delawares and other Ohio Indians and sided with the French.

Most Indians fought for the French—or, more to the point, against the British. The Anglo-Americans seemed perhaps the greater of the two European threats because of their huge and increasingly predatory population; Indians did not need census figures to know that land-hungry Anglo-Americans were pressing westward. Especially in the Ohio region, where the Delawares and Shawnees still smarted from their forced removal from Pennsylvania a generation earlier, anti-British sentiment had been high even before the war. Now the outbreak of open conflict between the two European powers gave the Ohio Indians a new opportunity to settle old scores—which the Delawares and Shawnees did to frightening effect, raiding settlements in Pennsylvania and creating a serious western threat to the British colonies. As Richard White explains, the Ohio Indians pursued a "parallel war" against the British. They were not enamored of the French by any means, but in the immediate context of the conflict, the French seemed much the lesser of two evils.

That anti-British stance eventually underwent a dramatic change, however. Beginning in 1756, worried Pennsylvania officials had begun negotiations with the Delawares to try to stop the attacks on their western flank. Two years later, they restored previously ceded lands west of the Appalachian Mountains to the Iroquois in an effort to enlist their help in pacifying the Delawares. At the Treaty of Easton, Pennsylvania, in October 1758, the Delawares agreed to give up their pro-French position, and the Iroquois promised to keep an eye on their Delaware dependents. It helped, too, that the British had begun to run up a string of critical victories against the French. The Indians understood which way the winds of war were blowing, and it took little coaxing for them to turn in the more desirable direction.

Yet, when the French presence receded more fully in the wake of the Seven Years' War, the limitations of the Indians' parallel war policy became especially evident. They could no longer play one European power off against the other but had to deal directly with the British. For some, that meant trying to work out new terms of trade, albeit in a less competitive market. For others, it meant war.

No sooner had the British signed the Treaty of Paris than they had to face a frontier uprising of Indians in the Ohio country in 1763. Pontiac, a leader of the Ottawas, is generally credited with being the main motive force behind this revolt, but he was only the most famous figure in what was really a pattern of widespread resistance to the increased British presence. Throughout the region of former French influence, native groups had become wary of the new European power in their midst, especially since the British did not seem to be generous trading partners. The British commander in the Ohio country, General Jeffrey Amherst, had little respect for Indians and even less interest in the customary rituals of mutual respect that had traditionally defined dealing with Indians. As Richard White has put it, Amherst "blustered into Indian affairs with the moral vision of a shopkeeper and the arrogance of a victorious soldier." He put an end to gift-giving and the sale of rum, and he restricted the amount of gunpowder Indians could obtain. Indians, understandably, felt resentful and even fearful of this new imperial policy. The French may have had their faults, but the British had almost no discernible virtues.

Another underlying cause for conflict lay below the surface of anti-British sentiment, deep in the souls of the Indians themselves. In the early 1760s, just as the British were establishing themselves in the Ohio country, a Delaware Indian named Neolin had begun to gain prominence as a prophet among the peoples of the region. Neolin had had visions in which the Master of Life spoke to him about how far the Indians had strayed from the proper way of living. They drank too much, the Master said, they fought among themselves, and they prayed to evil spirits. Moreover, they had become so dependent on European trade goods that they had lost the ability to live on the natural abundance the Master had given them.

> Before those whom you call your brothers had arrived, did not your bow and arrow maintain you? You needed neither gun, powder, nor any other object. The flesh of animals was your food, their skins your raiment.

The Master now called upon the people to reject the foreign goods and the people who brought them.

> Drive them away; wage war against them. I love them not. They know me not. They are my enemies, they are your brothers' enemies. Send them back to the lands I have made for them. Let them remain there.

Neolin was by no means the first Indian prophet to preach spiritual and cultural renewal, but he was suddenly one of the most effective. Coming at a time of transition in the political and economic order of the Ohio country, especially when Amherst's policies had made the terms of trade comparatively rigid and disadvantageous for Indians, Neolin's call for change fell on receptive ears. For Pontiac and other leaders, it served as a call to arms.

The series of uprisings known collectively as Pontiac's Rebellion threatened to drive the British out of the Ohio country even before they had become firmly established. Indians launched devastating attacks, overwhelming several British outposts and turning on the larger garrisons at Forts Detroit, Pittsburgh, and Niagara. But those three forts held out, and a worried British government dispatched reinforcements of regular troops. Facing a larger military force and suffering from limited supplies, Pontiac and his allies could not dislodge the British. They carried on the struggle into 1764, but the war had become essentially a stalemate. Indian groups began to make separate peace treaties with the British, and in 1765 Pontiac likewise accepted a settlement.

The British had survived another round of frontier warfare, but they had no assurance that peace would be permanent. In the aftermath of the uprising, the best they could do was to avoid creating more Indian unrest in the Northwest. That depended, they reasoned, on keeping their own colonists out of the region. For years, British and provincial officials had been worried about land-hungry squatters who moved westward into Indian country; such people were commonly characterized as "scum," the "dregs of society," lawless "banditti" who only stirred up trouble among the Indians. Accordingly, in October 1763, in the face of the sudden Indian uprisings that threatened the army's very existence in the Northwest, the British government issued a proclamation that prohibited Anglo-American settlers from living west of the Appalachian Mountains. In effect, the authorities in London drew a line on the map running down the Appalachian ridgeline from Maine to Georgia, thus creating two separate zones of settlement: the western part would be Indian territory, regulated by the British Army; all other British subjects would be limited to the eastern part.

What seemed like sensible regulation in London seemed more

like restrictive confinement in the colonies. Land-hungry Anglo-Americans felt that they had fought effectively in the late war, and now they deserved to reap the benefits of the peace. No prize looked more appealing than the land across the mountains. No official proclamation could deter them from claiming that prize, nor could the British Army. In the decade after the conclusion of the Seven Years' War, tens of thousands of Anglo-American colonists pushed through the Proclamation Line with impunity and took up land in the trans-Appalachian frontier. To those officials who called them "scum" or "banditti," they remained a resentful and potentially resistant force on the frontier. By the 1770s, they would add their resentment to the more widespread unrest that was pushing the Anglo-American colonies toward revolution.

Of all the images and associations brought to mind by the American Revolution, the frontier must be fairly far down the list. Almost immediately, popular memory conjures up rowdy crowds assaulting tax collectors and dumping tea; silk-stockinged statesmen delivering speeches and writing declarations; sturdy farmers leaving their plows and marching off in minuteman companies; and, finally, shabbily dressed soldiers shivering through the winter and occasionally winning a battle. If anything, the almost ridiculous Indian disguise of the participants in the Boston Tea Party makes the frontier seem even more distant from the drama of the Revolution. It was the urban mob, not the Mohawks, who made the defiant move toward conflict with Britain. Moreover, it was in the cities and settled areas that the most dramatic actions were played out.

Yet the American Revolution, like all other colonial wars fought on the continent up to that time, had its frontier front. Admittedly, the fighting on the frontier was essentially a sideshow to the main event, and sometimes a seemingly unrelated one at that. People living in frontier regions, both Native American and Euro-American, usually took a decidedly localistic approach to the broader conflict; different frontier groups took different sides in order to promote their own immediate interests. The intensity of these local conflicts seems all the more striking because they had so little apparent connection to the larger ideological or imperial

issues. In many cases, the standard designations of Patriot and Loyalist provided only a thin cover for Anglo-American factions that
often engaged in a brutal guerrilla war of plunder, murder, and
revenge. When General Nathanael Greene arrived in the South
Carolina backcountry to take command of the Continental troops
there in 1780, he was shocked at the savagery. The local militia
factions "pursue one another with the most relentless fury killing
and destroying each other whenever they meet," he wrote. "Indeed, a great part of this country is already laid waste and is in the
utmost danger of becoming a desert."

On one level, the interaction of these various local struggles with
the larger conflict reflected the complex mix of alliances and brutal
rules of battle that had marked earlier frontier wars. But this war
seemed somehow different, with a more momentous meaning and
more permanent implications. The fighting on the frontier may
have had only a marginal impact on the outcome of the Revolution,
but the Revolution had a dramatic impact on the future of the
frontier. It effectively removed the major European players from
the scene and created a new nation, the United States, that would
soon establish itself as the dominant Euro-American power on the
continent.

From the outset, it was almost inevitable that the war would
expand to the frontier. Both the British and the rebellious colonists
understood the potential importance of the exposed western flank
of the thirteen colonies, whether as a staging area for attacks or as
a refuge for retreat. They likewise understood the potential importance of the various Indian groups of the interior, whether as
allies or as enemies. To be sure, both the British and the American
rebels sought at first to keep Indians out of the fight, preferring to
confront each other directly without stirring up trouble among
people they could not easily control. Before long, however, neither
side could resist the temptation to recruit such strong allies—or
perhaps neither could overcome the fear that the other side would
do so first.

Indians had little immediate interest in joining a war over issues
that meant little to them. They had had no opportunity to hear
the stirring oratory of Patriot leaders like Patrick Henry or read
inspiring pamphlets like Thomas Paine's *Common Sense*—although
they could no doubt appreciate the stance of Henry, a man who

claimed to prefer liberty to death, and they could certainly endorse the argument of Paine, a man who insisted that a far-off king on a small island had no right to claim ownership of a whole continent he had never seen. But Indians were not Whig ideologues. They were pragmatic people with homelands to protect, and for that reason most Indians of the interior became allied with the British. They understood that the British, whatever their faults, had formulated and tried to enforce a policy of keeping land-hungry settlers out of Indian territory. Now confronted with a war between two evils, most Indians decided, as always, to side with the lesser of the two. It was a reasonable but not altogether successful decision.

The Iroquois confederacy is again a good case in point. As Anthony F.C. Wallace has explained, the Six Nations tried to maintain their earlier position of neutrality toward European and Euro-American conflicts and "had, in effect, implemented the classic play-off policy again; they would fight *against* whoever first invaded their territory, interfered with their trade and travel, injured their people, or demanded their alliance, and *for* whoever had not upset the *status quo*." Almost inevitably, Wallace adds, it was the Patriots who first ran afoul of the Iroquois, because "they were revolutionaries attacking the established system and could not tolerate a neutrality that maintained the *status quo*."

Playing on Iroquois outrage caused by increasing Patriot incursions into Mohawk territory, an influential Mohawk leader called Joseph Brant (Thayendnaegea) convinced most of the Iroquois to fight on the side of the British and the American loyalists. (Two of the Six Nations, the Oneida and the Tuscarora, gave their support, but not many warriors, to the Patriot side.) Together with a group of loyalist Rangers under Major John Butler, Brant led Iroquois warriors on devastating raids in central New York and the Wyoming Valley of Pennsylvania in 1778. They not only defeated Patriot militia in battle, but they also laid waste numerous settlements, burning houses and barns, destroying crops, slaughtering farm animals, and, in at least one atrocious incident at Cherry Valley, killing men, women, and children who had been taken prisoner.

The Patriots retaliated in kind. In 1779, George Washington ordered General John Sullivan to march a force of three thousand

Continental soldiers into Iroquois country, drive back Brant's and Butler's forces, and launch a scorched-earth campaign against Iroquois villages. "The immediate objects are the total destruction and devastation of their settlements," Washington wrote, "and the capture of as many prisoners of every age and sex as possible . . . parties should be detached to lay waste all the settlements around . . . that the country may not be merely overrun, but destroyed." Sullivan and his troops did what they were told. Within less than a year, all but two of the thirty villages in Iroquois territory had been largely depopulated and destroyed.

In fact, for the remainder of the Revolutionary War, a similar pattern of pillage shaped the strategy of both sides in the North. Throughout the region that stretched from the Mohawk Valley in New York through western Pennsylvania to the Ohio country, no settler, whether Indian or Anglo-American, could feel secure. Everyone suffered, but perhaps no one more than the Iroquois. The war they had not wanted to fight left them greatly weakened and divided if not defeated, and they survived the war only to suffer more during the peace.

In the South, frontier fighting was equally savage on all sides. The outbreak of the Revolution only rekindled hostilities that had been smoldering for years. In 1776, when the Cherokees launched attacks against white settlements in the Virginia and Carolina backcountry, Patriot militia units retaliated by raiding and burning Cherokee villages. This campaign did not defeat the Cherokees, but it did help discourage other Indian groups in the South, most notably the Creeks, from entering the war on the British side.

To take even further steps to protect its vulnerable frontier— and to strengthen its claims to western lands—Virginia sent an expedition led by George Rogers Clark deep into the interior to challenge the British and their Algonquian Indian allies in the Illinois and Indiana territories. By late 1778, Clark had ventured as far as the Mississippi, to the site of the ancient Indian metropolis of Cahokia, which was now a small French settlement. By setting up small forts at Cahokia, Kaskaskia, and Vincennes, Clark established the first Patriot presence in the West, far across the old Proclamation Line.

The leading British official in the Great Lakes region, Henry Hamilton (who bore the grisly nickname of "Hair Buyer"), soon got wind of Clark's presence. Quickly mobilizing a force of British, French, and Indian fighters, Hamilton marched south from Detroit to dislodge the Patriot intruders. Hamilton took Vincennes in December 1778, but that was as far as he got. No sooner had he fortified himself for the winter than most of his French and Indian allies began to drift away, unhappy with his leadership and with the prospect of serving garrison duty so far from home. Then, in February 1779, Hamilton was surprised to find that Clark, who had led his men in a grueling wintertime march from Kaskaskia, had surrounded the fortress with a force of over two hundred men. Realizing that his undermanned garrison had no chance to survive a siege, Hamilton hung out a truce flag.

But Clark was not yet in the mood to offer Hamilton the honor of a proper military surrender. First, he wanted to exact a measure of revenge for all the frontier settlers whose scalps had gone to the "Hair Buyer." To show Hamilton that two could play at butchery, Clark had four captive Indians brought before Hamilton's fort, held down, hacked to death, and thrown into the river. Only then, as Hamilton later described the scene, was Clark ready to talk terms, with his "hands and face still reeking from the human sacrifice in which he had acted as chief priest." After the surrender, Hamilton was carried off to Virginia, and Clark carried on his western campaign, trying to claim greater control of the frontier for the Patriot side.

In reality, though, neither side could claim control of the frontier, at least not through military means. The area was too vast and the armies too small. In the end, the fighting on the frontier, for all its viciousness, proved inconclusive. As had been the case in previous wars, the decisive battles were fought elsewhere, and the final division of land was determined around a treaty table in Europe.

When the Treaty of Paris was finally concluded in 1783, it gave the new American nation what England had fought for over a century to obtain: the vast interior region that reached westward to the Mississippi and ran from the upper Great Lakes almost to the Gulf of Mexico. (Spain obtained all of Florida, which included the coastal region as far west as the Mississippi.) The treaty erased the Proclamation Line from the map and opened the trans-Appalachian frontier to eager settlers. After independence itself, the American interior was the greatest prize of the Revolution.

Still, the prize existed only on paper, on the maps that showed the broad bands of old colonial claims running straight to the west. Gaining actual control of those claims would be one of the most challenging tasks facing the new government, for it meant subduing not just the native inhabitants who lived there but also many of the new settlers who had moved there.

Even before American military forces had won the war, in fact, the American government began planning for the future of these frontier regions. The first step was to wrest control of the West from other American claimants, which turned out to be quite a task. The original colonial charters had given some of the early English colonies huge (and sometimes overlapping) grants of western lands. Virginia, for instance, claimed all the territory beyond the Alleghenies as far west as the Mississippi River and north of the Ohio River to the Canadian border. Massachusetts and Connecticut also possessed (on paper, at least) part of the same territory. So, too, did several private companies of land speculators. Led by well-connected promoters and prominent politicians (including George Washington, who had a very substantial interest and investment in western lands), these land companies had acquired hundreds of thousands of acres during the late colonial period, either by purchase from Indians or by grant from the royal or colonial governments; with the prospect of peace, they looked forward to selling their lands to settlers and turning a tidy profit. The only players apparently left out of the race for the West were a handful of states whose colonial charters had been less generous and had not given them a claim on the trans-Appalachian territory.

But one of these land-poor states, Maryland, had a powerful trump card to play. Knowing that the Articles of Confederation, which had been devised by the Congress in 1777 as the framework for the national government, required unanimous acceptance by all the states, Maryland officials announced in December 1778 that their state was withholding its approval. The requirement for ratification would be that all states holding western lands would have to cede their territory to Congress. After several years of debate and dealmaking, New York and Connecticut reluctantly agreed to cede their lands in 1780; Virginia soon fell in line, but only after stipulating that the Congress nullify all the purchases private land companies had made from Indians. The speculators howled in protest and, more quietly, tried to buy key congressmen's votes, but to no avail. On March 1, 1784, Congress finally gained formal control of most of Virginia's lands north of the Ohio River. The internal political struggle over the disposition of western lands was essentially over; it had lasted longer than the war itself.

The next step for Congress, of course, was determining what to do with the land it had just acquired. The promise of future westward expansion held an undeniable appeal: new states would strengthen the new nation. But at the same time the new lands held dangers that might weaken the nation. Lurking on the frontier were not just Indians, but agents of European powers as well, always ready to take advantage of any instability among new settlers. To avoid any possible collapse into renewed conflict or social chaos, American expansion had to be controlled; the new territories would have to be settled properly, according to a predetermined plan, with due regard for order and authority.

In March 1784, a committee chaired by Thomas Jefferson put forth such a plan, which called for dividing the Old Northwest Territory into ten new states. The erudite Jefferson gave them impressive-sounding names, some of which eventually came into use (Michigania, Illinoia) while others (Assenisipia, Pelisipia, and Polypotamia, for example) were too much even for classically educated congressmen. More important, he underlined the principle of republican self-government in the territories and outlined a process whereby the territories could eventually become states in the Union. Congress approved the essential elements of Jefferson's plan but failed to act on it immediately. The following year, Congress did provide for a systematic survey of the territory. According to the land ordinance of 1785, the Old Northwest Territory would be divided into a regular gridwork of townships, each one six miles square, with thirty-six sections of 640 acres each. Once the land had been surveyed, it could be sold to land companies or individuals, thus creating not just a source of revenue for the government but also a pattern of orderly settlement in the territory. Sir Robert Mountgomery might well have been pleased had he lived to see these plans so much in the spirit of what he had proposed for his Margravate of Azilia almost seventy years earlier.

Finally, in 1787, Congress revived and slightly revised Jefferson's

1784 plan for organizing the territories into new states. The Northwest Ordinance of 1787 called for a modified system of republican government, with a territorial governor and judges appointed by Congress and, once the territory had five thousand free adult male voters, a bicameral legislature. Eventually, when the free population reached sixty thousand, the territory could enter the Union "on an equal footing with the original states in all respects whatsoever." Thus, while the delegates to the Constitutional Convention in Philadelphia were hammering out a plan for a new national government, members of the Congress in New York were laying out a plan for future national expansion.

Yet, once again, actual settlement would not be so neat and orderly. One of the main obstacles to settling the newly acquired American interior according to the congressional plan was that people were already settled there—Indians, of course, but also white squatters who had occupied small plots of land without paying any purchase price or taking out legal title. Congress tried to deal with both groups, even as it was devising the final plans for the Northwest frontier.

In its dealings with Indians, Congress took the role of conqueror: after all, so the government's reasoning went, the United States had defeated not only the British but also Britain's Indian allies, and now the triumphant new nation claimed sovereignty over their territories. In October 1784, in the Treaty of Fort Stanwix, federal commissioners got the Iroquois to cede all their lands west of the Niagara River. To do so, the government agents surrounded the Iroquois with armed troops and held hostages, causing some Iroquois delegates, including Joseph Brant, to depart in outrage and disgust. The commissioners came away with the written agreement they wanted. A few months later, in January 1785, in the Treaty of Fort McIntosh, another group of commissioners used less coercive means, especially liquor, to get a large part of the Ohio country from the Wyandot, Delaware, Chippewa, and Ottawa peoples. A third treaty, with the Shawnees in 1786, completed the diplomatic conquest of the West, relegating Indians to reservations and opening a huge expanse of land to white settlers.

The white settlers who had already taken up land there were quite another matter. For years, long before any European or American government had established authority over the western lands, squatter families had begun carving small farms out of the frontier; by 1785, there were reported to be more than two thousand families in the Ohio territory. In the eyes of government officials, elite landowners, and other promoters of proper settlement, these squatters were a blight on the landscape. They lived off the land with little concern for legal title or proper surveys, and they stood in the way of orderly settlement and profitable land sales. They were disdained, in a commonly used eighteenth-century phrase, as "white Indians." (That term, which became commonplace from Maine to Georgia to Ohio, was not intended to connote honor, courage, and other positive qualities that could be associated with Native American culture. Rather, it drew upon demeaning stereotypes of Indians as lazy, drunken, and devious.) Moreover, the "white Indians'" constant encroachment on the lands of real Indians stirred up trouble just when the government was trying to maintain peace.

In a sense, the new United States government was in much the same situation as the British government twenty years earlier. In both cases, the government wanted to keep squatters and other unauthorized settlers away from the Indians and promote future settlement on its own terms. Congress did not draw a Proclamation Line around the Northwest Territory, however, but took a much more direct approach. In 1785–86, federal troops marched into the region to evict squatters by burning their houses and fields. A few years later, the Reverend Manasseh Cutler, a leading land developer in the region, noted with some satisfaction:

> It is a happy circumstance that the Ohio Company are about to commence the settlement of this country in so regular and judicious a manner. It will serve as a wise model for the future settlement of all federal lands . . . leaving no vacant land exposed to be seized by such lawless banditti as usually infest the frontiers.

But the "banditti" did not go away, and neither did the Indians. Neither, for that matter, did the British or the other European powers. The new United States government would quickly learn, as European governments had before, that military and diplomatic victories often had a short lifespan on the frontier. Designs for national integration almost invariably ran up against desires for local independence among both Native American and Euro-American inhabitants of the frontier. As the eighteenth century drew to a close, the political reality remained the same as it had been at the beginning of the century: no nation could truly control the land and the people living on it.

THREE

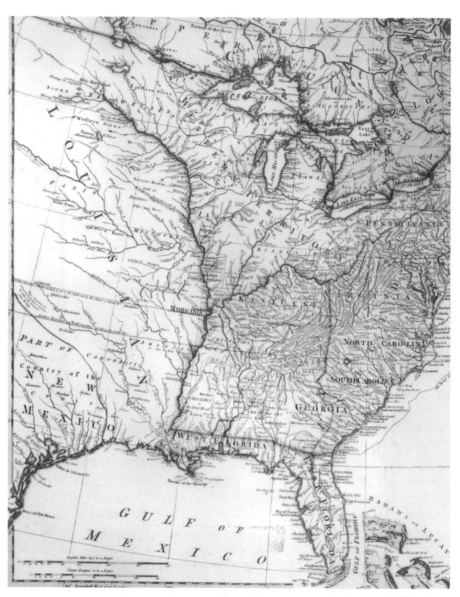

William Faden, "The United States of North America: with the British Territories and those of Spain, according to the Treaties, of 1784," 1796, portion.
Courtesy Hargrett Rare Book and Manuscript Library, University of Georgia Libraries

FORGING A FRONTIER POLICY IN THE NEW NATION

E arly on the morning of September 30, 1794, George Washington set out from Philadelphia for western Pennsylvania, a region he knew well from his earlier exploits in the Seven Years' War. Once again, Washington was leading a military expedition, this time not as a young militia colonel but as President of the United States and Commander in Chief of the Army. And this time he rode not on horseback but in a carriage—a display of dignity, perhaps, but also a concession to his advancing years and, more specifically, to a recent back injury. With him in the carriage was his most trusted political advisor, Alexander Hamilton, the Secretary of the Treasury. These two men had much at stake. Frontier farmers in the western regions were refusing to pay a federal excise tax on whiskey, and they had taken up arms in protest. These dissident citizens posed a direct challenge to the newly formed federal government's authority to impose and collect taxes. Moreover, Hamilton, who had proposed the tax, and Washington, who had supported it, took the farmers' refusal to pay almost as a personal affront. Therefore, they took it as their personal responsibility to respond. For support, they brought along almost thirteen thousand militia troops to quell the uprising.

Later that night, after Washington and Hamilton had journeyed twenty-five miles and stopped at a tavern to sleep, a messenger rode up with news of another frontier conflict, this one involving Indians. In mid-August, almost six weeks earlier (news never traveled fast on the frontier), General Anthony Wayne's army of fewer than a thousand unseasoned troops had defeated a much larger force of over two thousand Indian warriors in a tornado-swept forest along the banks of the Maumee River in the Ohio Territory. Wayne's victory at the Battle of Fallen Timbers was the army's first significant military success in a region where the government had felt vulnerable since the end of the Revolution. Not only had the British refused to relinquish their forts in the Old Northwest, but the Shawnees and other Indian groups in the region had begun making raids on settlers in the late 1780s. When Washington sent troops to fight them, the Indians had inflicted humiliating losses on federal forces under Colonel Josiah Harmar (1790) and Ohio territorial governor Arthur St. Clair (1791). Washington desperately needed a victory, and Anthony Wayne finally gave him one.

Washington always worried about the frontier. He had spent a large part of his life (and a good deal of his money) in the wilderness as surveyor, soldier, and land speculator. Now, as president, he had the added responsibility of making sure that the western flanks of the new nation remained stable for orderly settlement and secure from foreign intrigues. The frontier unrest he faced in 1794, both from Indians and from his fellow citizens, was a threat he would not take lightly.

The news of Wayne's success allowed Washington to turn his full attention to the farmers' uprising in western Pennsylvania, which came to be known as the Whiskey Rebellion. Indeed, the sizable number of troops Washington led against the rebels—far more than he had ever sent against the Indians—testified to his concern and determination. He knew from recent history that backcountry farmers could be a disruptive and dangerous lot.

In the 1760s, for instance, backcountry settlers in North Carolina had complained about unfair representation and taxation to their provincial government. By 1766, the Regulators (so named because they took it as their right to regulate the actions of the government) had organized themselves into local associations that resorted to armed force to disrupt the political and legal system in the western counties. The provincial government sent the militia out to suppress them, and at the Battle of Alamance in 1771—the largest single instance of armed conflict between opposing groups of Anglo-Americans before the Revolution—the government effectively put an end to the Regulator movement. Regulator resentment continued to smolder, however, and throughout the Revolution many former Regulators remained disaffected toward the new government.

Then, just after the Revolution, in 1786–87, another Regulator movement (which came to be known as Shays's Rebellion, after its alleged leader, Daniel Shays) arose in parts of western and central Massachusetts among farmers in the newly settled hill towns of the "near frontier." Like their backcountry counterparts elsewhere, the so-called Shaysites felt unfairly taxed and generally oppressed by the eastern mercantile interests that controlled the state government. For a while, there were rumors that a farmers' army was going to topple the Massachusetts government, but a hastily organized (and merchant-financed) state militia force broke the insurgents' strength and eventually forced the Shaysites to surrender.

Even though these frontier resistance movements had been suppressed, the record of repeated unrest remained a matter of serious concern to political leaders—chief among them, George Washington. And now in 1794, less than a decade after Shays's Rebellion, frontier farmers in Pennsylvania were up in arms against the new United States government and George Washington himself, protesting his policies, abusing his officials, and challenging his government. Washington had no intention of letting the Whiskey Rebellion survive, much less spread.

And spread it could, Washington feared. Ever since the end of the Revolution, foreign intrigues and frontier independence movements had created the specter of secession from a fragile new nation. At the time of Shays's Rebellion, Washington had warned: "There are combustibles in every State, which a spark might set fire to." And Britain, he suspected, always lurked in the background ready to stir up trouble: "That she is at this moment sowing the Seeds of jealousy and discontent among the various tribes of Indians on our frontier admits of no doubt, in my mind. And that she will improve every opportunity to foment the spirit of turbulence within the bowels of the United States, with a view to distracting our governments, and promoting divisions, is, with me, not less certain."

Washington was not just imagining things. In Vermont, Ethan Allen had gained a widespread reputation as a popular leader of the Green Mountain Boys during the Revolution, but he and his brothers had also engaged in discussions with the British to keep Vermont an independent state rather than join the United States. Similarly, local leaders and settlers in Franklin (a post-Revolutionary "state" formed out of Kentucky and the western parts of North Carolina) were talking of independence and even foreign alliance with Spain. The Spanish, who still had control of the Mississippi, were only too happy to lure western settlers away from the United States and into a separate economic and political sphere. Clearly, the end of the Revolution and the creation of the Constitution had not by any means guaranteed the territorial integrity of the United States. As Washington moved toward western Pennsylvania, it was with the not unreasonable fear that the frontier might fall away, and perhaps fall again into foreign hands.

In the end, though, nothing much came of this federal foray into the frontier. After about three weeks, Washington went back to Philadelphia to return to his other duties as president, leaving Hamilton to accompany the army as his personal representative. The main force, now under the command of General Henry Lee, marched on, but by the time it arrived in the rebellious region, the insurrection had essentially fallen apart. Although the army encountered a few signs of defiance, it never faced mass resistance. Dozens of suspected rebels were captured, interrogated, and imprisoned, but only twenty were actually put on trial for treason, and all but two of them were acquitted. (The two condemned men received a presidential pardon.) At Hamilton's urging, Washington left a force of fifteen hundred men to police western Pennsylvania, but by late November the main body of militia began the march home. With that, the Whiskey Rebellion had come to an end.

Thus, the crisis of 1794 turned out well for Washington—but it had still been a crisis. That is, it brought into immediate focus the frontier issues facing the federal government in the post-Revolutionary era. There were, of course, the two most obvious obstacles to frontier security, the Indian and European nations still intent on preserving their North American claims. Yet, because they were so obvious, so much the "other," the government could attempt to deal with them through the familiar means of diplomacy or warfare. Indeed, in the half century after the Revolution, treaty-making and warmaking were two of the most important tasks of the national government.

The post-war rebellions in Massachusetts and Pennsylvania revealed a third threat: the citizen-settlers themselves. Years of experience had shown that they could be fiercely independent, intent on defending their economic interests and their notions of local identity, often in direct defiance of external authority. They, no less than Indians or other Europeans, could resist and seriously disrupt the government's plans for determining the future of the American frontier.

And the government did have plans. In the early years of the Republic, the United States took its first significant steps down a path of purposeful national expansion that would eventually end in the conquest of the continent. To a great extent, expansion would depend on hundreds of thousands of common citizens who would move west to settle, staking their claim to the land and thereby reinforcing the claims of the nation. Yet, in the eyes of government leaders, it was not enough that these settlers simply occupy the land; they also had to promote the economic and political interests of the whole nation. The challenge was to combine human migration with government direction, to make frontier pioneers the agents, not the opponents, of national policy. That would be one of the more critical issues facing George Washington and the men who followed him in the presidency.

———◆———

Most political leaders and policymakers in the post-Revolutionary era came from a cultural background that gave them little faith in frontier settlers. Despite later literary attempts to create a romantic image of the noble pioneer, the standard eighteenth-century assumptions about backwoods people were anything but encouraging. Anglo-American writers had commonly described frontier folk as the dregs of otherwise decent society, a deviant and sometimes dangerous element hardly worthy of tolerance. Virginia's William Byrd II referred to the Scotch-Irish settlers who swept down the Shenandoah Valley in the second quarter of the eighteenth century as being like "the Goths and Vandals of old." He often snickered at their uncouth behavior and criticized their apparent indolence in a land of abundance. "The more they are befriended by the soil and the climate," he observed, "the less they will do for themselves." The Reverend Charles Woodmason, an Anglican clergyman who searched the southern backcountry for suitable converts, was even more disdainful, calling settlers there "the Scum of the Earth, and Refuse of Mankind" who lived a "low, lazy, sluttish, heathenish, hellish Life." Woodmason offered a stinging indictment of frontier society: "Behold on ev'ry one of these Rivers, What Number of Idle, profligate, audacious Vagabonds! Lewd, impudent, abandon'd Prostitutes Gamblers Gamesters of all Sorts— Horse Theives Cattle Stealers, Hog Stealers—Branders and Markers Hunters going Naked as Indians." In general, slurs against settlers became an almost essential part of the formula for writing about the frontier.

Nowhere did the negative picture of frontier folk find a more extensive expression than in the eighteenth century's most famous analysis of Anglo-American culture, *Letters from an American Farmer* (1782), by Michel-Guillaume-Jean (better known as J. Hector St. John) de Crèvecoeur. When it came to writing about the frontier, Crèvecoeur was no literary dilettante. Although born into the French nobility, he left his native Normandy at nineteen and emigrated to Canada in 1755—just in time for the outbreak of the Seven Years' War. During the early years of the war, he served as a militiaman and mapmaker for the French, but he later left French Canada for British New York, where he assumed a new identity as J. Hector St. John. There he began a new chapter in his life as surveyor and Indian trader. During the 1760s, his travels took him throughout the frontier regions of the British-American colonies, from Vermont to western Virginia to the Great Lakes. At one point, he was adopted by the Oneidas in New York, who gave him yet another name, Cahio-Harra. Crèvecoeur himself adopted a new nationality by becoming a naturalized citizen of New York. Finally, late in 1769, he married a young woman named Mehetable Tippett, bought some land in Orange County, New York, and settled down to make a farm out of the forest. He also began to write.

Given Crèvecoeur's remarkable personal odyssey in North America, it is especially worth noting that *Letters from an American Farmer* has comparatively little good to say about the frontier—or the people who lived there. In the book's most famous passage, after asking, "What, then, is the American, this new man?" Crève-coeur takes his reader on a whirlwind tour of the new nation. Start-ing on the East Coast, he offers a quick glance at the "bold and enterprising" people who live by the sea, the merchants and mar-iners whose love of trade keeps America in touch with the rest of the world. Next he moves on to the "middle settlements," the familiar farmlands of the near interior of the northern states. The people there were Crèvecoeur's (and implicitly God's) chosen people. "[T]he simple cultivation of the earth purifies them," Crèvecoeur explains. Whatever mild vices they might have, like selfishness or litigiousness, are far overshadowed by their virtues; these farmers are industrious, well informed, independent-minded, and reasonably tolerant on matters of religion. They seem the quintessential citizens of the new society.

When Crèvecoeur moves farther inland toward the frontier, his observations take on an ominous note of darkness, danger, and depravity. "There men appear to be no better than carnivorous animals of a superiour rank," he writes. "There, remote from the power of example and check of shame, many families exhibit the most hideous parts of our society." People might have moved to wilderness regions because of a number of personal problems or opportunities—"misfortunes, necessity of beginnings, desire of ac-quiring large tracts of land, idleness, frequent want of economy, ancient debts"—but in Crèvecoeur's eyes, they have little power to resist the effects of the frontier environment: "By living in or near the woods, their actions are regulated by the wildness of the neighborhood."

The very notion of "neighborhood" loses most of its traditional meaning on the frontier, as settlers revert to savage and antisocial behavior. The frontier farmer inevitably becomes a hunter, first to defend his crops from animals, then to feed his family: "The chase renders them ferocious, gloomy, and unsocial; a hunter wants no neighbour, he rather hates them because he dreads the competi-tion." Moreover, Crèvecoeur notes, "their success in the woods makes them neglect their tillage. They trust to the fecundity of the earth and therefore do little." The frontier farmer's sloth affects the whole family, undermining the education of the children and leaving them to "grow up a mongrel breed, half civilized, half savage."

Violent, indolent, ignorant, and isolated, Crèvecoeur's frontier folk are hardly model citizens. They are depraved people, a far cry from the paragons of republican virtue Crèvecoeur found in the farmers of the "middle settlements." In fact, for the frontier to fulfill its role in America's future, these first pioneers have to give way to a better sort of settler:

> They are a kind of forlorn hope, preceding by ten or twelve years the most respectable army of veterans which come after them. In that space, prosperity will polish some, vice and the law will drive off the rest, who, uniting again with others like themselves, will recede still farther, making room for more industrious people. . . . Such is our progress; such is the march of the Europeans toward the interior parts of this continent. In all societies there are cast-offs; this impure part serves as our precursors or pioneers. . . . Thus are our first steps trodden, thus are our first trees felled, in general, by the most vicious of our people; and thus the path is opened for the arrival of a second and better class, the true American freeholders, the most respectable set of people in this part of the world.

Crèvecoeur's categories represent the kind of near-caricature that should make historians cringe. True, he did anticipate by about a century Frederick Jackson Turner's notion of successive frontiers, where the hunter's frontier gave way to the farmer's frontier and so on. But just as Turner's rigid, racially biased distinction between Indian "savagery" and Euro-American "civilization" serves no useful analytical purpose, neither does the socially biased division of frontier settlers into "cast-offs" and a "better class" of people. Perhaps a better approach is to read Crèvecoeur and other unsympathetic observers of backcountry culture much as we now read Euro-American observers of Native American culture—with great care, with some skepticism, and always with an eye to finding an element of truth between the lines. By recognizing that geographically, politically, and economically marginal people could still have legitimate interests, we can appreciate them as independent actors who played an important part in an emerging new nation.

Moreover, they played their part against some of the most prominent actors of their era. In the years after the American Revolution, there were basically two groups of Euro-Americans who confronted each other in the frontier regions of the United States:

the prosperous and powerful, and the poor and vulnerable. Men
of wealth and influence, of whom George Washington was the
most famous, saw the frontier as a source of personal and national
benefit—generally in that order. They acquired huge holdings of
land by grant or purchase, but usually not with the intention of
settling on the frontier themselves. Rather, they hoped to sell or
rent the land to sturdy, stable, hard-working, law-abiding farmers
who would improve the land (and the land values) and produce a
marketable commodity. Henry Knox, a hero of the Revolution and
one of the most prominent proprietors of post-Revolutionary
Maine, explained his role as being the settlers' "father and guardian
. . . their close friend and protector." By promoting their notions
of orderly settlement of the frontier, the large landowners felt they
would enhance not only their own fortunes but those of the settlers
and of the nation as a whole. Profit, paternalism, and patriotism
mingled in the minds of the landowning elite.

Those proprietors were often dismayed by the reality of frontier
settlement. Above all, they found the people who settled their lands
to be a destitute and generally disappointing lot. They should
hardly have been surprised. People who had property or other decent opportunities in older, long-settled areas had little incentive
to brave the dangers of the "howling wilderness." Those who did
confront the frontier usually did so out of necessity because they
had run out of options elsewhere.

Most people came poor and stayed poor. By almost all accounts,
living conditions in such settlements would quickly disabuse anyone of the notion that the early frontier was a land of opportunity.
Thomas Slaughter has described the frontier of post-war Pennsylvania as an area "where poverty was the standard in 1780 and
where living conditions declined over the next fifteen years." The
frontier was a land of equality only in the sense that poverty defined the least common denominator.

In another respect, most frontier regions were areas of striking
inequality. A comparatively small number of property-owners, including non-resident proprietors and speculators, controlled vast
amounts of land; in parts of western Pennsylvania and western Virginia, the portion of property owned by the top ten percent of
landowners actually increased in the 1780s, in some cases to over
thirty-five percent. By comparison, a substantial percentage of

settlers—ranging from twenty-five percent to over fifty percent in some areas—owned no land at all. Some of them were renters, but many others were squatters, people who could not (or would not) pay the price of land but simply took possession and hoped to hold on as long as possible before being detected and evicted.

Government officials, proprietors, and other promoters of proper settlement considered squatters a bothersome blight on the landscape. People who lived on the land without paying for it represented not just the cost of unpaid rent but an obstacle to attracting other settlers who would be able and willing to pay. Accordingly, landowners tried repeatedly to remove squatters, using every means at their disposal, ranging from persuasion to litigation to armed force—usually without much success. For seemingly transient people, squatters could be a persistent lot.

Squatters posed a direct challenge to the economic and political designs of the lawmakers and landowning elite, and sometimes they articulated a defiantly independent ideology that found widespread support within the broader backcountry community. In Ohio, for instance, a squatter leader, John Amberson, led a short-lived independence movement in 1785. Claiming that common people had the right "to pass into every vacant country, and there to form their constitution," Amberson urged settlers to call a special convention and create a separate government. In Maine, James Shurtleff, an equally influential local leader, developed a set of political principles that spoke directly to the situation of squatters. Following ideas laid out a century earlier in John Locke's *Second Treatise of Government* (1690), Shurtleff asserted in a 1798 pamphlet that the frontier remained a state of nature. The wilderness belonged originally to no one, and only the settler who actually worked and improved the land could claim title to it: "In order to detach any part of the common mass and give it the stamp of exclusive right, he must not only claim it, but annex his labor to it, and make it more fit for the use of man; till this is done it remains in the common stock, and anyone who needs to improve it for his support, has a right." Or, as Shurtleff's fellow squatters in the Sheepscot Valley put it, "possession was the best title."

To impoverished people who lived in a Hobbesian environment where life sometimes seemed "nasty, brutish, and short," such a proto-Lockean approach to property had an understandable appeal.

The assertion of fundamental rights of personal possession and local self-government offered an alternative to the written laws established by the political and economic elite. More specifically, it threatened the prior claims of land-rich proprietors, whose title often rested on dubious Indian deeds in the first place.

Shurtleff's followers even undertook some "Indian deeds" of their own. Calling themselves "Liberty Men" or, increasingly, "White Indians," they took collective action against surveyors and land agents, occasionally threatening them with bodily harm. Resistance to the authority of absentee landowners challenged them to employ the full weight of the law, even though both sides knew it was not always easy or successful. But equally important, their resistance had a symbolic value that extended beyond legal proceedings. In part, the moccasins and blankets the White Indians usually wore helped keep them from being identified by the authorities, but as Alan Taylor has suggested, "White Indians set themselves apart from the outside world that harbored their proprietary foes and was not privy to the culture of the resistance. Thereby, the White Indian counterculture encouraged the settlers to stand together rather than with external authorities and laws." The settlers had taken a term, "white Indian," commonly used as a slur against frontier folk, and turned it into a source of local pride.

Proprietors and settlers often had very different notions of land use. Large landowners wanted to develop their frontier holdings into productive parts of a far-reaching national and international market. They expressed deep disappointment, even disdain, at what they took to be the low economic aspirations of the pioneer farmers. Wealthy landowners complained that frontier farmers not only grew corn for home consumption rather than wheat for the market, but they also devoted too much time to felling (or stealing) logs, hunting, and generally avoiding farm labor as much as possible. The solution lay in encouraging settlers to be better, more productive farmers—or, as David Cobb, a proprietor's agent in Maine put it, "teaching the Yahoos here, these log stealing scoundrels, how to get their living by cultivating the soil."

Although most frontier farmers knew well enough how to cultivate the soil, they were not always up to date on the latest developments in eighteenth-century scientific agriculture, as were many of the large landowners. Neither were they closely attuned to the economic opportunities of the international market for agricultural products. They used traditional agricultural practices that wasted resources but saved time and labor and generally produced just enough food to provide for their families.

To create farmsteads of five to ten acres, frontier farmers usually clear-cut the forest. Sometimes skilled woodsmen would topple a whole row of trees by cutting partway into the trunks and then chopping down a large tree at the end of the row to start a domino-like line of falling trees; other times, farmers took a simpler approach by "girdling" a strip of bark around the trunk to kill the tree. Both methods prepared unwanted wood for burning, which also cleared away underbrush and left a coating of ash for fertilizer. On the newly cleared ground they built their cabins and planted their crops, usually a small plot of garden vegetables and a few acres of corn.

Corn was the crop of choice for good reason. Most important, it grew well in poorly prepared ground and produced a good return from only a small quantity of seed. Winter wheat, by comparison, the grain most commonly promoted by agricultural reformers and large landowners as a marketable commodity, tended to be much more expensive as seed and much less prolific as plant; a successful wheat crop produced only a quarter to half as much grain per acre as corn. Moreover, corn was hardy enough to store over the winter and versatile enough to feed both people and farm animals. And even though corn had a limited market value as a grain, it could be turned into whiskey; as the western Pennsylvanians so clearly demonstrated, it was both potable and more easily portable.

In general, frontier farmers did not have their eyes fixed on the fickle movements of the market. That is not to say that they were obstinately opposed in principle to producing for the market; if they had something to sell—surplus bushels of grain or a few barrels of whiskey—they would sell it. For the most part, though, they did not make the market their primary focus. They stuck to a safe and simple strategy to ensure their subsistence in an uncertain world. Admittedly, their approach to farming was neither environmentally nor economically advanced, and it almost always failed to fulfill the broader vision of the large landowners. Still, it served its purpose for impermanent people with a sometimes suspect claim on the land.

Farming practices were not the only way in which settlers' customs clashed with those of the landowning elite. Compared to the norms of genteel society, theirs was a fluid, often fierce, and almost always male-centered society where hard living, hard drinking, and hard fighting were well within the bounds of socially accepted behavior.

The standard institution of conflict resolution and social control, the court, held little sway in frontier settlements. As Richard Beeman has noted in his study of Lunenburg County in the Virginia backcountry from the 1740s to the 1830s, the local court exerted only scant authority over the people's daily lives. Its business consisted primarily of laying out roads and licensing taverns—admittedly important tasks in an undeveloped region—but the court had little to do with regulating behavior or resolving conflict. "The conditions of life in frontier counties like Lunenburg made it hardly likely that the absence of such routine civil and criminal business before the court was a reflection of the chastity, sobriety, piety, and law-abiding character of the citizens of the area," Beeman wryly observes. "Rather, the justices were either unable to exert their discipline in such matters or were unconcerned with them altogether."

If people had personal disagreements, they sometimes worked them out or fought them out on their own. A casual insult, for instance, might trigger a challenge for one-on-one combat held within a circle of fellow frontiersmen. Maimed and mutilated bodies provided the most striking evidence of the outcome. Especially in backcountry regions of the South, men commonly resorted to "rough-and-tumble" fighting with no holds barred, in which biting, gouging, and clawing were all part of a fair fight. Such bloody and seemingly barbaric battles, explains Elliott Gorn, reflected the larger conflicts of frontier culture. In an unsettled society where harsh conditions made everyday life a constant struggle, "men came together and found release from life's hardships in strong drink, tall talk, rude practical jokes, and cruel sports." While gentlemen in older, more developed areas used gambling, dancing, horse racing, and the occasional duel to define manly prowess and defend their honor, frontiersmen turned to gouging. As Gorn explains, "They craved one another's recognition but rejected genteel, pious, or bourgeois values, awarding esteem on the basis of their own traditional standards. . . . Reputation was everything, and scars were badges of honor." In short, the motivation was the same; only the methods were different.

Outside observers were almost always appalled at such violence and vicious behavior, and they expressed even greater distress at the lack of an established church to control the boisterous behavior of the settlers. One eighteenth-century critic of frontier culture observed that most inhabitants came together on Sundays not to worship but "to drink, to settle their differences, and to try their manhood in personal conflict." People in distant settlements lived beyond the reach of organized religion, and many seemed happy to have it that way. The Reverend David Thurston warned his fellow ministers in the Maine Missionary Society that the frontier was not always fertile ground for the planting of orthodox churches. During the early years of settlement, when people were struggling to clear fields and build rude cabins:

> they are from necessity without schools, without ministers, without any of that influence, or those institutions which contribute so essentially to form the sober, steady, sterling character of the older parts of the country. . . . In such a soil, we should naturally suppose, that infidelity and every species of error would take root and flourish. Every account represents the state of these settlements, as deplorable for ignorance and irreligion.

Many backcountry communities, however, did have regular religious gatherings—albeit often with the kind of spiritual practices that established ministers like the Reverend Thurston would define as prime evidence of "error" and "irreligion." Frontier congregations generally preferred the more emotive, expressive style of evangelical sects to the subdued, stately order of the orthodox churches. Church gatherings offered a release from the rigors of this life, an opportunity to sing and celebrate, to hear about the hope of escaping from hardship to heaven. People came together as equals in a setting where there was no sense of hierarchy, no rigid division between pulpit and pew. Evangelical ministers made no claim to theological education or erudition; they looked upon book-learning as an obstacle to true religious feeling. Both preacher and congregation gave themselves over to the inspiration of the spirit, letting the emotions of the moment take them into otherworldly ecstasy. Small wonder, then, that the top-down, didactic, and often dreadfully dull sermons of the learned clergy had little appeal among poor settlers.

More to the point, the distance between the extreme evangelical sects and the religious establishment accommodated a wide continuum of churches—Separate Baptists, Freewill Baptists, Calvinist Baptists, New Light Congregationalists, New Side Presbyterians, Old Side Presbyterians, Quakers, Methodists, Mennonites, Moravians, to name a few of the most prominent. They had striking differences of doctrine and style, but all served the important purpose of giving dispersed settlers a sense of community in an otherwise isolated existence.

In many cases, the church came to be the main institution of social cohesion and control: it was the congregation, not the court, that defined acceptable social standards, and the charge of "unchristian behavior" covered a multitude of sins—drunkenness, fighting, wife-beating, cheating, stealing, slandering, and lying. The censure of the church did much more to regulate social relations than the infrequent appearance of the sheriff.

The role of the church in defining bonds of community and promoting neighborly behavior points to other forms of reinforcing communal relationships among frontier inhabitants. Life was not just a violent struggle of individuals against the environment —or against each other. It offered numerous opportunities for human connection and cooperation. In addition to church meetings, people came together for other social and ceremonial events such as weddings, barn raisings, cornhuskings, and quilting bees. Usually well lubricated by liquor and accompanied by music, these gatherings helped settlers get to know their neighbors and sometimes helped get work done. On a more personal basis, people often exchanged goods and services with each other. Men helped their neighbors clear fields and harvest crops; women helped each other make cloth, prepare food, and give birth. In frontier settlements, probably even more than in older rural communities, reciprocal exchanges and other forms of mutual support became an important part of a locally based, cash-poor economy. No matter how independent they may have claimed to be, people needed each other. That common need defined a sense of common identity among members of a legitimate, albeit often loose-knit, community.

In this as in many other respects, frontier settlers were considered a perplexing part of the new Republic. They formed the ragged fringe of the social fabric, living at the outer edges of Euro-American society where genteel standards of order appeared to unravel. Isolated and impoverished, they took for granted none of the common comforts of "civilized" society. In the harsh conditions of the frontier, they had to fashion their farms, churches, and communities as best they could. They resented and usually resisted the efforts of outsiders, especially landowners and lawmakers, to impose their notions of propriety and profit. In some cases, when they felt mistreated or threatened by those external forces, they took up arms to defend their communities and their customs; organized movements of Regulators and Whiskey Rebels had made that point clear on a large scale, and smaller collective actions repeatedly reinforced it.

Yet these people who were so often thought to be the nation's outcasts were also the nation's agents of expansion. Restless settlers would eventually carry the institutions and aspirations of their fellow citizens across the continent, creating family farms, churches, and communities not just for themselves but for their government. No bureaucracy, no army, no matter what its size (and, in the early years of the Republic, both were tiny) could occupy and hold new lands long enough to establish firm control. Only common people could make good the government's claims by settling and securing the land for others to follow.

Therein lay the dilemma for policymakers in the Early Republic. George Washington never fully trusted the common people who pioneered expansion. He shared the suspicions men of his class harbored about the poor, especially the poor who lived beyond the reach of formal government. He had too much invested, both economically and politically, to feel comfortable with the consequences of the settlers' self-determination. His mobilization of militia forces to put down the Whiskey Rebellion was only the most open manifestation of his insistence that frontier settlement be under close governmental control. But military repression would destroy the democratic foundation essential to the long-term future of national expansion. Promoting new settlements in the new century would require a new approach and new policies. And as the nineteenth century began, the presidency

passed to the national leader who best embodied the benign belief
in the common people, Washington's fellow Virginian Thomas
Jefferson.

In some respects, Jefferson seemed an unlikely candidate to play a
prominent role in westward expansion. He had lived and traveled
throughout much of Europe—France, England, Holland, Italy,
and Prussia—but he had never been west of the Shenandoah Valley
of his own Virginia. Yet Jefferson had developed a deep intellectual
curiosity about the land beyond the Appalachians, and quite unlike
Washington, he professed a "peculiar confidence in the men from
the western side of the mountains." Moreover, unlike Crèvecoeur,
Jefferson did not make a sharp distinction between the settled
farmer and the "savage" frontiersman. That sense of uncompro-
mised connection with common folk became an increasingly critical part of Jefferson's thought in the 1790s, one of the several
factors that set him and his political party, the Democratic-
Republicans, increasingly far apart from the Federalist faction of
Washington and Hamilton. In Jefferson's mind, the future of the
Republic lay with the common farmers, "the chosen people of
God," and their future lay in the West. Jefferson, of course, had
already laid the plans for settling the western lands in his proposals
for the Northwest, with the neoclassically named new states of
Assenisipia and Pelisipia and the rest. When he became president,
he took the opportunity to do even more.
    At the time Jefferson assumed office in 1801, the western coun-
try was already filling up with frontier farmers. Two new western
states had recently entered the Union—Kentucky (1792) and Tennessee (1796). (Their names did not derive from ancient Greek or
Latin, but from Indian tongues.) The 1800 census counted 220,959
and 105,602 non-Indian inhabitants, both free and slave, in those
states, respectively. The Ohio Territory, which was poised on the
brink of statehood, contained 45,365, and the recently created Mississippi Territory accounted for another 8,850.
    Because of the mountainous barrier that separated them from
the eastern United States, many of these western settlers had a
southern orientation. They turned the way their rivers flowed, toward the Mississippi, for trade; every year a growing flotilla of

flatboats went downstream to the port at New Orleans, where western goods found an outlet into the Atlantic economy.

The flatboats that arrived in New Orleans entered a foreign land. In 1763, at the end of the Seven Years' War, France had surrendered its claims to New Orleans and all the Louisiana territory west of the Mississippi River to Spain; throughout the remainder of the eighteenth century, all the lands surrounding the Gulf of Mexico, from Mexico to East Florida, were under Spanish control. "Control," however, was hardly the word for Spain's role in the region. The lower Mississippi was a focus of frontier exchange among Indians (Choctaws, Chickasaws, Creeks, Chitimachas, Houmas, Tunicas), Europeans (French, Spanish, and English), and African-Americans, both slave and free. At the beginning of the nineteenth century, New Orleans was probably the most culturally diverse city in North America, a compact contact zone at the mouth of the Mississippi that knew no national identity. As long as it stayed that way, an open city under a weak government, it served a useful purpose for the frontier farmers so favored by Thomas Jefferson.

Jefferson had hardly taken office, however, when he heard a rumor that Spain was giving the vast Louisiana territory, including New Orleans, back to France. That worried him, especially when the French denied any such arrangement. In April 1802, he wrote his minister to France, Robert Livingston, that the United States had much to fear in a renewed French presence in the lower Mississippi region, especially with control of New Orleans. "There is on the globe one single spot, the possessor of which is our natural and habitual enemy," he wrote. "It is New Orleans, through which the produce of three-eighths of our territory must pass to market." With France in a position to threaten the interests of western farmers, the president concluded, it seemed "impossible that France and the U.S. can continue long friends."

Jefferson's fears mounted a few months later when the Spanish Intendant of New Orleans closed the port to the deposit of goods from the United States, thus cutting off the only trade outlet from the north. He suspected, as did almost everyone else in the government, that French machinations lay behind the provocative move. Jefferson's political opponents in the Federalist Party began to make noises about going to war. Jefferson put them off, but he quietly shored up his forces along the Mississippi frontier. Jefferson wanted another way to acquire New Orleans, though, and he appointed his fellow Virginian and Republican, James Monroe, to join Robert Livingston in France and negotiate the purchase of New Orleans and West and East Florida. Congress agreeably appropriated $2 million but did not publicize the purpose of the mission.

On April 11, 1803, the day before Monroe arrived in Paris, Napoleon's minister of foreign relations, Charles Maurice de Talleyrand-Perigord, suggested an even bigger deal to Livingston: France was willing to sell all of Louisiana. Without first sending word to Jefferson or anyone else in Washington—communication was impossible in so short a time span—the two representatives agreed that the United States would pay France sixty million francs ($11,250,000) for Louisiana, including New Orleans. (The French could not properly sell the rights to the Floridas, since they were claimed by Spain. The United States would acquire them in 1819, through the Adams–Onís Treaty.) As an additional sweetener, the United States would assume another twenty million francs ($3,750,000) of its citizens' claims against France. The total price thus came to $15 million for a piece of real estate so big that there was no precise measure of its dimensions.

When word of the treaty reached the United States in the summer of 1803, both the Jeffersonians and their opponents lost little time in shaping the Louisiana Purchase to fit their political purposes. As Drew McCoy has noted, Jeffersonians endowed the acquisition of New Orleans with moral as well as economic implications. Access to foreign markets would not only stimulate trade, it would also stimulate the industrious habits of the western inhabitants. "Without it," wrote one supporter of the Purchase, "even the natural luxuriance of the soil, would produce the worst impression on the morals of the people. Without commerce to yield a market to the products of agriculture, that agriculture would languish, and the mass of society be thrown into a state of listless indolence and dissipation." Thus the old concerns about the frontier settlers' descent into sloth and savagery found a solution in Louisiana.

Jefferson himself took a longer view, envisioning the Republic expanding in stages from the Mississippi. In 1803, he was not yet ready to release settlers to roam at will throughout the new territory; for the time being, he wanted to keep the West as a peaceful preserve for Indians. But population growth made future frontier settlement inevitable: "When we shall be full on this side, we may lay off a range of states on the western bank from the head to the mouth, and so, range after range, advancing compactly as we multiply." It was as if Jefferson were already drawing the map in his imagination. Like the Old Northwest, the Louisiana territory would provide another opportunity for the orderly extension of the United States.

Federalists saw different implications for the Republic. Many raised the very legitimate objection that the president had far overstepped his constitutional bounds by acquiring so much land for so much money with so little congressional involvement. Others questioned the value of the purchase in the first place, dismissing the whole territory as a "great waste, a wilderness unpeopled with any beings except wolves and wandering Indians." In truth, no one in the government, Republican or Federalist, knew what the nation had bought, much less what it would mean for the future of the nation.

Jefferson was determined to find out. Even before the Louisiana Purchase was consummated, he initiated plans for western exploration far beyond the bounds of Louisiana into Spanish territory. Beginning in 1803, he secured funding from Congress to support four expeditions to the West: Meriwether Lewis and William Clark (1803–6); William Dunbar and George Hunter (1804–5); Thomas Freeman (1806); and Zebulon Pike (1805–7). Jefferson had long had a deep curiosity about the West, and now his position as president gave him the opportunity to indulge one of his many avocations, that of scientist. Knowing that Congress would never spend good money on science alone, Jefferson couched his appeal for appropriations in economic terms. The expeditions, he said, would provide useful geographical information that might someday promote settlement and trade. Congress could be persuaded to spend money to make money.

In the end, it was the first of these missions to the West, the Lewis and Clark expedition, that proved to be the most successful. Meriwether Lewis, the president's personal secretary at the time, was a veteran of military service in the Whiskey Rebellion, and he was familiar with frontier life in western Pennsylvania and the Old Northwest; moreover, he shared Jefferson's passion for knowing more about the lands beyond. To get him ready for the expedition, Jefferson sent him back to Pennsylvania, but this time for a quick education in mathematics and science under the guidance of some of the leading lights in Philadelphia's scientific community. Jefferson then gave him the charge "to explore the Missouri river, & such principal stream of it, as, by it's course and communication with the waters of the Pacific Ocean, whether Columbia, Oregan, Colorado or any other river may offer the most direct & practicable water communication across this continent for the purposes of commerce." Thus educated, directed, and financed, Lewis set off from Washington on July 4, 1803, the day after the news of the Louisiana Purchase reached town.

While spending the winter of 1803–4 in Illinois and Missouri getting his expedition ready to venture into uncharted territory, Lewis had the good fortune to be joined by his friend William Clark. Clark could claim little of the formal (or even force-fed) education that Lewis had, but his Kentucky background had prepared him for life in the wilderness. Together, they made remarkably competent and compatible co-leaders, taking their party north to what is now North Dakota, across the plains and mountains to the Pacific Northwest, and finally, in November 1805, to the Pacific Ocean. They could probably not have done so well, however, without the help of a young Shoshone woman they encountered along the way, Sacajawea. Though not the girl guide that later legend made her out to be, she was an effective interpreter in the expedition's encounters with native peoples, and she also helped find wild foods to feed the party. Perhaps most important, she played a critical role in establishing peaceful relations between Lewis and Clark and her own Shoshone people, who in turn helped the expedition reach the Columbia River, their access route to the Pacific.

By the time they returned to Saint Louis, in September 1806, stories of their success had long preceded them. The explorers sent back numerous specimens of plant and animal life, almost enough to satisfy the intellectual curiosity of their sponsor, the president. They also brought back enough written material—maps, drawings, and Indian vocabularies—to keep eager researchers busy for years.

In general, the Lewis and Clark expedition provided a huge store of information about the landscape, the natural history, and the native peoples of the West. No other expedition before the first human landing on the moon did as much to ignite interest in the unknown. The West had become the landscape of the nation's imagination.

Yet the expanding nation still had to come to terms with the other peoples who inhabited North America: Indians. Since the Washington administration, the government had adopted an official policy of recognizing Indians as legitimate inhabitants of their tribal territories. The United States did not have the right simply to take Indian lands by force, except in the case of "just war"; otherwise, those lands could be acquired only by treaty based on the "free consent" of the people who possessed them. Many political leaders, perhaps most notably Thomas Jefferson, liked to look upon Indians as noble savages who embodied basic traits of cleverness, courage, loyalty, and honor that would, as Jefferson observed, "place them on a level with Whites in the same uncultivated state."

But that was the catch: no one, neither Euro-American nor Native American, could be allowed to live for long in an "uncultivated state." To do so would impede national expansion and development. Government policy did not call for the extermination of Indians, only their cultural transformation. That is, in order to live peaceably in the United States, Indians would be pressured to give up their language, their way of life, and much of their land. In the minds of Jefferson and other leaders, such a policy was in the Indians' best interests, offering them incorporation into "civilized" society. Yet, as the government extended this open hand of philanthropy, it kept in the background the closed fist of force.

Some Indian groups did attempt to accommodate to the increasingly powerful presence in their midst. Most notable of these were the Cherokees, whose territory had once covered much of the Southeast. By the first decade of the nineteenth century, the Cherokees had already ceded over half of their homeland to the United States—partly the price they had been forced to pay for their earlier opposition during the Revolution and partly the result of poor, perhaps even corrupt leadership. Faced with a diminished territory and a declining population, some Cherokee leaders argued that accommodation, if not assimilation, was the only way to survive the inevitable expansion of white society. They eventually won control of the tribal councils and committed their people to a process of cultural change in which Christianity, settled farming, private property, and even chattel slavery became common components of Cherokee life. In general, it appeared as if Cherokees were aspiring to live, as Jefferson had put it, "on a level with Whites." For a while, the whites grudgingly allowed them to do so.

Other Indians adopted quite the opposite strategy. In some cases, they felt they had already gone too far toward accommodation, and they tried to go back to their traditional ways, even if doing so meant making war. No one did more to turn that sentiment into a broad-based movement than the Shawnee leader Tecumseh. Since the Battle of Fallen Timbers in 1794, the Shawnees had seen both their territory and their traditions threatened by soldiers and settlers from the United States. Moreover, government agents, missionaries, and traders had also increased in number in the Ohio–Indiana country, and with them they brought all the influences that had undermined Indian culture in the past: new legal and religious systems, manufactured goods, guns, and alcohol. Tecumseh and his followers had moved several times to keep their distance from these newcomers, but they could not move far enough or fast enough.

Then, during the summer of 1805, they began to resist. Tecumseh had a younger brother, Tenskwatawa (or the Prophet), who spent much of his time in the spiritual world. Like the Delaware prophet Neolin in the 1760s, Tenskwatawa called for his people to reject the evil influences of the Euro-Americans and return to their traditional ways. Together, Tecumseh and Tenskwatawa became a powerful pair of leaders, and they began to forge a movement among Indians throughout the Midwest. In addition to preaching cultural renewal, they also called for intracultural confederation. Above all, they urged all native people to oppose further cession of their lands: no one, they insisted, had a right to give away what belonged to all.

That message attracted hundreds of Indians—Kickapoos, Potawatomis, Winnebagos, Wyandots, and others—to the Shawnee village called Prophetstown, on the Tippecanoe River in the Indiana Territory. Not surprisingly, it also attracted the attention of wary government officials. The governor of the Indiana Territory, General William Henry Harrison, was concerned about the possible implications of Tecumseh's movement. The Shawnee chieftain was a natural leader, Harrison admitted: "If it were not for the vicinity of the United States, he would perhaps be the founder of an Empire that would rival in glory that of Mexico or Peru." Harrison's task, though, was to thwart Tecumseh's influence and prevent the creation of just the kind of pan-Indian empire he described. In 1811, while Tecumseh was in the South recruiting converts among the Creek, Chickasaw, and Choctaw people, Harrison marched toward Prophetstown with a force of around a thousand militiamen and ordered the Indians there to disperse.

Tenskwatawa, more a mystic than a military leader, had a vision in which the Master of Life told him that his warriors would be invulnerable to the soldiers' bullets. That proved to be bad advice. On November 7, 1811, Tenskwatawa's warriors attacked Harrison's encampment and fought the militiamen for about two hours, only to be pushed back. Harrison staged his own attack on Prophetstown and burned it. The victory gave Harrison sudden stature as a military hero, and from the site of the battle he took the nickname "Old Tippecanoe" into a later political career, which reached its ultimate peak with his election as president in 1840. The defeat cost Tenskwatawa his town and much of his credibility; forced into flight, he was never a trusted leader again.

Tecumseh still had his credibility, but little else. When he returned to his homeland in January 1812, he found his confederacy broken and his Indian allies scattered. A sustained pursuit by Harrison might well have brought about his end right then—except that right then Harrison had greater concerns on his mind.

The United States was about to go to war again with Great Britain. The cause had to do with long-standing economic ill will between the two nations, which had led to British attacks on United States ships and sailors on the high seas. But aggressive political leaders in the South and West, the "War Hawks," saw the possibility of war as an excellent opportunity to take even more dramatic action on land as well. If the United States could defeat the British again, the new nation might take control of Canada and

Florida and solidify its hold on the eastern half of the continent. With such a potentially monumental struggle brewing, both sides recalled the single most important lesson of frontier diplomacy learned during the long series of colonial wars: Indians could be crucial allies.

Like his predecessors in the Old Northwest in the eighteenth century, Tecumseh bought time by playing one side off against the other. While he entertained overtures of amnesty from General Harrison, he also met with British agents who were eager to secure his support. Then, with the outbreak of war and the United States' invasion of Canada in the summer of 1812, Tecumseh took sides with the British and played an important role in bringing other Indians into their camp. But in the following year, with a series of British setbacks, Indian enthusiasm for the British cause began to wane. Tecumseh stayed with the British, but many of his Indian allies either changed sides or decided to sit out the rest of the war. In the wake of British defeat, a discouraged Tecumseh joined the British Army's retreat into Canada. There, in a brief battle on the banks of the Thames River on October 5, 1813, Tecumseh was shot and killed. His death meant the end of his confederacy as well, and with it, the demise of the movement for cultural renewal he and his brother Tenskwatawa had forged only a few years before.

In the South, a similar movement for cultural renewal among the Creeks led to division within, attack from without, and the ultimate destruction of a once-powerful confederacy. Like the Cherokees, many Creeks had begun to accommodate to the encroachment of white people, and they had begun to accept settled farming and the Christian religion. Like Tecumseh, many young Creeks had become alarmed at the intrusion of new settlers and the resulting erosion of the old ways. These champions of traditional culture, called Red Sticks, challenged the authority of the older, more accommodationist tribal leaders. The arrival of Tecumseh himself on a recruiting mission in Creek territory in 1811 only intensified the internal antagonism. By that time, the confederacy was in a state of civil war, and bloodshed broke the bonds that had held the people together.

When the bloodshed spread beyond the Creeks themselves, when rebellious Red Sticks also attacked white settlers, killing women and children, the whole confederacy paid a heavy price.

War fever had already risen to a high point in the Southern states, and angry leaders had no trouble raising troops to attack the Indians. Outraged and ready to fight, Andrew Jackson of Tennessee fumed that "when we figure to ourselves our beloved wives and little prattling infants, butchered, mangled, murdered, and torn to pieces, by savage bloodhounds, and wallowing in their gore, you can judge of our feelings. . . . [We] pant for vengeance."

Jackson certainly did not hold his breath long before taking decisive action. In August 1813, a group of Red Sticks attacked Fort Mims, a poorly guarded stockade that provided refuge for around five hundred settlers, including many peaceful Creeks, and slaughtered over 250 men, women, and children. Immediately after hearing news of the massacre, Jackson mobilized his Tennessee militia and went on the warpath against the Red Sticks, promising death to the "cowardly dogs." He carried out the promise in March 1814 at the Horseshoe Bend in the Tallapoosa River in Alabama. With a combined force of about fourteen hundred militiamen and six hundred Cherokee and Creek allies, Jackson attacked a Red Stick stronghold of around a thousand warriors and killed eight hundred of them. Never had there been more Indian blood shed in a single battle.

That was not enough for Andrew Jackson. Acting on his own, over the protests of federal authorities and friendly Creeks, Jackson demanded fourteen million acres of Indian land, the largest single cession in the South. He even took land from his Creek allies. "Listen," he told them:

> the great body of the Creek chiefs and warriors did not respect the power of the United States—They thought we were an insignificant nation—that we would be overpowered by the British. . . . They were fat with eating beef—they wanted flogging—they had no idea they could be so easily destroyed. They were mad—they had a fever—we bleed our enemies in such cases to give them their senses.

Whether or not Jackson's actions engendered respect among the Creeks (or any other Indians, for that matter) is debatable, but they certainly gained him favor among his fellow citizens. Like Harrison, he was hailed as a war hero, the architect of one of the United States' few significant victories in the War of 1812.

The next year, Jackson cemented his status with a second victory, an even more thorough rout of the British Army at the Battle of New Orleans on January 8, 1815. What is noteworthy about the battle is not so much its military importance as its popular imagery, especially the portrayal of Jackson as the frontier hero. A congressman from Georgia congratulated not just General Jackson but his fellow frontiersmen from Tennessee, Kentucky, Mississippi, and Louisiana: "It was the yeomanry of the country marching to the defense of the City of Orleans. . . . The farmers of the country triumphantly victorious over the conquerors of the conquerors of Europe. I came, I saw, I conquered, says the *American Husbandman*, fresh from his plough." And on and on it went, from Congress to concert halls, a stirring celebration of a new kind of national hero: the frontier farmer-fighter, the common man committed to defending the nation's honor. And it was Jackson's self-conscious association with that image that helped him become not just war hero, not just president, but, as John William Ward has put it, "Symbol for an Age."

It was an ill-fitting image, however. As Ward and other historians have noted, Jackson could by no means claim to be the embodiment of the common man. True, he had been born into comparative poverty in the South Carolina backcountry, and as a young man he moved west (with a young slave woman in tow) to Tennessee almost a decade before it became a state. And he was a ferocious fighter, both as an individual and as a military leader, on the southern frontier. The Creeks who fought him at Horseshoe Bend could testify to that, and, later, so could their cousins, the Seminoles, when Jackson invaded Florida in 1818. But by the time Jackson entered presidential politics, land speculation and slaveholding had made him a wealthy man, and he was certainly far from a common farmer.

Yet many voters appeared not to notice, or perhaps not to care, and they accepted the image of "Old Hickory" that his political allies promoted:

> *He's none of your old New England stock,*
> *Or your gentry-proud Virginians,*
> *But a regular western fighting-cock*
> *With Tennessee opinions.*

A "western fighting-cock/With Tennessee opinions"—that was the critical last piece in Jackson's political persona. The jingle's regional distinctions set Jackson apart from his predecessors in the presidency, all of whom had come either from Virginia (Washington, Jefferson, James Madison, and James Monroe) or from Massachusetts (John Adams and his son, John Quincy Adams). By the 1820s, when Jackson entered national politics as a profession, the trans-Appalachian West was still a new part of the nation, but it now contained nine states to challenge, or at least balance, the dominance of the original thirteen. A "western fighting-cock" like Jackson could be the perfect symbol of their political maturity.

Exactly how Jackson turned those "Tennessee opinions" into a national victory makes a wonderful story, but not one to be retold here. Suffice it to say that when Jackson finally entered the White House in 1829, he had become a self-conscious symbol of the common man in national politics and an unapologetic promoter of the western interests. Jackson claimed to be a political descendant of Jefferson, and he was in a sense a coarser second coming of the yeoman president. Jefferson saw the yeoman as an admirable abstraction; Jackson knew him as a fellow soldier from the frontier wars. Jefferson wanted to assimilate Indians; Jackson was willing to kill them. Jefferson looked to the frontier and envisioned orderly land allocations for future national expansion; Jackson lived on the frontier and engaged in land speculation for future personal profit. Jefferson bought the West with money; Jackson bought it with blood.

Yet, while Andrew Jackson was the self-conscious man of the West, one could argue that he did not so much create new policies of national expansion as benefit from policies already in place. Beginning in the Washington administration, Congress had passed a series of Land Acts to make it easier for settlers to acquire acreage in the trans-Appalachian regions; between 1796 and 1820, the price of government land fell from $2 an acre to $1.25, and the minimum purchase had been reduced from a whole section, or 640 acres, to eighty acres. During the Jacksonian era, the government not only continued a policy of providing cheap land but also made it possible for squatters to acquire land by the right of preemption. Moreover, both the state and federal governments had promoted transportation policies to help people move west to new land and to ship their surplus produce back to eastern markets. Beginning in the 1790s, state governments took the lead in chartering road- and canal-building projects that lay the foundations for a national transportation network. In 1806, Congress authorized funds for a National Road to extend this infrastructure into the frontier. By the time Jackson became president, the government had already made a major commitment to westward movement.

There was one important part of expansionist policy, however, that Jackson embraced and made almost emblematic of his presidency: Indian removal. Again, there was nothing altogether new about the policy. The federal government and individual state governments had long pursued policies that encouraged or coerced Indians to cede their lands and move out of the way of westward expansion; even Jefferson had assumed that unassimilated Indians would probably be best off on reservations west of the Mississippi. But more than any other president before him, Jackson had the power and certainly the will to pursue this policy to its conclusion, or at least to finish this first stage by securing all the land east of the Mississippi for white settlement. No other United States president, before or since, could surpass Andrew Jackson for the dubious distinction of being the most anti-Indian leader of the nation.

Jackson focused most of his energy for Indian removal on the South, the region where he had lived, farmed, and fought almost all his life. The major Indian groups who lived there—the so-called Five Civilized Tribes: the Cherokees, Chickasaws, Choctaws, Creeks, and Seminoles—had already been forced, through both military or diplomatic means, to cede much of their homelands to the federal and state governments. By the 1820s, however, those earlier cessions seemed insufficient in the eyes of southern settlers and speculators. Their hunger for land led them to look longingly, almost lustfully, at the Indian territories from Florida to the Mississippi.

The main stimulus to land hunger was cotton. In the 1790s, the development of a cotton gin for cleaning cotton revolutionized the production process and suddenly created a new cash crop for the lower South. Now even small farmers could grow a few acres of cotton along with their corn, take it to the gin, and send it on to market. Large slaveholders could grow even more on their plantations. By 1820, cotton production had risen dramatically, to almost seventy-five thousand bales a year, and the end seemed nowhere in sight. If cotton was not yet king in the South, it was certainly crown prince.

But just as cotton gave new life to the southern economy, it also took the life out of southern soil. Many cotton growers, large and small, worked their land to exhaustion and then had to look for new land. They found it in the vast expanse running from central Georgia through Alabama to the Mississippi region, which in the early part of the nineteenth century came to be known as the "cotton frontier." As had been the case in other frontier regions, the land was already occupied by Indians—and some, like the Cherokees, had begun to grow cotton themselves.

Political leaders in the Deep South states laid out a straightforward plan of dispossessing the Indians. As Richard Wilde, a congressman from Georgia, put it, "We should take direct control of Indian land." He shed no sentimental tears about the Indians' loss of land or identity:

> When gentlemen talk of preserving the Indians, what is it they mean to preserve? Is it their mode of life? No. You intend to convert them from hunters to agriculturists or herdsmen. Is it their barbarous laws and customs? No. You promise to furnish them with a code, and prevail upon them to adopt habits like your own. Their language? No. You intend to convert them from their miserable and horrible superstitions to the mild and cheering doctrines of Christianity.

Small wonder, then, that such state leaders saw bright prospects for national support in a Jackson presidency. No sooner had Jackson been elected than Georgia, Alabama, and Mississippi asserted that Indians would now be subject to the laws of the respective states, and that tribal laws and legislative assemblies no longer had legitimacy. Although Indians could neither vote, file suit, nor testify in court, they were subject to court proceedings for debt. In general, these southern states declared open season on Indian rights, inviting settlers to intrude upon Indian lands with virtual impunity.

In response to Indian protests, Jackson made an uncharacteristic claim of weakness:

> Say to my red Choctaw children, and my Chickasaw children to listen —my white children of Mississippi have extended their law over their

country. . . . Where they are now, say to them, their father cannot prevent them from being subject to the laws of the state of Mississippi. . . . The general government will be obliged to sustain the states in the exercise of their right.

Jackson thus allied himself not just with states' rights but also with settlers' appetites. By saying he was unable to stop them, he was in reality telling them to make the most of their movement onto Indian lands. And by doing so, he made both the states and the settlers instruments of an increasingly aggressive national policy of dispossession.

Jackson offered Indians only two options. They could stay put and accept subjugation to state laws, or they could sell their lands and move west of the Mississippi into open territories where they could live without state interference. This second option, offering Indians money in exchange for removal, helped avoid the appearance of coercion. As Michael Paul Rogin notes, "Jackson successfully combined paternalism with the doctrines of market freedom." Indeed, Jackson argued that the deal he offered Indians was no different from, and even better than, the opportunities available to whites. "Doubtless it will be painful to leave the graves of their fathers," he admitted, but thousands of United States citizens did that every year; the pain of separation and the cost of moving west seemed insignificant compared to the benefits to be derived from living where "our young population may range unconstrained in body or mind, developing the power and faculties of man in their highest perfection." How could Indians, a wandering people anyway, complain about moving?

Indians did not rush to embrace the opportunity Jackson offered. The Cherokees met the southern states on their own cultural and legal ground by appealing to the United States Supreme Court, arguing that state laws could have no effect on an independent Indian nation. In the first of two decisions, *Cherokee Nation vs. Georgia* (1831), the Court ruled that the Cherokees did have an "unquestionable . . . right to the lands they occupy," but they were not in fact a separate state or nation; rather, they were a "domestic dependent nation" whose "relation to the United States resembles that of a ward to his guardian." However, in a second decision the following year, *Worcester vs. Georgia*, the Court took a much firmer stand on the issue of state authority over Indian lands. The Constitution and the laws of the United States, wrote Chief Justice John Marshall, had always considered Indian nations as "distinct, independent political communities" and their "territory as completely separated from that of the states." Only the federal government could make treaties and otherwise define relations with Indians. Therefore, Marshall concluded, the Georgia laws that extended state jurisdiction over the Cherokees were "repugnant to the constitution, treaties, and laws of the United States and ought, therefore, to be reversed and annulled."

Indians may have had a supportive friend in John Marshall, but they had a powerful enemy in Andrew Jackson. When he heard of the Court's ruling, Jackson is reputed to have scoffed, "John Marshall has made his decision; now let him enforce it." Moreover, by the time the *Worcester* decision came down, Jackson's allies in Congress had already pushed through the controversial Indian Removal Act (1830), which gave the federal government authority to move Indians westward, by force if necessary. Many Creeks, Choctaws, and Chickasaws had already ceded their land to the states and had begun moving west. Those who resisted—some groups of Seminoles, Creeks, and Cherokees in the South, and the Sac and Fox in the Old Northwest—faced the armed force of the federal government. By the late 1830s, thousands of Indians had been marched to reservations several hundred miles west of the Mississippi.

Many never made it. A rickety steamboat carrying over three hundred Creeks sank in the Gulf of Mexico, drowning all the men, women, and children aboard; hundreds of other Creeks fell victim to cold, hunger, and disease on the overland trek. Similarly, up to a quarter of the sixteen thousand Cherokees who walked the "Trail of Tears" died en route. Those Indians who survived the forced migration found themselves on an unfamiliar landscape of open plains quite different from the eastern woodlands they had known before. Contemporary maps labeled the area the "Great American Desert."

In the space of fifty years, the United States had taken major steps toward gaining control of the continent. In 1790, at the beginning of the Washington administration, the government felt vulnerable

on its western frontier. Indians still held the majority of the territory west of the Appalachians, and they did not look forward
to further encroachment on their lands. The European colonial
powers—France, Spain, and Britain—also maintained footholds in
frontier regions, and they often worked with Indians to undermine
the interests of the United States. Even some citizens of the United
States were suspect. Independent-minded inhabitants of the frontier had repeatedly shown themselves resistant to external direction, defiant of government authority, and susceptible to foreign
intrigue. Small wonder, then, that a wary George Washington
looked westward with concern.

By 1840, the problems that faced the first administration were
not altogether resolved, but were certainly reduced. Through a
variety of means—war, treaty, and intimidation—the government
had removed most of the native inhabitants from the region between the Appalachians and the Mississippi. So, too, had the area
been cleared of the European powers. Now settlers from the
United States had almost free rein to take over the western territories and turn them into states. In the first fifty years of the
new Republic, eleven new states were carved out of the trans-
Appalachian West, not to mention Vermont and Maine on the
northern frontier of New England.

Somewhere in this process of national expansion, presidents and
other policymakers apparently developed a new perception of the
people who made it possible. No longer were frontier settlers dis-
missed so easily as "white Indians," indolent people to be ridiculed
but also regulated. Rather, they became symbols of an energetic
new society, the human agents of national growth. To Jefferson,
of course, they had always been something of an abstraction, idealized images to inhabit future frontiers. Although he purchased a
huge territory for their eventual expansion, he was not ready to
release them for a pell-mell push toward the Pacific. Andrew Jackson, on the other hand, who shared many of the rough customs
and boisterous behaviors of frontier folk, knew them as real flesh
and blood. He made their aggressiveness and antagonism toward
Indians part of federal policy. In a sense, settlers became the shock
troops of national expansion, moving into Indian territory in advance of federal authority and effectively forcing the government
to follow with military force. Jackson was only too happy to oblige.

It was during the Jacksonian era that these westward-moving settlers set the stage for the next step in expansion. In the late 1820s and early 1830s, while the first groups of southeastern Indians were on their forced march to the reservations west of the Mississippi, a small but steadily growing stream of United States citizens began heading into the region just south of the reservations—out of the United States, in fact, and into territory controlled by another new American nation, Mexico. Their immediate destination was Texas, Mexico's easternmost province in North America. In the end, they would help propel the people from the United States across Mexican territory all the way to the Pacific.

FOUR

W. H. Emory, "Map of Texas and the Countries Adjacent," 1844. *Courtesy Hargrett Rare Book and Manuscript Library, University of Georgia Libraries*

WESTWARD EXPANSION: POLITICAL CONTROVERSY AND POPULAR CULTURE

"Are there any Negroes here?"

When the young black man named Joe heard the voice call out the question in Spanish, he knew there could be no escape. Summoning up his courage, he stepped out of his hiding place and said firmly, "Yes, here is one."

As soon as they saw him, two soldiers turned their guns on him; one shot at him, grazing his side; and the other nicked him with a bayonet. Fortunately, an officer intervened and no doubt saved Joe's life. He knew Joe was an important prisoner—the only surviving defender of the small Texas mission known as the Alamo.

As the soldiers led Joe across the courtyard, he saw in the Sunday-morning sunlight the grisly results of the battle that had just ended. On the ground and along the walls of the mission lay a tangle of bodies, some in the plain clothes of frontier farmers and hunters, even more in the uniform of the Mexican Army. Joe saw one dead woman lying between two guns, but he could not even guess the number of dead men. (In fact, no one could ever provide an exact count. Over 180 of the defenders died in the battle or were executed immediately afterward; the casualty estimates for the attacking Mexicans ranged anywhere from three hundred to over a thousand.) Joe knew, though, that one of the dead men was the commander of the Alamo garrison, Colonel William Barret Travis, who happened to be his owner.

Joe had become Travis's slave in February 1834, soon after both of them arrived in Texas. Joe had originally come as the property of the man who sold him to Travis, and he had had little choice about making the move. Travis, on the other hand, had come to Texas of his own volition, both to escape his past and to secure his future. After a successful early career as a teacher and lawyer in Alabama, Travis suddenly headed west in 1831; his wife had been unfaithful, he claimed, so he left her and a child behind. In Texas he took up work as a lawyer, and he did well enough to buy Joe and to support a life laced with sex, alcohol, and gambling.

Travis also fell in with fellow settlers from the United States who were soon intent on making Texas independent from Mexico. By 1835, they had begun organizing an army, and Travis, a dashing and active figure, quickly rose to the rank of lieutenant colonel. In February 1836, he was assigned to take a handful of men to the small town of San Antonio de Bexar to reinforce the rebel garrison holed up inside the Alamo. Within a week, he had become the Alamo's commander. Within a few weeks more, he and his men were besieged by a Mexican force of over two thousand. During that time, Joe's status changed too, from officer's orderly to fellow soldier.

At dawn on March 6, when the final Mexican assault began, Travis roused Joe from his sleep, and the two rushed to a battery position on the north wall, where they began to fire down on the Mexican soldiers trying to scale the wall. Within a few minutes, Travis took a bullet in the head and slumped down behind the wall, while the Mexicans scrambled over, as Joe later put it, "like sheep." One of the Mexican officers, General Mora, struck at Travis with a sword, but Travis had just enough strength to thrust his own sword into his attacker, and then the two died next to each other. By that time, Joe, like most of the other defenders, had retreated from the walls into the courtyard and buildings of the mission compound. He found shelter in a small barracks room and began firing. When he ran out of ammunition, he waited for the soldiers to come for him, all the while listening to the horrible sounds of the battle as men fought hand to hand from building to building and room to room. Finally, the shooting subsided, and after a few volleys from firing squads, everything was quiet. All the defenders were dead—except for Joe. Somehow, the Mexicans had missed him during the melee.

Later that morning, after the Mexicans had found Joe, they took him out into the courtyard, where the bodies of the dead defenders lay stacked in a pile, ready to be burned. He watched as the soldiers assembled before their commander, General Antonio López de Santa Anna, the President of Mexico, who gave a fiery victory speech; his dramatic gestures and animated oratory reminded Joe of a Methodist preacher's. Joe soon got to meet Santa Anna personally, when he was brought before the Mexican general for interrogation. Santa Anna wanted to know about the size of the rebel force, but he also wanted to make sure Joe knew the size and strength of the Mexican Army; with Joe as a prominent spectator, he staged a formal review of his troops, about eight thousand in all.

A few days later, Joe made his escape (or perhaps Santa Anna let him go) and headed for the rebel stronghold at Washington-on-the-Brazos. Along the way, he encountered an improbable group of travelers—a black man and a white woman and her infant child—who also turned out to have been at the Alamo on the morning of the battle. Joe knew the woman: she was Susannah Dickinson, the wife (now widow) of Almaron Dickinson, one of the officers in charge of the Alamo's artillery. She and her little girl, Angelina, had been spared by Santa Anna, and they rode away from the Alamo accompanied by the black man, Ben, who was a cook for Santa Anna's officers. (Unlike Joe, Ben was not a slave: the Mexican government had outlawed slavery in Texas.) When the party reached the rebel lines, Susannah, Ben, and Joe recounted what they had seen and heard the morning of the massacre; each of them confirmed that the leaders of the Alamo defenders—Colonel Travis, Lieutenant Dickinson, Jim Bowie, and Davy Crockett —had all died. According to one of his listeners, Joe told his part of the story "with much modesty, apparent candor, and remarkably distinctly for one of his class." Sam Houston, the rebel commander, cried when he heard the news.

Then they went on their separate ways into historical obscurity. Ben signed on as cook for Sam Houston, and he soon had the opportunity to see his old employer, Santa Anna, soundly defeated and captured by Houston's vengeance-minded army at the Battle of San Jacinto on April 21, 1836, just six weeks after the Battle of the Alamo. After that, there is little record of Ben's life. Susannah

Dickinson's life took some difficult turns. As a single parent, she had few financial resources, and she had to resort to prostitution to survive. She eventually remarried and lived the rest of her life in Texas, telling anyone who would listen about her adventures in the Alamo; in 1878, in fact, she was a noted member of the audience when the popular Alamo melodrama, *Davy Crockett: Or, Be Sure You're Right, Then Go Ahead*, played Austin.

Joe got out of Texas. Although he was a survivor of the celebrated battle, his skin color precluded his ascension to hero status along with the rest of the defenders. He worked in Washington-on-the-Brazos for about a year, and then, on April 21, 1837—a year to the day after the Battle of San Jacinto—he stole a horse and headed for Alabama, to the Travis homestead. According to Travis family legend, Joe was the first person to bring the news of Travis's death. Some years later—the records are not clear about exactly when—Joe died in Alabama and was buried in an unmarked grave.

Since then, Joe has remained a minor and mostly forgotten figure in the Alamo drama. The traditional telling depicts the battle as a massacre—as indeed it was—but massacre stories have more emotional impact if they do not have survivors. Moreover, if the only survivor happens to be a black man who fought alongside whites, the assumption of a common fate (much less a common racial identity) of the combatants becomes a bit less compelling. Joe was, thus, an inconvenient exception that needed to be either ignored or explained away. Well into the twentieth century, those few historical accounts that did mention Joe almost always referred to him as a "boy," the standard southern slur used to diminish the manhood of black males. Even Hollywood had trouble placing Joe in the picture: as late as the 1960s, movies about the Alamo depicted Joe either as a young boy, about ten or twelve years old, or as an old man, too feeble to fight. In fact, he was in his early twenties at the time of the battle, only a few years younger than Travis himself. Yet while Travis and the other Alamo defenders grew to mythic proportions as martyrs in popular memory, Joe has had a hard time finding his proper place in history alongside them.

Still, Joe's presence at the Alamo points to one of the most important factors in the nineteenth-century history of the North

American frontier: the connection between westward expansion and slavery. Joe may have been forgotten, but "Remember the Alamo" became a national battle cry that reached far beyond the borders of Texas. In the years following the fall of the Alamo, the steady stream of settlers moving out of the United States into Texas became a human flood flowing across contested western territory toward the Pacific. To assert its claims to the rest of the continent, the United States confronted not just Mexico but also Great Britain, not to mention the Indians who inhabited the interior. The attempt to acquire territory became a national passion; politicians and other promoters of westward expansion—including some of the nation's leading artists and writers—developed an ideology of inevitability, a notion that the nation's "manifest destiny" exerted a powerful pull all the way to the Pacific. By 1850, that destiny seemed fulfilled; by warfare and diplomacy, the United States had removed all "foreign" nations from competition. Indians were the only remaining source of resistance.

The struggle against external forces only covered up a growing internal struggle about the future of the western frontier. Like Joe, thousands of African-American slaves had moved west with their masters, and southern slaveowners looked hopefully down the paths to the Pacific. Northern opponents of slavery looked on with alarm and tried to stop them before they could get far beyond the Mississippi. Thus the westward movement divided into two competing political movements that struggled for supremacy and ultimately turned on each other in civil war. The question that brought Joe out of hiding in 1836—"Are there any Negroes here?"—took on a much broader meaning as it echoed across the continent for the next twenty-five years.

———•———

The United States and Mexico came into conflict over Texas in large part because both were new nations trying to define a frontier policy. In 1821, when an indigenous independence movement finally succeeded in throwing off three centuries of Spanish control, Mexico entered the era of independence with many of the same problems that had faced the United States four decades earlier. Above all, Mexico was land-rich and cash-poor. Getting loose from Spain meant losing Spanish capital; as David J. Weber notes, Mexico was "born bankrupt," and it stayed that way for over fifty years. At the same time, the new Mexican government inherited a huge northern frontier that ran from the Gulf of Mexico to the Pacific Northwest, and even that was a mixed blessing at best. In the years before independence, the old presidios and missions established by the Spanish had become forlorn outposts in a distant, disadvantaged, and economically undeveloped region. As had been the case in the Anglo-American experience, the Hispanic settlers who lived on the frontier often evoked scorn for their apparent indolence and independence. According to an eighteenth-century official of New Spain, "They love distance which makes them independent in order to adopt the liberty and slovenliness which they see . . . in their neighbors the wild Indians." Moreover, many local officials in frontier regions allowed for rather lax enforcement of governmental policies, preferring to promote peace and quiet among their neighbors. Therefore, one of the most difficult tasks facing the new government of Mexico was regulating these frontier regions and integrating them into the national political and economic system centered in Mexico City.

That proved to be an especially difficult task in Texas. The Hispanic inhabitants of the province, the *tejanos*, felt little loyalty to the central government, whether it be Spanish or, now, Mexican. Although Spanish government officials had intended the Texas frontier to be a buffer zone abutting the United States, it had become instead a contact zone, a meeting ground for settlers from both societies. Frustrated by the restrictive trade policies of the colonial government and, more generally, by the lack of manufactured goods available on the frontier, *tejanos* had begun trading with Louisiana merchants long before Mexican independence. By the same token, Anglo-American outsiders had been drifting into Texas since the eighteenth century, squatting on land under the indulgent gaze of local officials. On the eve of independence, in fact, the Spanish government began offering a few legitimate land grants to selected Anglo-American *empresarios* who came to establish colonies of Catholic (or at least nominally Catholic) settlers. Spanish officials figured that a limited influx of immigrants from the United States could help fill up the frontier, build up the economy, and provide additional protection against hostile Indians. At the time of Mexican independence, then, more than two thousand *norteamericanos*, both legal and illegal immigrants, lived in Texas.

During the 1820s, the new Mexican government tried to continue this cautious policy of controlled settlement. With a wary eye on westward-moving Anglo-Americans, a government commission warned in 1821 that unwanted outsiders might swarm into Mexico "just as the Goths, Ostrogoths, Alans, and other tribes devastated the Roman Empire." Mexican officials saw these aggressive immigrants as insidious agents of United States expansion, and they feared that their uncontrolled increase would eventually undermine the Mexican government's authority over its northern frontier—as indeed turned out to be the case. But the central government proved powerless to stop them, and local officials hardly even tried. By the late 1820s, the Anglo-American population of Texas was approaching seven thousand, which was more than double the estimated Mexican population of three thousand. Moreover, these settlers resisted assimilation into Mexican society and lived apart as a separate (and, in their own minds, superior) segment of the frontier population; they wanted to establish their own colonies and cotton plantations, extending into Texas the slave-labor system they had known in the southern states. To discourage the arrival of even more outsiders, the Mexican government outlawed slavery in Texas in 1829. The following year, it took an even more direct step by closing the Texas borders to additional immigration from the United States.

Neither approach worked. Frontier officials in Texas, always more loyal to their local interests than to the policies of the central government, generally failed to enforce the immigration laws and quietly encouraged the arrival of additional illegal aliens. They also tolerated slavery, or at least seemingly accepted the polite fiction that the black people on the plantations were not slaves but contract laborers. In general, no matter what Mexico's central government wanted to do to keep Texas Mexican, its own frontier officials opened the gates to slaveowning settlers from the United States; by 1836, the immigrant population, including slaves, had risen to over forty thousand—more than ten times the number of *tejanos*.

As the Mexican government had feared, these *norteamericanos* did not aspire to Mexican citizenship; they wanted their own independent state. Texas was fast becoming the sorest spot on a frontier already festering with separatist sentiment. From Yucatán in the south to California in the far west, inhabitants of Mexico's outlying provinces had been grumbling about the government's attempts to establish a system of centralized control, and in a few cases grumbling had turned to localized revolt. President Santa Anna, a strong centralist, attempted to squelch such unrest before it got out of hand: he personally led government forces on a brutal punitive expedition against Zacatecas, one of the northern states, in April 1835, and the following month he got the Mexican Congress to give him almost dictatorial control over the Mexican states. Santa Anna's actions only intensified the frustration of frontier settlers. In Texas, there were now enough Anglo-American immigrants to make the possibility of a large-scale revolt a serious concern.

During the early 1830s, however, not all Anglo-Texans had favored total independence. A moderate faction, the "peace party" under the leadership of the influential *empresario* Stephen F. Austin, sought only to reduce the restrictions on relations with the United States, especially with regard to trade, immigration, and slavery. As late as 1833, they petitioned Santa Anna to make Texas a separate Mexican state and even drafted a state constitution based on the 1780 constitution of Massachusetts. They did not call for breaking away altogether.

But while the peace party petitioned, other Anglo-Texans turned to armed resistance. The "war party"—which included the young lawyer and ladies' man William Barret Travis—made ready to oppose Mexican authorities and force the government to grant Texas its independence. Santa Anna's dictatorial actions in 1835 played into their hands, giving them added justification for taking dramatic steps. In June 1835, Travis and others launched a successful attack on the small garrison at Anahuac, the main tariff-collection point on Galveston Bay. Not surprisingly, the capture of Anahuac only confirmed in Santa Anna the need to meet force with force, and he launched a full-blown military campaign to crush the "war party" and discipline all unruly Texans.

It was not as easy as Santa Anna had anticipated. The march of the Mexican Army convinced Austin and the other proponents of peace that the time for petition had passed; they threw in with Travis and the radicals. Rebellious settlers—mostly Anglo-Texans but some *tejanos* as well—defied Santa Anna's army at the small town of Gonzales, and they later took Mexican military outposts at Goliad and San Antonio de Bexar. After the loss of San Antonio, an enraged Santa Anna assumed personal command of his army. He became even more enraged when the main body of his force reached San Antonio in late February 1836 and he found the small band of rebels inside the Alamo blocking his northward march. After a thirteen-day siege—much longer than he thought he should have to spend on such an annoying obstacle—Santa Anna ordered his men to take the Alamo at all costs. They would offer no quarter to the defenders inside. Thus it was that on the morning of March 6, after an assault lasting less than ninety minutes, the Alamo garrison was crushed.

Within six weeks, so were Santa Anna's dreams of retaking Texas. On March 2, 1836—just four days before the fall of the Alamo—a convention of rebellious Texans had declared their independence from Mexico and formed the Lone Star Republic. The subsequent destruction of the garrison at the Alamo and, a few weeks later, the massacre of another rebel force at Goliad only reinforced the Texans' desire for independence with the demand for revenge. After word of the events in Texas reached the United States, hundreds of volunteers poured into Texas to join Sam Houston's rebel forces. Houston had originally thought Travis a fool for trying to defend the Alamo, and he was furious when Travis ignored his orders to abandon the garrison. But with Travis now dead rather than disobedient, Houston could call on the memory of the Alamo martyrs to inspire his men. On the afternoon of April 21, while Santa Anna and his men were taking a siesta near the banks of the San Jacinto River, Houston launched a ferocious surprise attack that routed the Mexicans in a matter of minutes. Awakened by cries of "Remember the Alamo!" and "Remember Goliad!" Santa Anna barely managed to escape as his force fell into chaos. Captured later, disguised as a common soldier, the Mexican general was brought before Houston and forced to accept terms recognizing the independence of Texas. Although Santa Anna and the Mexican government would never admit that the treaty was legitimate, Houston and his fellow Texans had all they needed to claim complete victory. Like the United States and Mexico, Texas was now an independent republic.

Still, Mexico's loss was not yet the United States' gain—at least, not immediately. Despite the outpouring of acclaim for the Texans' victory in the press, in political circles, and among the people at large; despite the Texans' desire to join the Union as a new state; despite the obvious attractions of so vast and comparatively vacant an expanse of land; in short, despite all the signs that pointed to annexing the Lone Star Republic and making it a new state, Texas was too hot for the United States to touch. Although the United States would grant formal diplomatic recognition to the Lone Star Republic—as did Britain, France, Holland, and Belgium—the government played a cautious hand by not pushing for possession. For almost a decade, Texas remained in a state of what might be called suspended annexation, no longer part of Mexico, but not yet part of the United States.

Two important political considerations kept the United States from taking Texas under its wing immediately. First, government leaders knew that annexing Texas would lead to war with Mexico, which, even given Mexico's military weakness, no one was yet ready to risk. The Mexican government still claimed to control Texas, insisting (quite rightly) that Santa Anna had acceded to the Texans' demands for independence only to escape being hanged by Houston's men after the Battle of San Jacinto. Moreover, Mexican officials suspected Texans of instigating insurrection along Mexico's northern frontier, and they were not altogether wrong. In 1841, the president of Texas, Mirabeau Buonaparte Lamar, sent a force of three hundred men into New Mexico, certain that a substantial number of New Mexicans would leap at the chance to become part of Texas. His attempt to export revolution failed, and his men suffered miserably as they endured starvation, thirst, captivity, a forced march, and imprisonment. Lamar's expedition did nothing but increase Mexico's enmity toward *norteamericanos* in Texas, and the annexation of Texas by the United States would only have increased it more.

Second, and even more worrisome, was the growing antagonism within the United States itself over the issue of slavery. The United States government, no less than the Mexican government, had to be concerned by the emergence of the Lone Star Republic as a region dominated by slaveholding interests. East Texas had vast amounts of rich cotton land, and slaveowners from the southern states looked longingly toward bringing Texas into the Union as a slave state. Their anti-slavery opponents understood the implications of such a move, and they had already made clear their determination to block any attempt to take in Texas. Everyone could see that forcing the Texas question would lead to a divisive fight in Congress.

The government had faced such an issue before, with the struggle over Missouri statehood in 1819–20. When the settlers of the Missouri Territory first petitioned Congress to join the Union, they wanted to enter as a slave state, just as other new states—Louisiana (1812), Mississippi (1817), and Alabama (1819)—had done. It was no longer that easy, however. The admission of Alabama had created a numerical balance between slave and non-slave states, with eleven of each, and that balance became crucial in the Senate, where each state had two votes. If Missouri entered the Union as a slave state, the balance in the Senate would be upset. Accordingly, northern members of the House, not willing to see pro-slavery politicians get the upper hand in the Senate, attached a proviso to the Missouri statehood bill calling for the eventual abolition of slavery in Missouri. Congressmen from slave states rose up in outrage, and Congress remained deadlocked for months. Finally, a series of political agreements known collectively as the Missouri Compromise cut through the controversy. Missouri would enter the Union as a slave state in 1821, but it was preceded in 1820 by Maine, a new non-slave state that had formerly been part of Massachusetts. Thus the balance was preserved, at least for the time being; so, in the minds of many relieved observers, was the Union itself.

The balance held throughout the 1820s and 1830s, when another pair of slave/non-slave states—Arkansas (1836) and Michigan (1837)—joined the Union. By 1836, though, the national debate over slavery had become increasingly strident, and Congress had heard enough: to shield itself from the flurry of anti-slavery petitions coming in each year, it imposed a Gag Rule in 1836, whereby all petitions regarding slavery would simply be tabled and never brought to the floor for debate. Clearly, with the government and the nation as a whole in such a conflict over the future of slavery, the timing was not good for Texas statehood.

In another sense, the Texas question could hardly have been more timely. No matter what the government did to avoid diplomatic crises with Mexico or debates over slavery in Congress, it could do virtually nothing to hold back the increasing enthusiasm for national expansion. Throughout the second quarter of the nineteenth century, while official government policy called for caution, popular culture became fascinated with the frontier. Literature, painting, and other forms of artistic expression reflected (and thus reinforced) a new awareness of the North American wilderness, especially the vast, unexplored expanses in the West. The people who lived there—or, more to the point, the Anglo-Americans who lived there—became intriguing new figures in the eyes of easterners. Suddenly, it seemed, the people of the United States had overcome the fear of the frontier that had been so common in eighteenth-century culture. In the "Young America" of the Jacksonian era, the frontier seemed the new hope for the nation's future, and the frontiersman took center stage as a new kind of national hero.

In the first half of the nineteenth century, painters began to put this more favorable image of the frontier on canvas, and in doing so they helped define the artistic identity of the United States. Asher B. Durand, Thomas Cole, and the other painters of the Hudson River School focused on the forests of the Northeast, where they still hoped to capture the American environment as it had existed before being touched by human hands. As Cole explained in his "Essay on American Scenery" (1835), "The most distinctive, and perhaps the most impressive, characteristic of American scenery is its wildness." Even though New York's Hudson Valley had become an economically well-developed region by the 1820s, dotted with farms, forges, and mills, these eastern artists recorded a romanticized image of wilderness that reminded the viewer of what the East had been—and suggested what the West still was. Other American artists actually went west. In the 1830s and 1840s, George Catlin, George Caleb Bingham, Charles Deas, Alfred J. Miller, and William Ranney became the most prominent painters of western scenes, and the images they painted found an increasingly appreciative reception among eastern patrons and audiences.

None had a greater impact than Catlin. The Pennsylvania-born Catlin began his career as a portraitist of average if not outstanding talent—good enough, at least, to have his work shown at the Philadelphia Academy of Fine Arts in the 1820s. It was not until the

1830s, however, that he found his true calling as an artist of the American West and, most important, of the American Indian. For six years he traveled throughout the West, from the Dakotas to Texas, living among Indians and painting a remarkable number of portraits. Catlin often had Indians literally lining up to have their likenesses done. Working quickly, he would sketch in the face and capture the basic character of his subject and then fill in the details later. The finished result was a powerful portrayal of the individual Indian, dignified in demeanor but exotically dressed and decorated, "all in a state of primitive wildness . . . picturesque and handsome, almost beyond description."

When Catlin brought his collection of Indian paintings back to "civilized society" in the East, he became an instant success. In 1837, he displayed several hundred works in a traveling exhibit that opened in New York to packed houses and appreciative reviews and then moved on to Philadelphia, Washington, London, and Paris. In addition to the paintings, Catlin also included in his show a tipi and other Indian artifacts, and he had actors (including himself) dress up as Indians to enhance the exotic ambiance of the exhibit. Always in need of money to keep the show on the road, Catlin crossed the line from artist to entrepreneur and revealed himself, as Herman Viola has observed, a "born showman . . . [who] preceded Buffalo Bill as impresario of a Wild West show by half a century." And even if the exhibit itself became tainted by commercial excess and cultural exploitation, the paintings themselves remained powerful images of the Indian, and they helped stimulate increased interest in western subjects.

Some critics, however, wanted to see more white people in the picture. In an 1845 review of a painting called *The Indian Guide* by Charles Deas, a Brooklyn newspaper expressed uneasiness with Catlin's emphasis on Indians: "Pictures of pure savage life, like those by Mr. Catlin, cannot excite our sympathies as strongly as do the representations of beings who belong to our own race." The reviewer went on to note with approval that the subject in the Deas painting appeared to be of mixed blood. Unlike the Indian, who "stands at an impassible remove from civilization . . . the half-breed forms a connecting link between the white and red races . . . for we see that he has a tincture of our own blood, and his trappings show that he has taken one step toward refinement in civilized life." Here, then, was the darker side of art appreciation, a racist reaction to Indians on canvas that reflected a larger hostility toward Indians on the continent itself. In art as well as in life, the future of the frontier pointed to the increasing presence of whites.

If critics wanted western subjects that reflected "refinement in civilized life," they could find them in the works of another of Catlin's contemporaries, George Caleb Bingham. Born in Virginia but raised mostly on the Missouri frontier in the 1820s, Bingham was essentially a self-taught artist. In his early career he made a modest living painting portraits and political banners, but he eventually gained his greatest fame for Missouri landscapes and genre paintings, especially scenes of life on the river. Bingham created what the art world wanted: images of an inviting environment settled by common white people. Bingham painted a West that easterners could easily imagine living in themselves. Unlike the artists of the Hudson River School, he did not romanticize the landscape by depicting the dramatic power of nature; his river paintings tended toward the pacific, portraying both people and the environment in moments of calm. Unlike Catlin, he did not focus on the far-western wilderness inhabited by Indians; he stopped at the farthest edge of Euro-American settlement inhabited by fur traders, rivermen, and, eventually, farm families. As Nancy Rash, one of the more recent students of Bingham's art, has observed, his vision of the West was "a place of families with ties to the land, of cultivated fields, of domestic animals, of towns." It was the West already possessed by the United States.

While painters were framing the frontier on canvas, writers were putting it into print. One of the earliest and most enduring forms of frontier writing was the captivity narrative, which became popular as early as the seventeenth century; two of the most famous examples of the genre, Mary Rowlandson's *The Sovereignty and Goodness of God* (1682) and John Williams's *The Redeemed Captive Returning to Zion* (1707) remained best-sellers well into the nineteenth century. Such tales typically told of white people who were taken by Indians in raids or in battle; were held in, and sometimes adopted into, Indian villages; and then, after being rescued or redeemed, were returned to white society. Playing on the tension between notions of the "civilized" and the "savage," captivity narratives were intended to be didactic as well as dramatic, reinforcing among Euro-American readers a sense of their cultural superiority when their beliefs and behaviors were placed in stark contrast to those of native peoples. But on another level, as June Namias has noted, captivity narratives also reveal "a fascination with both the other and the self" that sometimes betrays Euro-American anxieties about ethnic and gender identities. Especially when the story dealt with a woman captive, which was quite often the case, the interplay between the specter of sexual violation and the display of female strength could create an unsettling counterpoint to the norms of frontier womanhood. If nothing else, captivity narratives offered an alluring, at times even lurid, alternative to the long list of sermons, advice manuals, and other sorts of prescriptive literature available to early American readers.

At the end of the eighteenth century, frontier literature took a new turn when John Filson, a young Pennsylvania schoolteacher, published a seemingly unexceptional book, *The Discovery, Settlement and Present State of Kentucke* (1784), to which he attached *An Appendix, Containing the Adventures of Col. Daniel Boon*. Filson had come to Kentucky in the wake of the Revolution not just to teach school but to deal in land, and his book reflected the mixed motives of scholar and speculator. Like most quasi-scientific surveys, Filson's description of Kentucky painted a promising picture of this frontier region, highlighting nature's abundance and embellishing the benefits the land offered the new settler. But with the section on Boone, Filson's book went beyond the standard promotional literature of land speculators. The ghost-written autobiography of the frontiersman contained tales of wilderness exploration and Indian fighting, complete with a captivity narrative. Whether Boone's story was actually true or not—and Boone always insisted that it was: "Not a lie in it!"—Filson had written an exciting tale of adventure in the American wilderness, in which Boone became the embodiment of the backwoodsman. Unfortunately, Filson perished soon after he published, killed in an Indian attack in Kentucky in 1788. *Kentucke* never became a best-seller in book form, but a much-abbreviated pamphlet version stayed in print in the United States for years, contributing to the emerging image of the frontiersman as a new kind of literary hero.

It was in the 1820s—at the beginning of the Jacksonian era—that frontier fiction fully entered the mainstream of American literature. In 1823, James Fenimore Cooper published the first of his "Leatherstocking" novels, *The Pioneers*, which was followed by *The Last of the Mohicans* (1826), *The Prairie* (1826), *The Pathfinder* (1840), and *The Deerslayer* (1841). Even though Cooper published over a dozen other novels and several works of non-fiction, he expressed this hope: "If anything from the pen of the writer of these romances is at all to outlive himself, it is, unquestionably, the series of *The Leatherstocking Tales*." Cooper could rest easy. The five "Leatherstocking" novels gained him both immense popularity in his lifetime and a prominent place in the history of American literature. (By the time he began writing the "Leatherstocking" novels, however, Cooper was living in comfortable circumstances in New York City and, for a while, Paris, Florence, and other European cities. He would be by no means the last American artist to depict the frontier from an urban outpost.) More than any other writer before or, arguably, since, Cooper infused the frontier with mystery and meaning, elevating it to mythical proportions in the national psyche. He made no claim to writing an altogether accurate historical account of frontier life; he wanted to capture the essence of the American frontier and, above all, the *beau ideal* of the frontiersman.

Everything came together in one central character carried through all the novels: Natty Bumppo, the honorable frontiersman whose various sobriquets—Leatherstocking, Pathfinder, Deerslayer, Hawkeye—clearly identified him as a man of the wilderness, a common man of heroic and inescapably symbolic stature. Born to Anglo-American parents but raised among Indians, Natty was a man of nature, neither savage nor civilized. Although Natty had deep affection for "good" Indians, like his friend Chingachgook, Cooper is careful to remind his readers that this frontiersman was no half-breed; his untainted Anglo-American blood symbolizes the racial purity of the pioneer. Moreover, his untainted morality symbolizes the purity that those of his race can achieve. "In Natty Bumppo," Richard Slotkin has observed, "all of the good qualities of the Frontier hunter and yeoman are concentrated and all the bad left out."

Yet, as much as Natty stands for his fellow Anglo-Americans, he often stands apart from them. In a famous scene from *The Pioneers*, he criticizes the frontier settlers' "wasty ways" of abusing the abundance of the American environment; in *The Prairie*, he feels regret when he hears "the sound of axes, and the crash of falling trees." His personal harmony with nature separates him, both physically and psychologically, from the rest of Anglo-American society. Still, he can never escape. At the end of his life (in *The Prairie*) Natty has moved west to the Great Plains, where he lives out his final days among the Pawnee Indians. But even then, as Annette Kolodny notes, "the very fact of Natty's being a white man, skilled in tracking and woodlore, and having, as a result, at least *some* ties to advancing settlement, puts him always in danger of somehow aiding that settlement's violating process into nature's enclosures." As he witnesses the arrival of wasteful white men on the plains, his melancholy is tinged with guilt: "I might have know'd it . . . I brought them to the spot myself." He dies among the Pawnees, sitting in a chair facing east, looking back with ambivalence over the path that led him west, a path that so many of his fellow countrymen would follow, both in fiction and in fact.

Nowhere are the complexities facing the simple man more evident than in *The Deerslayer*. In this last book of the "Leatherstocking" series, which is set in Natty's early life, Natty kills an Indian for the first time. Although an act of self-defense, it is an inevitable, almost necessary, rite of passage: "I know'd it—I know'd it!" Natty says, both echoing and anticipating his later realization in *The Prairie*, "I know'd it must come to this." When the Indian finally expires, Natty understands the broader implications of his actions:

> Well, this is my first battle with a human mortal, though it's not likely to be the last. I have fou't most of the creatur's of the forest, such as bears, wolves, painters, and catamounts, but this is the beginning with the redskins.

And so it was. By the 1840s, a century after the action in the novel, Cooper and his readers clearly knew where the "beginning with the redskins" would end. Looking back over the earlier novels and ahead in Natty's life, Cooper's readers could rest assured that Hawkeye would remain an honorable individual inescapably caught up in a larger drama in which the motives and methods of his fellow Anglo-Americans were not always as noble as his own. Although he occasionally regretted the aggressive expansion of the whites, he was powerless to prevent it; in fact, he did not even try. Still, the personal dignity and decency of this single figure helped sanitize the past, offering a moral alternative that enabled Cooper's readers to accept the often unsettling implications of their national history.

While Cooper was working out the complexities of his fictitious frontiersman, an equally fascinating figure emerged from real life: Davy Crockett, the classic common man likewise elevated to heroic stature. Even before he died a martyr's death at the Alamo, Crockett had become a living legend, larger than Daniel Boone. He was a creature of popular culture who was half man and half myth, half fact and half fiction, a frontier favorite who received as much acclaim in eastern cities as he did in the western settlements.

In his 1834 autobiography, *A Narrative of the Life of David Crockett, of the State of Tennessee* (which was, like Daniel Boone's, ghost-written by a more literate collaborator), Crockett opened with a self-effacing admission of wonder at his widespread popularity:

> I know, that obscure as I am, my name is making considerable deal of fuss in the world. I can't tell why it is, or in what it is to end. Go where I will, everybody seems anxious to get a peep at me. . . . There must therefore be something in me, or about me, that attracts attention, which is even mysterious to myself.

Yet there was no mystery about all the fuss, and Crockett knew it. He was a new Daniel Boone with better publicity, a true Natty Bumppo brought to life in almost superhuman size with homespun humor. In an anonymously written but enormously popular book, *Sketches and Eccentricities of Col. David Crockett of West Tennessee* (1833), the author first celebrated Crockett's skill in the woods with almost surprising restraint:

> To bear hunting, Colonel Crockett has ever been most wedded; first because it is profitable; secondly, because there is danger in it, and consequently great excitement. It requires a *man* to be a bear hunter.

But as the fabled exploits unfolded, Crockett the unfettered frontiersman burst forth, full of belligerent bluster.

I'm that same David Crockett, fresh from the backwoods, half-horse, half-alligator, a little touched with the snapping-turtle; can wade the Mississippi, leap the Ohio, ride upon a streak of lightning, and slip without a scratch down a honey locust; can whip my weight in wild cats,—and if any gentleman pleases, for a ten dollar bill, he may throw in a panther,—hug a bear too close for comfort, and eat any man opposed to Jackson.

Here was a man who, like "Young America" itself, knew no bounds. Not just another of nature's noblemen like Natty, fretting about the fate of the frontier as it filled up with white settlers, Crockett was the wild man of the wilderness, the brash and aggressive agent of expansion, the half-human hero who could conquer nature and claim the continent as his own.

Some of it was true. Crockett was a child of the frontier, raised in the remotest parts of Anglo-American settlement. Born in 1786 in eastern Tennessee, he spent most of his youth working to help pay off the debts of his father, a struggling farmer and tavern-keeper. By the most generous reckoning, Crockett had only a hundred or so days of formal education in his lifetime; later in life, when he was serving as a small-town magistrate, Crockett admitted (or bragged): "I never read a page in a law book in all my life." In the classic style of the Bumppo-like backwoods settler, Crockett always seemed uneasy with the approach of "civilization," and he moved farther west every few years.

He eventually moved into politics as well. In 1818, he made his first venture into electoral politics when he ran successfully for town commissioner in Lawrenceburg, Tennessee; he was later elected to the Tennessee state legislature, where he served from 1821 to 1825, and then to the United States Congress, where he was a member of the House from 1827 to 1831 and again from 1833 to 1835. Often mocked by his legislative colleagues as "the gentleman from the cane," Crockett was a backwoods Jacksonian who had a serious commitment to his constituents. One issue he championed throughout his legislative career, for instance, was a land bill to provide poor settlers with easier access to government lands. Unlike others who viewed squatters as slothful obstacles to orderly settlement and productive development, Crockett saw them as the advance agents of expansion, or at least as people who had a reasonable right to the land they improved. Crockett also had sympathy for Indian rights to the land, and he openly opposed Andrew Jackson's policy of Indian removal. This high-minded stance enraged the Jacksonians, and it did not play especially well back home among his constituents, who were both land-hungry and hostile to Indians. In 1831 he lost his seat in Congress.

Taking advantage of Crockett's anti-Jackson apostasy, the Whigs embraced Crockett and made him their man in the West. They not only helped get him reelected to Congress in 1833, but they also promoted him on the national scene, both in person and in print. His ghost-written *Autobiography* (1834) sold well, and the following year a Whig-sponsored junket to New England led to the publication of *An Account of Col. Crockett's Tour to the North and Down East* (1835). Crockett delighted eastern audiences as the wise-cracking western Whig, the consummate common man who poked fun at (and holes in) the Jackson image. Unfortunately, he was unable to make the message work again with his Tennessee constituents; in 1835 he lost the congressional election to a local Jacksonian loyalist, Adam Huntsman, who had both a woodsy name and a wooden leg. After the defeat, Crockett knew his political career in Tennessee had come to an end, and he bade farewell in classic Crockett style. "Since you have chosen to elect a man with a timber toe to succeed me," he told an assembly of Tennessee voters, "you may all go to Hell and I will go to Texas."

Crockett's trip to Texas cost him his life, but it gave new life to his legend. No sooner had word of his death reached the East than his publishers cranked out an ersatz autobiographical account, *Col Crockett's Exploits and Adventures in Texas, Written by Himself* (1836). Written in diary style, the book took Crockett right up to his final hours, when he recorded the sounds of battle—"Pop, pop, pop! Bom, bom, bom!"—and heroically signed off with his trademark slogan, "Go ahead!—Liberty and independence forever!" With earnest assurances that the diary was the genuine item, allegedly found in the rubble of the Alamo and sent to them soon after the battle, the publishers perpetrated a brazen fraud on the reading public. (A Texas newspaper editor went one step further a few years later, printing a fictitious letter asserting that Crockett was in fact still alive, working as a prison laborer in a Mexican mine.) When it came to Davy Crockett, the legend always mattered more than the literal truth. *Col. Crockett's Exploits* became a best-seller and even created additional demand for the earlier *Tour*, which had had disappointing sales up to that point. *Davy Crockett's Almanack*, which had first been published in 1835, likewise took off; for the next twenty years, various editions of this compendium of common sense and homespun humor remained a staple of popular literature, keeping Crockett alive in the national imagination. For a man with precious little formal education, Crockett had finally found his place in print.

Davy Crockett, Natty Bumppo, noble Indians, savage Indians, dramatic mountain landscapes, peaceful pastoral scenes—these were the increasingly common (and sometimes conflicting) artistic images that intrigued easterners looking west. The territorial expansion of the United States had stopped at Missouri in 1821, but the appeal of the western frontier continued to grow in the national imagination. Not many people living east of the Mississippi had actually seen the West, but thousands had envisioned it in their minds. They sensed the power of the landscape, the vast openness that offered the opportunity not only for a new start in life but also for a new type of life. There a common man could test and perhaps transform himself, becoming a hero in his own right and sharing in the mythic history of the American frontier. The West was the meeting point between the nation's past and future, America as it once was and as it should be.

By the early 1840s, when political leaders were still trying to avoid talking about taking Texas, a pent-up popular impulse for western conquest was growing around them. It was as if Davy Crockett's famous motto, "Be sure you're right, then go ahead," had become the slogan for national expansion. Whether right or not, thousands of people from the United States and Western Europe headed for Texas in the post-independence period, taking the lure of free land the Lone Star Republic had used to attract them; by 1845, the Euro-American population of Texas had risen to over 140,000. In 1845, in fact, a New York journalist, John L. O'Sullivan, would coin an even more powerful slogan of just two words: Manifest Destiny. The true mission of the United States, he claimed, was "to overspread and to possess the whole of the continent which Providence has given us" in order to bring the benefits of Anglo-

American culture to all people between the Atlantic and the Pacific. Thus inspired by the words of O'Sullivan and numerous other writers, many citizens of the United States assumed the West was already theirs by divine right; within a few years, they would make it theirs by force of arms.

But only the government could issue the call to arms, and the dangers of doing so remained daunting. Only a very bold, very foolish, or very desperate politician would take that risk.

John Tyler was, to be charitable, the third of those. He was a politically unpopular, Democrat-turned-Whig vice president from Virginia who had ascended to the presidency in 1841 when his running mate, William Henry Harrison, "Old Tippecanoe" of the War of 1812, died of pneumonia just a month after taking office. The man known best for following "Tippecanoe" in the political slogan as "Tyler Too" soon gained a new nickname, "His Accidency." Yet, once in office, he wanted to stay there by being elected on his own for a second term in 1844. Knowing that he had too few friends in either party to build a coalition, much less a campaign, on domestic issues, he took the more expedient path so often traveled by politicians seeking a way to look strong and statesmanlike: foreign affairs, where even an unpopular president could take on external enemies, defend his nation's freedoms and fortunes, and thus win the votes of a grateful electorate. To Tyler, Texas looked like a good place to start.

Texas was, in fact, the target of foreign machinations, and not just Mexico's. Both France and England opposed the annexation of Texas by the United States: each saw an independent Texas as a useful trading partner in North America, and perhaps a military ally as well. There was even some talk that England and France might join with Mexico to keep Texas out of the hands of the United States. Moreover, anti-slavery activists in England hoped that their government might pressure or persuade Texas to give up slavery at some point.

Armed with the reality, or certainly the rumor, of increasing European involvement in Texas, Tyler proposed immediate annexation. In late 1843, Secretary of State Abel P. Upshur began secret negotiations with the Texas government, and after Upshur died, John C. Calhoun succeeded him and concluded the negotiations. By April 1844, Tyler and Calhoun had a draft treaty to put before the Senate. Calhoun, the rabidly pro-slavery South Carolinian, promoted Texas annexation as a way to prevent English interference with slavery, to preserve the Southern way of life, and even to promote the welfare of slaves. Only a few senators fell in line with Tyler and Calhoun, however, and Calhoun's extremist stance actually served to galvanize anti-slavery congressmen. With a resounding 35–16 negative vote, the treaty quickly turned into another of Tyler's political failures. His short-lived 1844 presidential campaign, when neither of the major parties would have him, would prove to be the last.

Still, although the 1844 election brought an end to John Tyler's presidential career, it brought the Texas question to life. Suddenly, and somewhat surprisingly, Texas touched a national nerve, and annexation and expansion quickly became critical questions in political debate. As the eminent western historian Ray Allen Billington has observed, "Eighteen forty-four was America's year of decision."

At first, some members of the major parties tried to avoid having to make the decision openly. Henry Clay, the Whig nominee, was known to be an opponent of Texas annexation, but the party platform made no specific mention of Texas. The most likely Democratic candidate, Martin Van Buren, who had also spoken out against Texas annexation, tried to soften his position, but he ran up against opposition from southerners and a few pro-annexation northerners in his party. The Democratic convention fell into a deadlock, and it was not until the ninth ballot that the delegates turned to James K. Polk, an obscure slaveowner from Tennessee who had been suggested by former president Andrew Jackson, and made him their "dark horse" candidate. Thinking themselves secure behind the well-known Clay, the Whigs scoffed, "Who is James K. Polk?"

The answer was: the next president. Polk and the Democrats won (albeit just barely) by making a platform of aggressive expansion palatable to both northerners and southerners. Behind anti-British blustering about national ambitions, they tried to soft-pedal the slavery issue, suggesting that the westward extension of slavery could work to the advantage of North and South alike. Robert J. Walker, a Mississippian who, as chair of the Democrats' executive committee, was chief strategist for the party, asserted that if slavery were allowed to spread westward, the resulting dispersal of the black population, both slave and free, would help reduce racial tensions in the East and might even lead to the demise of slavery in some states. The only force standing in the way of this allegedly enlightened plan, of course, was Great Britain, whose desire to keep Texas independent was only the first step in stopping the spread of slavery.

The Democrats looked far beyond Texas, pointing to the simmering tensions in the Pacific Northwest. For over twenty years, Great Britain and the United States had maintained a joint occupation of the Oregon territory north of the Columbia River and south of the 49th parallel (the current northern boundary of the United States). During that time, a few thousand settlers from the United States had moved into the rich farmland of Oregon's Willamette Valley, just south of the Columbia River, and by the early 1840s the British seemed willing to concede that area. But the Democratic platform raised the bid by claiming that "our title to the whole of the Territory of Oregon is clear and unquestionable; that no portion of the same ought to be ceded to England or to any other power." The "whole" of Oregon extended as far as the southern border of Alaska, at the 54°40' line the United States had established as the northernmost point of its Pacific claims in a 1824 treaty with Russia. Thus, by calling for the "reoccupation of Oregon and the reannexation of Texas," the Democrats created the fiction that the United States would take control of land it already rightfully owned. Moreover, by making Great Britain as much a bogeyman as Mexico, they created just enough common ground among northern and southern voters to make Polk president.

In the minds of many politicians, the 1844 election served as a national referendum on expansion. The outgoing president, John Tyler, now saw another opportunity to annex Texas before his term was over. Not wanting to risk another treaty fight in the Senate, where he would once again need a two-thirds vote, Tyler adopted the new, never-before-tried tactic of having Congress approve the Texas treaty by a joint resolution, which would require only a majority vote. The measure passed easily in the House and won a bare majority in the Senate, allowing Tyler to sign the Texas annexation resolution on March 1, 1845, three days before he left office. The Lone Star Republic gladly accepted annexation in July, and when Congress reconvened in the fall, Texas became the twenty-eighth state.

In the meantime, the new president, James K. Polk, had begun to prepare for the inevitable conflict with Mexico. In June 1845, he sent General Zachary B. Taylor into Texas with orders to position United States troops between the Nueces River and the Rio Grande, in the territory claimed by both Texas and Mexico. Suddenly faced with the intrusion of almost half the United States Army on its own soil, Mexico countered with a troop build-up of its own. While the two armies made menacing gestures toward each other, Polk received word that the Mexican government might still be willing to negotiate its way out of war, and he sent John Slidell, a Spanish-speaking Louisianan, on a secret mission to Mexico City. Slidell was authorized to offer to buy New Mexico for $5 million and, for $25 million, California as well; in exchange, Mexico would agree to recognize the Rio Grande as the southern boundary of Texas. Confusion and a military coup kept the Mexican government from responding favorably, and in March 1846 Slidell returned to the United States empty-handed. An angry Polk made ready for war.

Soon enough, he got it. On May 9, he received word from General Taylor that a scouting party of sixty-three United States dragoons had been attacked by a large Mexican cavalry force operating north of the Rio Grande; sixteen dragoons had been killed or wounded, and others had been taken prisoner. Two days later, Polk sent a war message to Congress, claiming that "by the act of the Republic of Mexico, a state of war exists between that government and the United States." Some members of Congress objected that armed clashes did not make a war and that Polk himself bore at least some responsibility for provoking the Mexican attacks. But Polk got what he wanted: a declaration of war, a $10 million appropriation, and a call for fifty thousand volunteers.

But one war would be enough: Polk did not want to fight Great Britain and Mexico at the same time. His aggressive stance on the Oregon boundary had antagonized the British, and "54°40' or fight" had become a battle cry among Polk's supporters. On May 21, 1846—ten days after declaring war on Mexico—Polk gave the British notice that the joint occupation of Oregon must end and they had one year to leave. The British were unhappy with such belligerence, but they had other pressing problems to attend to much closer to home. They chose to negotiate. Polk did not get control of Oregon up to the 54°40′ line, but the British did cede all the territory below the 49th parallel—which was all Polk had really wanted or expected in the first place. Moreover, by resolving the Oregon boundary issue with bluff rather than bullets, he could turn the full military force of the United States on Mexico.

Both the United States and Mexico had seen the war coming, but neither side was fully prepared. On paper, the Mexican Army was much larger than that of the United States, but it was poorly led, poorly trained, and poorly supplied. Mexican gunpowder was of such poor quality, for instance, that artillery barrages often sent cannonballs bouncing slowly along the ground toward opposing troops, who merely had to step out of the way to avoid being hit. Although Mexican soldiers often fought ferociously in individual battles, the inherent weakness of their army doomed them to defeat. By the same token, the United States Army was not without its own problems at the outset of the war. The two leading generals, Zachary Taylor and Winfield Scott, both Whigs, never felt completely comfortable with the Democrat Polk. The regular troops under their command numbered just over seven thousand, and the rest of the fighting force consisted of hastily organized militia units made up of men on short-term enlistments, all eager to take part in the conquest of Mexico as long as it could be accomplished quickly. But the army also had a sizable number of younger officers, many of them recent West Point graduates, who provided excellent leadership against the Mexicans (and who learned valuable lessons they would later use against each other in the Civil War). In less than two years of fighting, the United States military would become increasingly professional as it rolled to a string of impressive victories.

By the end of 1846, the United States had taken almost all Mexican territory north of the Rio Grande. During the summer, just after the war started, General Taylor took his troops across the Rio Grande and gained control of two towns in northern Mexico, Matamoros and Monterrey. At the same time, a grizzled group of army surveyors under the command of Captain John C. Frémont was making the most of unrest in Alta California. Mexico's hold on its northernmost province had long been tenuous, since *californios* had frequently resisted the authority of the central government. During the early 1840s, the arrival of several thousand new settlers from the United States increased the number of unhappy inhabitants. In June 1846, even before they had heard about the official outbreak of war, a group of these Anglo emigrants around Sonoma staged a revolt against the local Mexican authorities and declared themselves an independent republic, complete with their own flag, which bore a single star and a brown bear. Frémont quickly moved in to take over the leadership of the Bear Flag Republic, but the days of independence were short-lived. In July, a United States naval squadron under Commodore John D. Sloat landed troops in Monterey and soon took San Francisco, Sonoma, and Sutter's Fort. Sloat's successor, Commodore Robert F. Stockton, declared California to be annexed to the United States, established himself as governor, and made Frémont an officer in the California Battalion.

While Frémont and Stockton were attempting to secure northern California, Colonel Stephen Watts Kearney was heading toward California from the south. Leaving Fort Leavenworth (in what is now Kansas) at the beginning of the war, Kearney led his Army of the West, a combined force of regular cavalry troops and Missouri frontier farmers, into New Mexico, finally reaching Santa Fe, the capital, in August. Like the *californios*, the *nuevomexicanos* had no great love for the central government of Mexico, and despite a show of token resistance from Governor Manuel Armijo, Santa Fe fell without a shot. Claiming New Mexico for the United States and establishing a territorial government, Kearney then began a long, hot, dry trek to California. He arrived in late November, just in time to face the last Mexican resistance in the south, an insurrection led by Captain José María Flores. After nearly being routed by Flores's forces, Kearney was able to reach Stockton, and together they broke up the insurgency, gaining control of Los Angeles in January 1847. At that point, the struggle for California was over, and for the second time in six months, Kearney established United States authority in territory taken from Mexico.

Then the United States turned its attention to the Mexican interior. President Polk had become frustrated with General Taylor, who seemed content to stay put in the northern part of Mexico after taking Monterrey, even offering the Mexican forces an eight-week armistice. Polk took part of Taylor's command from him and transferred nine thousand troops to the command of the more aggressive General Winfield Scott, who was planning an attack on the fortress at Vera Cruz, along the east coast of Mexico. During that time, Antonio López de Santa Anna—the man who had conquered the Alamo but lost Texas, who was recently returned from exile in Cuba—gathered an army of almost twenty thousand troops and marched northward to drive Taylor's depleted army back across the Rio Grande. When the two armies met at Buena Vista in February 1847, Santa Anna outnumbered Taylor almost four to one, but he could not dislodge him. Buena Vista would be the last significant engagement in the north, but the first of the final series of Santa Anna's losses. Later that month, Scott invaded Vera Cruz from the sea and began his march inland, defeating Santa Anna at Cerro Gordo, Contreras, Churubusco, Chapultepec, and finally, on September 14, 1847, Mexico City itself. The war was over.

In the United States, however, the political battles generated by the Mexican War did not come to such a neat conclusion. The skepticism and outright opposition that had greeted Polk's original call to arms continued to grow, leaving the nation increasingly divided over the war, the West, and slavery. To be sure, most people—and certainly most politicians—rallied to the cause of Manifest Destiny, but some questioned whether that destiny should be determined by pro-slavery Democrats. In Massachusetts, Henry David Thoreau went to jail rather than pay taxes to support the war. The Mexican War, he argued, was a pro-slavery plot, "the work of a few individuals using the standing government as their tool; for, in the outset, the people would not have consented to this measure." In Washington, anti-slavery or "conscience" Whigs kept up a chorus of anti-war criticism, and they began to sway more moderate members of their party. Opposition to "Mr. Polk's War" helped the Whigs gain control of the House in 1846. Even some Democrats had their doubts about the implications of the war. In August 1846, just three months before the congressional elections, a young Democratic congressman from Pennsylvania, David Wilmot, introduced a remarkable amendment to a routine military appropriations bill: slavery would be banned in any territory acquired from Mexico as a result of the war.

The Wilmot Proviso never became law—it was passed by the House but defeated in the Senate—but it brought to the forefront of American politics the debate over slavery in the West. Moreover, it provided a common point of connection for several strains of anti-slavery sentiment. One did not by any means have to be a staunch abolitionist to embrace Wilmot's position. Wilmot himself took pains to note that he had "no squeamish sensitiveness upon the subject of slavery, no morbid sympathy for the slave." Like many other northern politicians, he could tolerate the continued existence of slavery in the South; what he opposed was its expansion to new territories in the West. If the slave system was confined to the South, it might eventually wither and die. "Slavery has within itself the seeds of its own destruction," Wilmot opined. But that would be only a side benefit. The real issue, for Wilmot and for most of those who supported his position, was keeping the West open for free men—free *white* men, "the sons of toil, of my own race and own color." If slavery were kept out of the West, black slaves would be, too, and perhaps even free blacks as well. The Wilmot Proviso, he said, could in fact be called the "White Man's Proviso."

The appeal of a white man's West permeated anti-slavery politics for the next decade. In 1848, dissident New York Democrats, called "Barnburners," broke from their party and united with anti-slavery Whigs and former members of the Liberty Party to form a new third party, the Free Soil Party. Choosing former Democrat Martin Van Buren as their candidate, the Free Soilers ran on a platform opposing the expansive ambitions of the "Slave Power" and offering free western homesteads to settlers from the East. Although the Free Soilers gained only ten percent of the popular vote and no electoral votes in the 1848 presidential election, they kept the spirit of the Wilmot Proviso alive. Six years later, another new party, the Republicans, would revive the basic elements of the Free Soil Party message and even borrow its motto, "Free Soil, Free Labor, Free Men."

As Eric Foner has explained, a growing number of antebellum northerners considered free labor and free soil to be the essential ingredients of freedom itself. Personal independence depended on economic independence, on the ability of the shopkeeper, the artisan, or the small farmer to own property and make his way in life without having to work for wages. One way to increase the opportunity for free labor was to promote migration to open land. If the poor and unemployed of the East could acquire homesteads in the West, they not only could escape (and therefore lessen) the grim social conditions and class tensions of the cities but also could help spread a virtuous way of life. The simultaneous spread of slavery, however, would dampen and even destroy the prospects of free men to exercise their free labor on free soil. The slave system, so the argument went, undercut the economic viability of free labor and degraded all laborers, free as well as slave, white as well as black. If southern politicians and other promoters of slavery were to have their way, the "Slave Power" would conquer the whole land, West and North alike; in the end, all would be slaves.

The Wilmot Proviso and the Free Soil position offered whites a way to oppose slavery without necessarily embracing blacks. To be sure, many Free Soilers and Republicans did demonstrate sympathy for the plight of slaves, and some even accepted the possibility that black people were their equals, or at least deserving of equal rights. But self-interest and outright racism often lay beneath the anti-slavery rhetoric. The South had already made its choice for slavery, and many northerners were content to leave southern whites and blacks to deal with the consequences. But the future of the nation, or certainly of the North, lay in the West. If whites were to enjoy that future as free men, they would have to keep the region free of slaves. From that simple assumption grew an overarching anti-slavery argument that linked unlikely allies all across the continent.

On the other hand, one did not have to be a rabid supporter of slavery to oppose the Free Soil position. In 1848, mainstream Whigs and Democrats tried to avoid dealing directly with the expansion of slavery, and both parties took rather vague stances on the issue. The Whigs nominated General Zachary Taylor, a slaveowner but, more important, a popular war hero, a career soldier who had spent so much time in military service to his country that he had never voted in a national election. James K. Polk had never intended to run for a second term, and his fellow Democrats were no doubt relieved that they would not have to run on his record.

They nominated Lewis Cass of Michigan, a northerner who was soft on slavery. To avoid taking a firm stand on the expansion of slavery, Cass promoted "squatter sovereignty," the notion that the actual settlers of the West, not the national government, should determine the question of slavery in their respective territories. Taylor won the election, but Cass's "squatter sovereignty" (or, as it came to be more commonly called, "popular sovereignty") soon became the most important political alternative to "free soil."

"Popular sovereignty" had its first political test in 1850, when Congress had to do something with the territory it had acquired from Mexico. Under the Treaty of Guadalupe Hidalgo (1848), Mexico had ceded to the United States a huge swath of territory from Texas to California—over a million square miles of land that includes the present states of Texas, New Mexico, Arizona, Utah, Nevada, California, and parts of Colorado and Wyoming—all for $15 million. (The United States would get an additional section of southern New Mexico and Arizona with the Gadsden Purchase of 1853.) While the treaty negotiations were going on in Mexico, a mechanic, James Marshall, discovered gold in California's American River while building a sawmill for Johann Augustus Sutter, a large landowner-entrepreneur in the Sacramento Valley. When Sutter got this remarkable news, he tried to keep it quiet, but gradually the word got out. By the spring of 1848, the rush was on. Gold-seekers swarmed westward into California from all parts of the United States, and suddenly the Anglo-American population of California grew by as much as eighty thousand in 1849 alone. It was clear that the newcomers would want California to be a state. The question was whether or not they would want it to be a slave state.

The answer turned out to be much more than a local decision based on popular sovereignty. A territorial convention in Monterey in the early fall of 1849 drafted a constitution prohibiting slavery in California, and the voters ratified it in November. But this decision made in the West sparked a furious response among politicians in the East—specifically, in the South. Southerners saw the admission of a free-soil California as the beginning of the end for the slave system. Most immediately, California statehood would once again upset the balance between slave and free states in the Senate (there were fifteen of each at the time), putting pro-slavery politicians at a distinct disadvantage in both houses of Congress. More important, closing off the rich agricultural lands of California to slavery would block what southerners insisted was the necessary expansion of a system that was both economically beneficial and morally benign. If California entered the Union as a free state, they warned, the slave states might choose to leave. In March 1850, a dying John C. Calhoun, even in his last days one of the most militant defenders of slavery, told his colleagues in the Senate that the responsibility for saving the Union rested squarely on the shoulders of the North: "The North has only to will it to accomplish it—to do justice by conceding to the South an equal right in the acquired territory." If northern politicians were not willing to grant the South satisfaction, then they should say so, Calhoun argued, "and let the States we both represent agree to separate and part in peace." But then Calhoun added ominously, "If you are unwilling we should part in peace, tell us so, and we shall know what to do."

Most northerners were not yet ready to force a showdown over secession with the South, and during the first nine months of 1850 Congress struggled to reach a compromise on the California crisis. In January, Henry Clay had put together a package of proposals he hoped would resolve the problem to everyone's acceptance, if not to everyone's satisfaction. The main elements of Clay's compromise measures called for California to enter the Union as a free state, but the doctrine of popular sovereignty would be applied to Utah and New Mexico, the other territories acquired from Mexico, which could be organized without any congressional restrictions on slavery; as an additional concession to the South, Clay also proposed a stronger fugitive-slave law. Calhoun and other staunch supporters of slavery would have none of it, and neither would many anti-slavery northerners. Still, after months of fierce debate, with threats of sectional strife issued from both sides, Congress adopted the essentials of Clay's compromise. The Compromise of 1850 allowed California to enter the Union without tearing the Union apart—yet.

Four years later, however, an attempt to tie California into the national economy caused the thin threads holding the nation together to begin to unravel. Senator Stephen Douglas, an Illinois Democrat who was a strong promoter of both westward expansion and his own political career, put forth a plan for a transcontinental railroad linking California and Chicago, the burgeoning new midwestern metropolis (which just happened to be in his home state). The route would cross the vast, flat lands bounded by Iowa and Missouri in the east and Utah and New Mexico in the west, and Douglas figured it would facilitate settlement along the rail line if this expanse of the "Great American Desert" were organized into United States territory. Knowing that southern politicians had their own ideas about a transcontinental railroad terminus—St. Louis, Memphis, or New Orleans—Douglas devised a deal to gain support for Chicago and the northern route. In January 1854, he introduced a bill to create two new territories, Kansas and Nebraska, both of which would be open to the doctrine of popular sovereignty. Douglas knew that proposing even the possibility of slavery in these territories would be in direct violation of the Missouri Compromise of 1820, but he hoped that in the wake of the Compromise of 1850 people would overlook that technicality in the interest of national integration and expansion. Moreover, he doubted that slaveowners would find the plains environment suitable for plantation agriculture.

He was wrong. Southerners looked eagerly at Kansas, which lay just to the west of Missouri, a slave state, and they anticipated an easy extension of slavery into the new territory. To make their case clear, they insisted that Douglas include in the final version of his bill an explicit repudiation of the Missouri Compromise. He went along, knowing that doing so would create "a hell of a storm" among northerners. Douglas was roundly denounced in the North as a criminal, a conspirator, a traitor to his region, a tool of the "Slave Power." Even though he was still a good enough politician to guide the bill through Congress and guarantee its passage, he could not undo the political damage he had done, especially to his own party. In the aftermath of the Kansas–Nebraska Act, many anti-slavery Democrats split from the party and joined former Whigs and former Free Soilers to establish a new political party, the Republicans, which would offer the strongest opposition to the westward expansion of slavery. (In 1858, a comparatively unknown Republican politician in Douglas's home state of Illinois, Abraham Lincoln, would challenge the author of the Kansas–Nebraska Act for his Senate seat, taking him to task for his toleration of slavery.

Douglas defeated Lincoln in that race, but two years later, when the two were running for a much bigger prize, the presidency of the United States, Lincoln and the Republicans would make Douglas and his Democrat supporters suffer for their soft stance on slavery.)

Yet, important as they ultimately were, the political divisions created by the Kansas–Nebraska Act pale in comparison to the even more dramatic divisions within Kansas itself. This sparsely settled frontier state suddenly became the focus of an intense struggle, the moral and military battleground for pro-slavery and anti-slavery forces from all over the nation. The doctrine of popular sovereignty meant that whichever side could gain control of the territory long enough to elect a legislature and frame a constitution could determine Kansas's eventual entry into the Union as a slave or a free state. Accordingly, pro-slavery settlers from Missouri swarmed over the border to vote in the first election of the territorial legislature in November 1854, and they remained an imposing political presence for the next few years; whenever any election official dared challenge these "border ruffians" on the basis of a residency requirement, they simply cocked their guns and cast their ballots. In their eyes, any action was justified in order to stop wild-eyed abolitionists and slave-stealing scoundrels from making Kansas a free state or, even worse, a haven for free blacks. By the same token, anti-slavery emigrants from the North—many of whom had been inspired by the Reverend Henry Ward Beecher's assurance that sometimes people needed guns to do God's work—likewise relied on their rifles to reinforce their sense of right. They had no intention of letting any more land fall into the hands of pro-slavery "pukes." By 1856, Kansas had become a collection of armed camps.

It had also become a territory with two governments, neither of which was altogether popular or sovercign. The pro-slavery forces had bullied their way into winning the 1855 territorial election, and the resulting legislature created a constitution that required all officeholders to take an oath of support for slavery. Their anti-slavery opponents organized their own government and adopted their own constitution that prohibited slavery in Kansas. (It also prohibited any blacks, slave or free, from entering the territory: once again, opposition to slavery did not always mean opposition to racism.) Looking at each other with contempt and casting accusations of illegitimacy and corruption back and forth, the two sides stood on the brink of war.

Blood began to flow in May 1856. A mob of pro-slavery Kansans and their Missouri allies attacked the anti-slavery enclave at Lawrence, burning down houses, shops, and the Free State Hotel and destroying the offices and presses of two anti-slavery newspapers. Three days later, a recently arrived abolitionist named John Brown took it upon himself to avenge this "Sack of Lawrence." Armed with guns and broadswords, Brown and his four sons and two other men crept up to the cabins of five pro-slavery settlers along Pottawatomie Creek. They forced them out into the darkness, one by one, and slashed them with their swords as their wives and children cried in terror and begged them to stop. Leaving the mutilated bodies behind, Brown and his men washed their bloody swords in Pottawatomie Creek.

That was not the end of the killing. It was only the beginning. Over the course of the year, two hundred on both sides would die as guerrilla groups roamed the territory and Kansas fell into a state of savage civil war. This war in the West provided a foretaste (and forewarning) of a much larger civil war that would engulf the whole eastern half of the nation. The several hundred deaths in "Bleeding Kansas" would soon be followed by hundreds of thousands more.

FIVE

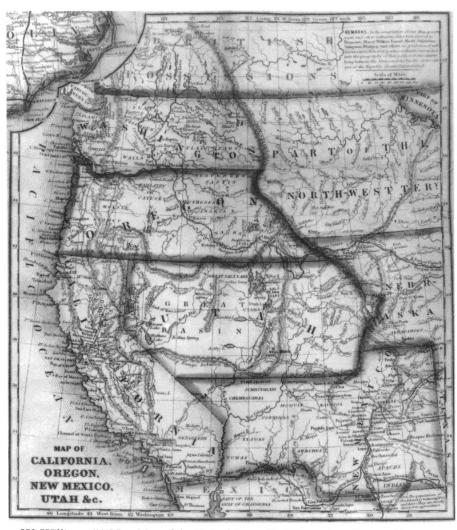

W. Williams, "A New Map of the United States," 1854, portion. *Courtesy Hargrett Rare Book and Manuscript Library, University of Georgia Libraries*

MOVING WEST
AND MAKING COMMUNITIES

I n the spring of 1862, people were reeling from the news of the
Battle of Shiloh. On April 6 and 7, Union forces under General
Ulysses S. Grant had faced a Confederate army under General
Albert Sidney Johnston at a small town in southwestern Tennessee,
just north of the Mississippi border—Davy Crockett's old region.
There, in a cataclysmic but ultimately inconclusive battle, over a
hundred thousand men had been thrown at each other time after
time, until eventually some twenty-four thousand Union and Confederate soldiers—about a quarter of all those who took the field
—were killed, wounded, or captured. The battle was by far the
costliest in American history to that time.

As millions turned their energies to the clash between North
and South, a few thousand set out that year for the West. Now
overshadowed by the Civil War, the westward trek was the con-
tinuation of a long-standing (and not unrelated) process of expansion that had been at the heart of American history as long as
slavery had been.

Jane Augusta Holbrook Gould, an Iowa farmwoman, was part
of that history—and she, like many other emigrants who headed
west, kept a diary that recorded the intimate history of her journey.
On Sunday, April 27, she and her husband, Albert Gould, and their
two young sons hitched up their wagon in Mitchell, Iowa, and
rolled out over the prairie, away from the war that gripped the
nation, headed for California. If she felt any immediate remorse

about the move, her first diary entry—"Left home this morning"
—did not elaborate on it. Perhaps her sense of separation was
soothed by the knowledge that, even though she was leaving home,
she was not leaving her friends and family behind. In addition to
her husband and sons, the emigrant party also included her father-
in-law, brother-in-law, sister-in-law, and several neighbors from
town.

In the first few days of the trip, Jane Gould learned some of the
trials of the westward trek—especially cooking outside without a
stove in the cold morning air, sometimes in a driving rain—but
she also learned how people could come together to make the best
of a bad situation. One morning during the third week on the trail,
she awoke and "found it raining hard as it could pour down."

> The men went out of the wagon, made some coffee and warmed some
> beans and brought the breakfast into the wagon, which we all crowded
> into. Used a trunk for a table and made out a very comfortable meal.
> After eating they put the dishes under the wagon where they remained
> until four o'clock, when the rain ceased and I left the shelter of the
> wagon for the first time today.

Being served food fixed by the men proved to be a rarity. On the
wagon train, just as on the farm, women did most of the domestic
work. Gould recorded the commonplace cooking and cleaning
tasks she and her fellow females performed, and on at least one
occasion she noted an exceptional achievement:

> I am baking. I made some yeast bread for the first time in three weeks,
> which tasted very good after eating hot biscuits for so long.

She also recorded recreational breaks in the routine. One Sunday
in mid-May, while "two gents and ladies of our company went out
horseback riding for their health," she and the children went out
to gather flowers and found hundreds of hazelnuts on the ground,
"quite a luxury this time of year." Two weeks later, while several
of the men in her group were taking turns playing the fiddle, some
people came over and suggested having a "little dance." On a July
evening, "The men had a ball-play. . . . Seemed to enjoy themselves
very much, it seemed like old times." She and her sister-in-law
even won approval from the men for their newfound skill at a

traditionally male activity: "Lou and I shot at a mark with a revolver. The boys said we did first-rate for new beginners."

In time, though, Gould's diary entries took on a more troubled tone. Her husband, Albert, had started feeling sick soon after the family set out, and his uncertain health was a source of concern throughout the trip. It also caused her to take on additional responsibilities: "Albert is not well today, so I drive." She not only attended to her husband, but she and Lou occasionally helped other women take care of sick children. More serious illnesses and injuries—a woman thrown from a horse, a child run over by a wagon—required the attention of the wagon train's doctor. Sometimes, no one could help. In late July, Gould's group came upon another train of emigrants in which a mother of six had died two days after giving birth. "They made a good picket fence around the grave," she noted. (On the trail, fences were not for decoration but to keep animals from digging up the body.) A few days later, the group had to dig more graves.

> They had just buried the babe of the woman who died days ago, and were just digging a grave for another woman that was run over by the cattle and wagons when they stampeded yesterday. She lived twenty-four hours, she gave birth to a child a short time before she died. The child was buried with her. She leaves a little two year old girl and a husband. They say he is nearly crazy with sorrow.

Death on the trail cast a pall over Jane Gould as well. Passing a "lonely nameless grave" with a rough wooden headboard

> called up a sad train of thoughts, to my mind, it seems so sad to think of being buried and left alone in so wild a country with no one to plant a flower or shed a tear o'er one's grave.

The sentiment expressed in that last line underscores Gould's growing sense of loss, her longing for a permanent home. On the trail, there was no time to linger over the dead, and certainly no opportunity to return later to mourn. The wagon train rolled slowly on, the connections to home receded further into the past, and the prospects of ever settling down again seemed a distant dream. On the Fourth of July, Gould noted that the men fired their guns in a truncated and apparently joyless celebration, but there was not even enough time to do extra cooking for the holiday; there was no holiday. "We wonder what the folks at home are doing," she wrote, "and oh, how we wish we were there." Six weeks later, she felt little better, even though she was closer to California.

> Oh dear, I do so want to get there. It is now almost four month since we have slept in a house. If I could only be set down at home with all the folks I think there would be some talking as well as resting.

The farther the emigrants traveled, the more the trail was littered with the remains of other expeditions, "wagon irons and keg hoops and piles of bones every five rods." Human bones were the worst, and Gould almost always attributed them to "Indian depredations." Once their group came upon an empty wagon surrounded by the body parts of three dead men sticking out of the ground.

> Some one had come along and thrown a little earth over them, but they were mostly uncovered again. One had his head and face out, another his legs, a third, his hands and arms. Oh! it is a horrid thing. I wish all the Indians in Christendom were exterminated.

Jane Gould was a distant descendant of William Bradford, the Puritan chronicler of the Pequot War, and she was expressing an anti-Indian sentiment that had been in the family for years. On the other hand, given what Yankees and Confederates were doing to each other on battlefields back east, she could well have reflected that Indians had no monopoly on depredation. But life on the trail offered little opportunity for a comparative perspective, and the hardships of the trip hardened her heart. In the early part of the trip, when the party had first encountered Indians, she looked upon them as something of a curiosity, but by the end, after having endured at least one attack and hearing rumors of others, she turned a hostile eye on Indians. Even peaceful Indians who came to trade with the emigrants met with disdain: "We are disgusted with the wretched creatures."

In fact, she was becoming disgusted with the whole trip. The rough roads, the lack of grass for the animals, the bad food for her family, and, always, the deteriorating condition of her husband made the trip seem endless, even as the emigrants reached California: "The road is the worst I ever saw. . . . We saw the trees on the Carson River and thought we were almost there but we kept going and going and it seemed as if I would never get there."

But she did. As she passed through the bustling mining camps of the Sierra Nevada, Gould noted the prospects for better food and a better life: "We see a great many fruit wagons here from Cal. . . . Money seems to be plenty. Buildings going up fast. Here is the place to make money." Finally she happened upon a woman in a settlement in the San Joaquin Valley who told her of a house to rent, "one block east of the Lunatic Asylum." (Apparently, Jane Gould was not the only one who had suffered psychologically on the trip west.) On October 8, 1862, she and Albert and Lou and Charlie moved in, and Jane Gould reported with some satisfaction: "Slept in a house for the first time in over five months."

Five months later, Albert died.

Jane Gould's diary is a small part of a huge historical record that chronicles the transcontinental movement of thousands of Euro-American migrants. In the early years of European exploration and occupation, Spanish, French, and English settlers had come onto the continent seemingly heading in all directions, but by the time the Gould family headed for California, westward migration had long since become the dominant and ultimately most decisive pattern of movement. Over the course of two centuries, a stream of settlers—individuals, families, sometimes whole communities— had pushed westward into the North American interior, stopping first in the shadow of the Appalachians, then crossing the mountains into the rich valleys whose rivers fed into the Mississippi, then across the Mississippi and out onto the prairies and plains, all the way to the Pacific Ocean. During the middle decades of the nineteenth century, more than a quarter-million migrants made their way across the continent.

Though based on thousands of individual or family decisions, this massive human movement also had the official sanction of the United States government. Since the founding of the Republic, the government had used the power of the pen and the sword to push native peoples off their land and, increasingly, onto government-regulated reservations. After the Civil War, the government directed virtually the full force of its military power to secure western land for settlement and to subdue Indians who resisted (a process that will be discussed in detail in the next chapter). Then the government made land available to settlers at a low price or to railroad companies essentially for free. Every cavalry column, wagon train, and railroad train that crossed the land contributed to the territorial expansion of the United States and thus became an agent of national policy.

In their own eyes, though, emigrants like Jane Gould had much more immediate and personal concerns. They were ordinary people moving west in pursuit of a vision of a better life—opportunity, adventure, even escape—and, in the process, trying to keep themselves and their families going. If some of them set out with a lofty, nationalistic notion of being part of the triumphal march of Manifest Destiny, the difficulties and dangers of daily existence soon brought them back to the reality of survival. The westward trek tested the emigrants' resourcefulness and resilience, challenged their traditional roles and relationships, and confronted them with numerous occasions for acts of courage, cowardice, compassion, or cruelty. Then, at the end of the trail, there was always the need to establish, or reestablish, settled life, some form of the social norms known before the trip. The creation of new communities across the continent was one of the most important parts of the frontier experience.

The oft-repeated phenomenon of settlement and community-formation has seemed such a comparatively peaceful process that it is almost taken for granted, or certainly is overshadowed by the more dramatic and dangerous saga of the westward migration. But each new western town was contested terrain. The creation of a new community almost always raised anew the central question about the frontier: who should live there, and how? Sometimes, the struggle to answer that question pitted recent emigrants against Indians, who fought to claim or reclaim the land from each other. Just as often, the contest involved the Euro-American settlers themselves, who became divided over how to define the terms under which people would provide for themselves and protect their respective interests. From the Great Plains to the Pacific, in mining camps, farming communities, and cow towns, considerations of

race, gender, and class contributed to tensions, even outright conflict, over the future of the western frontier. Getting there was only
half the battle.

—————•◆•—————

What would compel so many people like the Goulds to make so
long and dangerous a journey west? There was no single factor,
but a host of psychological and economic motives. In 1849, the
discovery of gold in California had created an epidemic of gold
fever, and thousands of emigrants—mostly men—took whatever
conveyance they could to get in on the rush. They went on ships
from eastern ports around Cape Horn, at the southern tip of South
America, to California, or they shipped to the Isthmus of Panama
in Central America, where they crossed on land to the Pacific and
caught another ship heading up the coast. Others headed straight
across the continent, most going in organized wagon trains but
some as individuals, a few even on foot, pushing wheelbarrows and
handcarts. Throughout the second half of the nineteenth century,
single men looking to be miners (and perhaps millionaires) formed
a mobile, sometimes seemingly volatile, part of the larger emigrant
picture. But aside from these single gold-seekers, the main emigrant stream consisted of farm families, members of the middling
levels of rural society who gave westward migration a generally
middle-class character. Unlike the very poor, they had just enough
economic resources to finance the journey. Unlike the more prosperous, they had just enough economic need to make such a move
necessary, or at least desirable. They were people who had faced
the frustrations of farming with too few acres and too many debts,
people who looked hopefully across the continent to a region
where they could find good, cheap land and start over again—this
time with a little more land and perhaps a little more luck.

They would have little trouble getting there, they were told. For
years, politicians and other promoters of westward expansion had
been making great claims about the trip—that it would be "easy,
safe, and expeditious," that the Rocky Mountains were "mere
molehills," that the road they would follow had been "excavated
by the finger of God." Moreover, the rhetoric of Manifest Destiny
assured the "hardy pioneers" that they were not just pushing west-

ward the boundaries of the United States; they were also "going to the wilderness like our first parents, when God sent them forth from the Garden of Eden to subdue the earth."

The role of the deity in defining the mission and paving the way may have been arguable, but the rest of the rhetoric was clearly untrue. The wide, arid prairies and the high, snowy mountains posed a formidable obstacle to any overland traveler. Some eastern skeptics suggested that people think twice before setting out across the "Great American Desert," especially with women and children in tow. Horace Greeley, the *New York Tribune* editor who would eventually become known almost solely for telling underemployed urban workers, "Go West, young man!", initially took a much dimmer view of the venture. In 1843, with the first great wave of emigrants heading west for Oregon, Greeley grumbled that there was "an aspect of insanity" in such a massive movement, and he argued that "it is palpable homicide to tempt or send women and children over this thousand miles of precipice and volcanic sterility to Oregon."

Such warnings may have caused some people to change their plans, but hundreds of thousands of others did go west, no doubt thinking that the American Promised Land lay just on the other side of the mountains. Watching a group of emigrants getting ready to depart from Independence, Missouri, one of the main jumping-off points for the westward trek, Francis Parkman looked at the "multitude of healthy children's faces . . . very sober looking countrymen, [and] . . . some of the vilest outcasts in the country" and "perplexed myself to divine the various motives that give impulse to this strange migration; . . . an insane hope of a better condition in life, or a desire of shaking off restraints of law and society, or mere restlessness." (Parkman, a twenty-three-year-old Harvard graduate, was also going west, but with a very clear goal "of observing the Indian character," intending "to live in the midst of them, and become, as it were, one of them." *The Oregon Trail* [1849], his account of six months spent among Indians, trappers, and hunters, is one of the classics of nineteenth-century writing about the West.) Mark Twain, who also went west in his twenties, took an upbeat, characteristically comic view of his own motives as a prospective emigrant in *Roughing It* (1872). When his brother received an appointment as Secretary of Nevada Territory in 1861, Twain was immensely jealous.

Pretty soon [Twain's brother] would be hundreds and hundreds of miles away on the great plains and deserts, and among the mountains of the Far West, and would see buffaloes and Indians, and prairie dogs, and antelopes, and have all kinds of adventures, and may be get hanged or scalped, and have ever such a fine time, and write home and tell us all about it.

(Fortunately for Twain—and his readers—he got to go along with his brother.) In only slightly more muted terms, a similar spirit of adventure and escape lay at the heart of Frederick Jackson Turner's later explanation of the appeal of the frontier, where, he argued, people exhibited "freshness, and confidence, and scorn of older society, impatience of its restraints and its ideas, and indifference to its lessons."

More recently, historians have suggested that, whatever motivated men to emigrate, whether a sense of adventure or a device to escape adversity, the same motives cannot be ascribed to women. As John Mack Faragher and Julie Roy Jeffrey have observed, the decision to move west was almost always made by the male head of the household; in his study of the diaries and recollections of women on the overland trail, Faragher concludes that "not one wife initiated the idea" of moving. Women's wishes hardly mattered, he adds. "It was fully within a husband's prerogative to move his family without consulting his wife." A woman might express reluctance and resistance, even outrage, in response to her husband's decisions—and some clearly did—but if a man was truly determined to move his family west, there was little his wife could do but accept the inevitable and start preparing for the trip. Still, Jeffrey warns against "the danger of viewing women solely as reluctant pioneers." They, too, could see the improved economic prospects the West offered their families; they, too, could feel the spirit of adventure in going to a comparatively uncharted, open country; they, too, could simply use a change. The point, though, is that many women tended to have somewhat ambivalent feelings about emigration. They went west with family members and friends, but they also looked back longingly at the kinfolk and communities they were leaving behind. As the diary of Jane Gould indicates, that sense of loss and regret could last the whole trip.

Aside from saying farewell to loved ones, one of the greatest pains of leaving home was saying goodbye to beloved possessions.

A family traveling in a covered wagon had to pare down its possessions to the bare necessities, or at least to those items that had enough utilitarian or emotional value to make them seem indispensable. Everything else had to be given away or, if possible, sold to help pay for the essential items: a wagon with a canvas covering; salt, flour, bacon, coffee, and other foodstuffs; cooking and farming utensils; gunpowder and shot. And even after the sacrifice of selling off nearly everything they had, some emigrant families found they had taken too much. Crossing the prairie, Parkman wrote about seeing numerous family treasures along the trail, the "shattered wrecks of ancient claw-footed tables, well waxed and rubbed, or massive bureaus of carved oak."

> Imported, perhaps, originally from England; then, with the declining fortunes of their owners, borne across the Alleghenies to the remote wilderness of Ohio or Kentucky; then to Illinois or Missouri; and now at last fondly stowed away in the family wagon or the interminable journey to Oregon. But the stern privations of the way are little anticipated. The cherished relic is soon flung out to scorch and crack upon the hot prairie.

Tracing the long history of westward migration through family furniture, Parkman showed the trans-Mississippi trek to be the most challenging and demanding of all, the one where keepsakes and other connections with the past would finally have to be thrown off. With a lighter load, but perhaps with heavier hearts, the emigrants would push on across the prairie, a slowly rolling household moving away from its roots.

Like most households elsewhere, the emigrant family was part of a larger community, in this case the wagon train, a mobile microcosm of rural society. As in the settled farm villages from which most migrants came, the social norms of the emigrant community consisted of a general equality undergirded by gender inequality. That is, each household shared a sense of responsibility and mutual support for the others, yet within each household and in the community at large, men and women were supposed to play distinct and decidedly separate roles—at least at the outset. Men made most of the decisions concerning the emigrant train, choosing leaders, setting schedules, determining where to go and when to stop. Such issues often occasioned considerable debate and disagreement, but the collective decisionmaking process ultimately reflected a rough democracy that gave each man a voice. Men also assumed separate standards of work and leisure. They took responsibility for driving the wagon, caring for the livestock, making repairs, standing guard, and, when time permitted, organizing hunting expeditions and other outlets for "manly" energies—even, as Jane Gould noted, playing ball. In short, men worked hard when they worked, but they also enjoyed various forms of rest and recreation at the end of the day—sometimes, as one woman observed, just "lolling and smoking their pipes and guessing, or maybe betting, how many miles we had covered in the day."

Women's work lasted longer into the night and left much less time for leisure. Helen Carpenter confided in her diary that *"we have no time for sociability."*

> From the time we get up in the morning, until we are on the road, it is hurry scurry to get breakfast . . . and at night all the cooking utensils and provisions are to be gotten about the camp fire and cooking enough done to last until the next night . . . so by the time one has squatted around the fire and cooked bread and bacon, and made several dozen trips to and from the wagon—washed the dishes (with no place to drain them) and gotten things ready for an early breakfast, some of the others already have their night caps on—at any rate its time to go to bed.

Women on the wagon train did essentially the same traditional tasks they did back home—cooking, cleaning, caring for children and the sick—but sometimes, especially as the trip wore on, they took on men's jobs as well—driving the wagon, tending livestock, and, in time of danger, defending the train. Necessity weakened the walls of gender segregation but did not break them down altogether. By the same token, men and women sometimes shared the same leisure activities—dancing, singing, storytelling, and the like—but women still took it upon themselves to see that such recreational behavior did not become too boisterous or, even worse, immoral. They discouraged swearing, fighting, and other forms of aggressive male behavior, and they often reminded the men to set aside time for worship. It was their special responsibility, they felt, to make the emigrant community a fit place for children. It was not enough to try to keep children content (or at least quiet) during a long, boring journey; women also had to attend to their moral and physical well-being, keeping them healthy and out of harm's way.

That last task was one of the most difficult, because the overland journey offered numerous opportunities for danger and sudden death. The most obvious threat—certainly the most often discussed—came from Indians. When Mary Jane Caples first encountered a group of Pawnee men, "the first Indians I had ever seen," she was terrified by their appearance: "dressed in their long mackinaw blankets and eagle feathers in their hair, they looked ten feet high—my thought was that they would kill us all, and take my baby in captivity." Caples's reaction was a conditioned response. When emigrants headed west, they carried considerable cultural baggage along with everything else; seldom could their prejudices be discarded as easily as their possessions. For years, an outpouring of paintings, press reports, and popular fiction, especially captivity narratives, had helped create a set of preconceived, sometimes quite contradictory, images of the Indian. Whether noble or bloodthirsty, the Indian was seen as a "savage" and always occupied the category of the "other," someone quite separate from "civilized" white society. Upon coming into actual contact with Indians and seeing them as human beings, some emigrants looked at them with awe and a kind of grudging admiration, taking note of their dignity and decency. Yet even the most well-meaning emigrant could hardly surrender the underlying fear of Indian misdeeds and "depredations," as Jane Gould put it. Rumors were almost as frightening as the real thing: tales of Indian atrocities spread from wagon train to wagon train, causing emigrants to keep their guns at the ready.

In some cases, those guns did more damage to the emigrants than the Indians did. Despite the then- (and now-) popular image of the frontiersman as sure-eyed sharpshooter, many emigrants were unfamiliar with their firearms, having acquired them just before setting out (sometimes buying them at low cost from a gun-promoting national government). The combination of being armed and inexperienced could be a recipe for disaster, or at least derision. Maria Shrode noted that the men in her party had "killed a beef," but added that "the boys shot at it about 50 times before they got it." Mark Twain remarked wryly that when he set out on his trip west, he had been "armed to the teeth with a pitiful little Smith

& Wesson's seven-shooter . . . [which] appeared to me to be a dangerous weapon"—except for one problem: "you could not hit anything with it." One of his traveling companions "practiced for a while on a cow with it, and as long as she stood still and behaved herself she was safe; but as soon as she got to moving around, and he got to shooting at other things, she came to grief." So, unfortunately, did many emigrants who became victims of accidental (or apparently accidental) shootings, especially in the early stages of the trip; some of them died a violent death without ever seeing an Indian.

Death came in many forms for the emigrant. Epidemics of deadly diseases, most notably cholera, were the greatest killers, sweeping through emigrant trains and taking people already weakened by the physical and emotional demands of the journey. The harsh environment likewise took its toll, subjecting people to long stretches of scorching heat or bitter cold that wore down and eventually broke their endurance. Some people died in common, albeit sometimes careless, accidents, falling under wagons, falling off cliffs, or falling, quite literally, dead drunk. Others just wandered away, got lost, and never came back.

Avoidable mistakes and other mishaps accounted for far more emigrant deaths than Indians did. In his sweeping study of westward emigration, John D. Unruh estimated that fewer than four hundred emigrants died at the hands of Indians between 1840 and 1860, and upward of ninety percent of those deaths occurred west of the continental divide, where the main overland trail split at South Pass in the Rocky Mountains (in what is now southwestern Wyoming) and sent emigrants along various—and very dangerous—paths to Oregon and California. Despite the fierce reputation of the Plains Indians such as the Sioux and Pawnees, emigrants had much more to fear from the much-despised Diggers along the Humboldt River of Nevada. (Some attacks ascribed to Indians were actually carried out by western outlaws posing as Indians. These "white Indians," as they were called—reviving a frontier term first used in the eighteenth century—sometimes committed atrocious acts of banditry, not just robbing their victims but also subjecting them to mutilation and killing them. The Indian disguise gave them a cover for their depravity and helped shift the responsibility to a culture commonly associated with "savagery.") Equally important, Unruh notes that Indians provided valuable, often vital, assistance to overland emigrants, helping them get through difficult parts of the journey by serving as guides, interpreters, and trading partners. In that sense, Indians may well have saved more emigrant lives than they took.

The point is not to trivialize the deaths of those emigrants who did get killed or to minimize the many other dangers overlanders faced from Indians. In the absence of direct attacks, emigrant parties still had to take care not to lose their livestock, especially horses, to theft. Moreover, even ostensibly friendly contact with Indians often left emigrants feeling harassed, sometimes threatened, by Indians who wanted to beg or buy goods that were not for sale. Sometimes, too, Indian assistance came at a price, as they charged tolls to cross streams on bridges or exacted tribute before allowing emigrants to cross their lands. The important point is that the threats and depredations ran both ways, and in the long run they weighed most heavily against Indians. Of all the dangers emigrants faced on the trail, Indians were by no means the worst; they only appeared so in the heightened anxiety and anger of uneasy overlanders. Perhaps given the impossibility of doing anything about epidemics, the environment, or even fate, emigrants focused their fears and frustrations on Indians, targeting them as the one factor on the frontier they could hope to control—and possibly eliminate.

Such perceptions shaped government policy as well. To protect emigrant parties—indeed, to promote further emigration—the United States government began in the late 1840s to build a string of forts along the main overland routes. To be sure, the government had established a military presence in the trans-Mississippi region earlier in the century, as expeditions had been sent out to explore the land and impress its inhabitants; in 1827, the army built its first western outpost, Fort Leavenworth, on the western bank of the Missouri River. But in the wake of the war with Mexico, when the nation's territorial claims expanded suddenly, the call for a more permanent and pervasive presence gained support. Between the Mexican War and the Civil War, the U.S. Army's troop strength ranged between seven thousand and eight thousand men, but around ninety percent of the soldiers were stationed in the growing number of garrisons in the West. After the Civil War, the size of the army finally settled at around twenty-seven thousand men, again with the vast majority in the West. Clearly, so few men spread out over a vast expanse of land could hardly hope to be everywhere at once, but patrols sent out from the forts provided armed support and other trailside services to grateful emigrant groups.

Emigrants were even more grateful for the forts themselves. What soldiers often saw as godforsaken garrisons in the middle of nowhere, emigrants saw as all-purpose stopping points, safe oases where they could get information, medical care, rest, refreshment, and repairs. Forts were much more than military outposts; they were frontier gathering spots for people of various descriptions— not just soldiers, but Indians, trappers, traders, tradesmen, and other hangers-on (or, as Parkman put it, "*engagés* of the establishment"). They also usually had at least a handful of women and, with them, some small antidote to the all-male military life. Frances Roe, the young wife of a recent West Point graduate, accompanied her husband, Faye, from fort to fort in the western territories, and her letters sent back East recorded some of the more genteel aspects of army life, with numerous descriptions of dances, dinners, and other forms of festivity. At Fort Shaw, a distant outpost on the far northwestern end of the Missouri River in Montana Territory, she described how the garrison got ready for the social season:

> Everyone is happy in the fall, after the return of the companies from their hard and often dangerous summer campaign, and settles down for the winter. It is then that we feel we can feast and dance, and it is then, too, that garrison life at a frontier post becomes so delightful. We are all very fond of dancing, so I think Faye and I will give a cotillion later on.

While few people would describe garrison life as "delightful," the forts did serve as intermittent reserves, or perhaps reminders, of the middle-class manners and diversions most emigrants had long since left behind. Small wonder, then, that emigrants often dawdled at the forts, sometimes staying the whole winter and thus taxing the provisions (and the patience) of the soldiers stationed there. When these "winter soldiers" finally moved on, they usually did so feeling that their government was indeed their friend.

There was another great oasis for the overland emigrants, but one of a very different sort—the Mormon settlement at Salt Lake City. The Mormons were themselves recent emigrants to the West, a people whose journey had been instigated not by expectations of wealth or a spirit of adventure but by religious intolerance back East. This is hardly the place to recount the history of early Mormonism—Joseph Smith's encounter with an angel who led him to two golden plates buried in a hill in upstate New York; his translation of the plates and the subsequent publication of *The Book of Mormon* (1830); his founding of the Church of Jesus Christ of Latter-Day Saints; the growing suspicion and persecution by Protestant groups; the resulting emigration of Smith and his followers from New York to establish new settlements in Ohio, then Missouri, then Illinois; and the arrest and lynching of Joseph Smith in Carthage, Illinois, in 1844. Suffice it to say that early Mormon history contains a long, ugly record of anti-Mormon prejudice, hostility, and violence. There seemed to be no place in the East that would allow the Saints to live in peace, so in 1846 they began to move west.

Brigham Young, Joseph Smith's successor as head of the Church of Jesus Christ of Latter-Day Saints, led the move. A man of great organizational talents, Young took his people on a year-long trek across the vast prairies and plains along a new trail that avoided the main Oregon Trail—and the intolerant emigrants who traveled it. Finally, despite all advice to the contrary, Young and his followers came to rest west of the Wasatch Mountains in the valley of the Great Salt Lake on July 24, 1847. The dry, desert-like environment was discouraging, but the valley had two important factors in its favor: water for irrigation, and isolation from intolerant Christians. To the Saints, the Salt Lake site seemed the place to plant Utopia in America.

The irrigation worked out better than the isolation. After a difficult beginning, complete with cold, hunger, and a plague of locusts, the Mormons managed to turn the dry soil into fertile farmland; under Brigham Young's direction, they devised a system of allocating and irrigating land that provided for successful agriculture and orderly growth. By 1849, after the arrival of a second band of Mormon emigrants, there were almost two thousand Saints settled at the southeastern tip of the Great Salt Lake. But 1849 also brought other arrivals, hundreds of emigrants bound for the California goldfields who had heard of the new stopping place by the lake. In the interest of keeping the Saints uncorrupted by outside influences, Young had tried to discourage "trade or commerce with the gentile world." But the steady stream of tired, hungry, and needy emigrants offered too tempting an opportunity for Mormon merchants to turn away. By the 1850s, Salt Lake City was by no means the only trading center on the trail between Saint Louis and San Francisco, but it was the biggest and best.

The Saints and Gentiles who did business together had ambivalent attitudes toward each other. To Mormons, the emigrants were representatives of the hostile Christian culture that had attacked their brand of Christianity and had driven them into the desert in the first place. On the other hand, now that they were in the Saints' home city, they were ripe for price-gouging. By the same token, the emigrants knew they needed the goods and services of the Mormons, but they also knew these people were very different, perhaps even dangerous. The result was a generally strained encounter between people who, although ostensibly of the same culture, could barely abide each other.

Of all the suspect practices of the Mormons—and in the minds of most mid-century Protestants, there were many—none was more upsetting than polygamy. Although Mormons did not openly declare polygamy to be part of church doctrine until 1852, rumors about Mormon men with multiple wives had been circulating widely since the 1840s. (The rumors were true, but at no time were more than a small minority of Mormon families polygamous.) To mainstream Christians, polygamy was barely a peg above prostitution; some called it human bondage. Harriet Beecher Stowe, whose *Uncle Tom's Cabin* offered the most effective fictional indictment of racial slavery in the South, also weighed in against this new form of female "slavery" in the West. Polygamy, she warned, was a system of sexual servitude "which debases and degrades womanhood, motherhood, and the family." Other writers in the East also contributed to the chorus against Mormonism, offering lurid tales of sexual exploitation and brutal abuse, asserting that Mormon women were beaten-down drudges who lived only to satisfy the lusts of their lecherous, overbearing husbands. In an era when sexuality was deemed a delicate, if not indecent, issue, such stories may have served to titillate as much as terrify their readers, but the message to middle-class Americans was clear: Mormons were strange, even satanic people who had best be avoided.

Emigrant parties that chose not to avoid them found that the Mormon settlements did not reflect the salacious rumors they had heard. Mormon women were willing converts to their religion, and they seemed generally content with their situation—even those wives who shared one husband. Mormons, both men and women, were quick to counter their critics by arguing that polygamy actually reinforced good health, good morals, and good family life. It enabled married men to fulfill their sexual needs within the family, without having to resort to marital infidelity or prostitution; it also allowed some wives to share (and therefore more easily avoid) the responsibility for satisfying those needs. In general, try as they might, people stopping over with the Mormons could find no compelling evidence of human degradation or moral decay. Upon arriving in Salt Lake City, Mark Twain noted rather playfully that he and his companions "felt a curiosity to ask every child how many mothers it had, and if it could tell them apart," but he, like many other visitors, remarked more on the orderliness and industriousness of the community.

Next day we strolled about everywhere through the broad, straight, level streets, and enjoyed the pleasant strangeness of a city of fifteen thousand inhabitants with no loafers perceptible in it; and no visible drunkards or noisy people; a limpid stream rippling and dancing through every street in place of a filthy gutter; block after block of trim dwellings, built of "frame" and sunburned brick—a great thriving orchard and garden behind every one of them, apparently—branches from the street stream winding and sparkling among the garden beds and fruit trees—and a grand general air of neatness, repair, thrift and comfort, around and about and over the whole. And everywhere were workshops, factories, and all manner of industries; and intent faces and busy hands were to be seen wherever one looked; and in one's ears was the ceaseless clink of hammers, the buzz of trade and the contented hum of drums and flywheels.

However much the beauty of this garden spot gave delight, the stable social order and "buzz of trade" sometimes turned out to be a mixed blessing for visiting emigrants, especially those who stayed the winter. Mormon merchants, farmers, and artisans could supply emigrants with almost anything they needed or wanted—not just fresh food and other supplies for the trail, but restaurant, hotel, and even mail service—but they were able to do so in what was decidedly a seller's market. The longer emigrants tarried, the more they traded, and they usually came out on the short end of the deal. Moreover, the longer they tarried, the more they treaded on local law. In 1850, Utah had become a United States territory and Brigham Young had been appointed governor, giving Mormons legitimate legal authority over all inhabitants, whether permanent or just passing through. Emigrants who were caught drinking, swearing, or fighting, or whose animals were caught wandering on Mormon property, wound up before Mormon magistrates and were forced to pay fines; even if they managed to beat the charges, they still had to pay court costs. Mormon officials also extracted cash (or its equivalent in goods) from emigrants who committed no crimes, charging them property taxes on the goods they had in tow. Although the degree of economic and legal extortion was sometimes overstated by anti-Mormon agitators, even a generally sympathetic historian like John D. Unruh scarcely sidesteps the issue. "How justly or benevolently the Saints had in fact treated the overland emigrants," he concludes, "remains the unanswered question."

There could hardly be any question about the brutal treatment accorded a group of emigrants in one of the worst chapters in Mormon–Gentile relations, the Mountain Meadows Massacre of 1857. Throughout the 1850s, tensions and antagonism had been building on both sides. Emigrants and officials of the United States government complained loudly about the abuse of Mormon power in the Utah basin, and the crusade against polygamy continued to cast Mormon morality in a lurid light. Mormons feared that their desert enclaves were going to be overrun and undermined by hostile emigrants, especially the malicious midwesterners who had harried them out of Missouri and Illinois. If the mutual vituperation were not bad enough, the United States government heightened Mormon fears by sending an armed expeditionary force into Utah to establish greater federal authority over the rule of the Saints. Led by Colonel Albert Sidney Johnston (the officer who, five years later, in an even greater clash between hostile white Americans, would lead his Confederate troops against Ulysses S. Grant at the Battle of Shiloh—and be killed in the effort), the federal troops never engaged in an open battle with armed Mormons. But Mormon guerrillas, aroused by intensified religious zeal as much as by the intrusion of hostile soldiers, did take deadly action against an equally unwelcome band of emigrants, many of whom came from that most-hated state, Missouri. Acting in collusion with Indian allies who surrounded and stopped the emigrant train, the Mormons persuaded the overlanders to surrender and then killed over a hundred unarmed men, women, and children; they spared a handful of young children and adopted them into Mormon families.

The Mountain Meadows Massacre was, fortunately, an isolated incident; it did not lead to more widespread violence between Mormons and emigrants or to the military suppression of the Mormons by the United States government. However, it did demonstrate quite dramatically the depth of Mormon–emigrant antagonism in the 1850s: just as Indians were not the only human threat to overland emigrants, neither were Indians the only frontier inhabitants to feel that the increasing intrusion of outsiders was serious enough to resist with violence. Although the Mormon leadership tried to deny responsibility for the massacre, the United States government soon sent a sympathetic negotiator, Colonel Thomas L. Kane, to reach a settlement with Brigham Young. According to the terms of the 1858 agreement, the Mormons would accept the presence of federal troops and a Gentile governor in the Utah Territory, but in general they would be left to govern themselves as they— or certainly Brigham Young—saw fit. Thereafter, the Mormons remained an unpopular yet important presence on the way west. No matter what people thought of the Saints, Salt Lake City was still a good place to stop.

Compared to what emigrants would find in other communities along the way, Salt Lake City might have seemed the last stop for order, morality, and equity. No matter how much the emigrants' middle-class sensibilities might have been seasoned, even eroded, by months on the trails, almost nothing could have prepared them for the fast, freewheeling life of the West's turbulent mining camps. Long after the initial influx of gold-seekers in 1849–50 had subsided, Gold Rush culture had left its stamp on the region.

Mining camps had spread quickly throughout California's gold country in the wake of the first strike at Sutter's Mill, and they continued to spring up almost overnight whenever there was a new strike—or sometimes just a reasonable-sounding rumor of one. Placer mining—washing gold flakes out of gravel—required little more than a pan and patience, and virtually anyone could do it just by standing in a stream. Virtually everyone did do it, in fact: the Gold Rush attracted eager wealth-seekers not just from the United States but from England, France, Germany, Mexico, Chile, China, and a host of other countries. The camps attracted a remarkably diverse group of people in every respect but one: over ninety percent of the population was male. Miners lived in a messy male world of ragtag appearance and ramshackle accommodations, where prices were high and life was cheap. They maintained a modicum of social control by creating local committees to certify claims and adjudicate disputes, but like everything else in this rough environment, law had a hard edge: vigilance committees were often little more than lynch mobs that dispensed justice by forgoing the rules of jurisprudence. In the get-rich-quick, fly-by-night atmosphere of gold country, miners had little time and less inclination to help establish courts and the other institutions of stable communities. They were there to find a fortune and to follow the next rumor.

The first bout of gold fever in California had scarcely begun to ebb when word of other mineral finds set prospectors off to the next rush. In 1858–59, gold strikes seemingly all over the West— along the Fraser River in British Columbia; at Pike's Peak, Colorado; in the Comstock Lode of western Nevada—sent miners scurrying to stake their claims, dip their pans, swing their picks, and make their pile. Then, in 1860, they heard about more gold and silver in Nevada, up north along the Humboldt River and down south at Esmeralda in the Washoe Mountains on the California border. Mark Twain was one of those swept up in the excitement.

Every few days news would come of the discovery of a brand-new mining region; immediately the papers would teem with accounts of its
richness, and away the surplus population would scamper to take possession. By the time I was fairly inoculated with the disease, "Esmeralda"
had just had a run and "Humboldt" was beginning to shriek for attention. "Humboldt! Humboldt!" was the new cry, and straightway Humboldt, the newest of the new, the richest of the rich, the most marvellous
of the marvellous discoveries in silver-land, was occupying two columns
of the public prints to "Esmeralda's" one. I was just on the point of
starting to Esmeralda, but turned with the tide and got ready for
Humboldt.

Twain eventually went to Esmeralda as well as Humboldt, but in
both places he found no more than most other miners did: "Nothing but rocks. Every man's pockets were full of them." In addition
to rocks, people seemed to have claims to supposedly rich underground veins, but they were suspiciously willing to sell them at a
moment's notice for the cost of the evening's meal. Twain ultimately took an alternative approach to getting regular food and
money: "I went to work as a common laborer in a quartz mill, at
ten dollars a week and board."

Such was the story of most men in the mining camps. Although
there were rich deposits of gold and silver in the western mountains, not much of it settled in the pans of individual placer miners
working the streams; most of it flowed into the corporate coffers
of companies that had the large amounts of capital needed to buy
large-scale mining machinery. In placer regions, mining companies
used high-pressure hydraulic sprays to force tons of gravel through
sluices, so that gold could be extracted more quickly. Much more
gold and silver lay deep underground, locked inside veins of quartz
that could be cracked open only by expensive mining machinery.
As a result, well-financed companies quickly came to control hard-
rock mining throughout the West by bringing in the best engineers
and the latest technology. Individual miners found themselves with
little choice but to work for the company, doing back-breaking,
extremely dangerous work underground and living in a company-
dominated community aboveground. Many men who left the mines
stayed on in the mining community. Some worked in the various
support services that were indispensable to mining—building construction, transportation, shopkeeping, saloonkeeping, gambling,

and even journalism. Others managed to buy land and take up (or go back to) farming, selling their crops to an always hungry community. Whatever their occupation, the men in the mining camps lived as their predecessors had in the early years of the California Gold Rush—mostly among men. In their leisure time, they loosened the restraints on their tempers and their appetites, brawling in the mud or, just as easily, splurging on oysters, eggs, and alcohol. The camps offered a depressing picture to moralists, but a seemingly boundless opportunity to merchants or anyone else with something to sell.

Not surprisingly, sex was for sale on an active and open market. Prostitution was one of the most pervasive services available in mining camps, and prostitutes often made up the majority of the handful of women who lived among the miners. Like male miners or merchants, women who worked as prostitutes hoped to make quick money in the most lucrative of available opportunities; they could work in other capacities in the camps—as cooks, seamstresses, and so forth—but in the short run, no other job could provide the earnings prostitution could. Yet, in the longer run, most prostitutes, like most of the miners, never came out of the mining camps with much money—if they came out at all. Prostitutes who worked in brothels were exploited by the madams who controlled their access to clients, and those who worked on their own faced the more difficult task of fending for themselves in a place with little concern for public safety. If men were vulnerable to violence in the camps, women were even more so; prostitutes were frequently beaten, sometimes killed, without any community outcry.

To be sure, mining camps were not the only communities available to overland emigrants as they neared the end of the trail. In fact, the influx of emigrant families helped transform the complexion and composition of Euro-American society in the West. The growing number of women who came west helped to alleviate the extreme sexual imbalance of the early settlements and, more important, increased the demand for decency and a stable social order. Women were always at the center of religious life. They could not serve as pastors—sexual exclusion stayed intact all the way across the country—but those who went west as missionaries' or ministers' wives played an important role in bringing other women under the wing of the church. Church women organized a host of auxiliary activities—prayer meetings, Sunday schools, sewing circles, community suppers—that supported the work of the ministry both financially and spiritually. Once women came to settle in a western community, whether a rough mining camp or, more commonly, a fledgling farm town, they helped establish not just churches but schools, libraries, and other amenities. Theirs was almost always an uphill struggle, because women were still a minority in a male society; although many married men shared their commitment to making frontier communities fit for family life, others, especially the young and single men, did not endorse their desire to spend time and money creating such "civilizing" institutions. Yet, without the pressure of mothers and the presence of young women willing to work as teachers, family-centered settlement would have been much slower.

The contrast between the raucous male culture of the mining camps and the genteel culture of middle-class communities became especially evident in the emerging new cities of the West, most of which owed their early growth to the mineral boom. The biggest and most successful of these new cities, San Francisco, was not a mining town, but it was the main port of entry and supply center for the California goldfields. In the early stages of the gold boom, it sometimes seemed like little more than an overgrown mining camp, with a wide offering of stores, barrooms, and brothels. Not surprisingly, it also had a widespread reputation for violence and disorder. The city's rapid population growth in the two decades after the Gold Rush—from around five thousand inhabitants in 1850 to 150,000 in 1870, about half of whom were foreign-born —made it anything but a stable community, especially given the even more turbulent turnover of transient men who moved in and out of the city so quickly. As in the mining communities, the city's vigilance committee remained the main source of local law enforcement throughout the early 1850s, and prostitution remained its main female occupation for even longer. But over time, with the arrival of middle-class women—and their middle-class husbands, who had the money to help finance refinement—the number of churches, schools, and theaters began to approach that of the barrooms and bordellos. Moreover, much to the dismay of many men (including, perhaps, some husbands of middle-class women), female reformers began to agitate for the suppression of prostitution, gambling, drinking, and other male amusements. Such was the pattern in other boom towns built on mineral wealth—Virginia City, Nevada; Denver, Colorado; Butte and Helena, Montana. As the community became transformed from a mining camp to an emerging metropolis, middle-class reformers tried to tame it. In the end, they had to face the apparent impossibility of imposing strict moral standards on such an open society. No matter how many reform-minded people eventually made their way west, San Francisco and the other cities would never be as sedate as Salt Lake City.

In 1862, the year the Gould family headed west to California, the United States government took two important steps that would both encourage and enable thousands of others to settle all over the trans-Mississippi West. On May 20, Congress passed the Homestead Act, which offered future settlers cheap land in the public domain—160 acres for $1.25 an acre after six months' residence or, if people promised to stay on the land for five years, for a small registration fee of around thirty dollars. Less than two months later, on July 1, the Pacific Railway Act authorized huge cash subsidies and land grants for private companies to build train tracks across the continent. Although both these acts were part of the unfinished business of the late antebellum era, they would have a profound effect on the post-war period. Even in the midst of a seemingly all-absorbing Civil War, the government made clear that its immediate commitment to national reunification had by no means diminished its long-standing commitment to national expansion.

Railroads had the most dramatic impact on the social and economic development of the West. On May 10, 1869, two railroad companies coming in opposite directions—the Union Pacific, whose largely Irish work force started laying track in Omaha, Nebraska, and the Central Pacific, which used Chinese laborers to take the slower, more difficult route from Sacramento, California, across the Sierra Nevada Mountains—joined their tracks at Promontory, Utah. California's Governor Leland Stanford, the dignitary given the honor of pounding in the ceremonial golden spike, created a single railroad route with a single stroke of a sledgehammer (actually, he needed a second stroke: he missed on his first try). With rails running between the Missouri River and the West Coast, goods and supplies of all sorts could now flow back and forth across the country; so, too, could settlers. In the quarter-century that followed, other railroad companies—the Northern Pacific; the Southern Pacific; the Texas Pacific; the Atchison, Topeka, and Santa Fe—would, as their names suggest, expand the national rail network throughout the West.

No western community better illustrates the significance of rail access than Denver. Established in 1859, Denver sat on the eastern edge of the Rocky Mountains, just where the high peaks rose up to mark the end of the Great Plains. Although Denver, like San Francisco, was not a major mining town, it, too, became a supply and service center for the nearby mining camps. For the first decade of its existence, though, it seemed to be a place where thousands visited but few stayed: although well over a hundred thousand passed through Denver each year in the 1860s, the population remained essentially 4,700 throughout the decade.

But, beginning in 1870, trains changed Denver for good. Denver had originally been bypassed by the railroads, when the Union Pacific line was routed a hundred miles to the north, through the Cheyenne Pass. The sudden emergence of Cheyenne, the new city in the new Wyoming Territory, threatened to doom Denver to second-class status. Not content to live in Cheyenne's shadow, a group of Denver merchants and political leaders formed a Board of Trade, and these boosters used all the influence they could muster, both in the West and in Washington, to get a rail line to run through Denver. Ultimately, the Kansas Pacific agreed to come west to Denver, and the local promoters, aided by a generous grant of 900,000 acres from the federal government, built the Denver Pacific line northward to connect with the Union Pacific at Cheyenne. Thus Denver, already well positioned adjacent to the Rocky Mountain goldfields, gained access to both the Midwest and the West Coast. While Cheyenne became the biggest town in Wyoming, by 1890 Denver became the biggest city between San Francisco and Omaha, with over a hundred thousand inhabitants.

Trains helped transform the eastern end of the Great Plains as well, accelerating settlement and community building in new Kansas cow towns created by the cattle boom. The western cattle industry had its origins in the antebellum era, when Texas cattlemen began to drive herds of hardy longhorn cattle west to California and Colorado, where they would feed the miners in the goldfields, or to Kansas City and St. Louis, where they could be shipped to eastern markets. It was not until the late 1860s, after the interruption of the Civil War and the expansion of the railroads, that the cattle drives reached their now-legendary scale. The old cattle trails from Texas intersected the new east-west rail lines in Kansas, and a handful of new towns—first Abilene, then Ellsworth, Wichita, Caldwell, and Dodge City—competed aggressively to attract cattle.

As they did so, the townspeople began to hold their noses in response to both the animals and the men who accompanied them. Like miners, cowboys were part of a rough, raucous male culture that appalled settlers who aspired to a more genteel society. At the same time, even the most conservative middle-class moralist had to admit that the annual arrival of the cattle drives was the one thing that not only sustained the community but enabled it to thrive. Cowboys may not have been model citizens, but they brought the money to town.

Cowboys have been so celebrated in popular culture that it is sometimes difficult to get a realistic picture of the lives they led. Despite the often romanticized descriptions of cowboy culture, the men who drove cattle to Kansas worked at a generally boring and sometimes suddenly dangerous job. Some were young men who had succumbed to the lure of dime novels and the romantic but inaccurate image of cowboy life, but most were men with few options—Civil War veterans, especially from the South, who had no post-war prospects at home; sons of farmers who saw the futility of staying on a failing family farm; blacks who faced discrimination and dislocation in the South (and often in the North as well); and Indian and Mexican *vaqueros* who had worked on ranches in Mexico and southern Texas. Drawn together for the duration of the cattle drive, a group of fifteen or twenty cowboys often reflected a remarkable racial and cultural diversity. Some cowboys had better long-term prospects than others—usually only whites could rise to the position of trail boss—but in the short run, they all endured the same long hours and low pay. While the owners of the herds might make a profit of up to twenty dollars a head for each of several thousand animals delivered to the shipping pens, the cowboys who drove them there usually received between one hundred and two hundred dollars for several months' work on the trail. In most cases, the end of the trail meant the end of their work, and they had no guarantee that they would find work in the next year's cattle drive.

In the meantime, they were free men in town with money in their pockets, and they typically went on a spree and spent it as long as it lasted—usually not very long. After getting a bath, a shave, and a haircut, they got rid of their dirty trail clothes and decked themselves out in an outfit that was sometimes almost a caricature of cowboy clothing. As one Kansas cow-town resident observed, "Dressed in gala attire, they wore high-heeled boots with large clanking spurs of various hues, shirts that bloused freely with no hint of suspenders, large colored handkerchiefs knotted loosely around their necks and large-brimmed Stetson hats. Some showed the influence of their Spanish neighbors and wore large brightly colored sashes." The shopkeepers who sold them these items were only too happy to have them as customers—as were local prostitutes, barkeepers, and boardinghouse owners—but hardly anyone wanted them as neighbors. Each year, the arrival of these dust-covered, saddle-sore summer visitors in a cattle community brought a sudden increase in vice and violence that created dismay among the town's permanent and presumably more proper inhabitants.

Many of the year-round residents of cattle towns were trying to create the semblance of civilized life. As was the case elsewhere in frontier settlements, women took the lead in establishing schools and churches, and they joined men in creating other outlets for intellectual enlightenment and decorous discussion. In 1872, for instance, men and women in Wichita organized the Union Literary Society, which quickly became the town's main forum for formal lectures and debates, tackling such topics as "Resolved, that Intemperance is a greater evil than Slavery." Slavery was no longer a problem in Kansas, of course, but intemperance certainly was. Reform-minded residents pushed to close down barrooms, brothels, and gambling dens, almost invariably without lasting success. As Robert Haywood points out in his study of Kansas cattle towns, local liquor dealers and their allies opposed the reformers, calling them self-righteous moralists and hypocrites who were out to ruin everyone else's pleasure, not to mention a few people's profits. The social divisions in cattle towns also became evident in occasional clashes over what constituted appropriate entertainment. Not everyone liked the lectures, lawn parties, croquet games, dramatic presentations, and church socials of the self-consciously sedate citizens; cowboys and the town's rowdier sort provided a ready audience for minstrel shows, burlesque, and baseball games.

It was one thing to offend people's sensibility, but quite another to threaten their safety. Unfortunately for many fearful residents, the cattle towns provided precious little organized law enforcement. At best, these towns hired a local sheriff—sometimes a former outlaw himself—to police the community, but just as often they relied on a local posse to provide protection. In some cases, the results brought the connection between Victorian gentility and vigilante justice into sharp focus. Florence Bingham, who moved to Abilene with her husband in 1871, soon saw the effects of local law enforcement:

> One morning a man was found murdered along the railroad tracks. The men suspicioned another man and that evening they searched him and found part of the murdered man's clothing and his money, so they forthwith took this man to the creek a little northwest of our house and hung him to a beam of the old mill. My husband did not tell me anything about it. The school was on the south side and the next morning, much to my surprise, the school children came running past our house, all excited. They were going to see the man who was still hanging at the mill. They seemed to think it quite a lark and swung him back and forth by his toes.

Clearly, lynching was not in the day's lesson plan, but it was part of the broader learning experience for children growing up in communities on the cattle frontier. The school could socialize children only so much; they also learned the code of community values from their fathers and other upstanding men like Mr. Bingham. Although Mrs. Bingham's own sensibilities kept her from looking at the dead man—"I could have seen him from my front gate," she noted, "but I certainly did not want to"—she did admit that it was "necessary that quick punishment be inflicted upon the criminal [in] those days."

"Those days" would last for most of the rest of the century, even after the great cattle drives. Kansas and the surrounding prairie regions remained rough-and-tumble territory where communities of farm families coexisted uneasily with cowboys and the coarser mores of the cattle industry. Farmers found that frail three-rail fences around their fields provided scant protection from the droves of cattle that lumbered by in the summer, just when crops were coming in. Sheepherders likewise saw that their animals had little chance of competing with cattle for grazing. To deal with cattlemen, customary farm security sometimes had to be supplemented with a shotgun. By the mid-1880s, the introduction of barbed wire offered a better means of keeping cattle from trampling crops and away from the sheep; fenced fields became increasingly common in the midwestern landscape. Cattlemen frequently cut through the farmers' fences and killed sheepherders' flocks without remorse. Cowboys had nothing but contempt for sheepherders—or "mutton punchers" and "lamb lickers," as they called them—and one of their preferred methods of ridding the ranges of sheep was to "rimrock" whole herds, driving the sheep over a cliff or into a river. Farmers and sheepherders fought back, using all the weapons at their disposal, from guns to government officials.

Eventually, economic and environmental factors dealt a near-fatal blow to the freewheeling ways of the cattle industry. By the mid-1880s, the extension of rail lines into Texas gave cattlemen a better way to get their animals to market, and there were fewer and fewer long cattle drives to Kansas. Cattlemen in Kansas and in other parts of the Great Plains kept big herds on the western grasslands, using barbed-wire fences themselves to defend their range land from encroaching homesteaders. But a significant spell of severe weather—abnormally cold winters in 1885–86 and 1886–87, and an extremely dry summer in 1886—led to the "Big Die-Up" among overstocked herds in 1887. From that point on, cattlemen turned to more scientific methods of animal husbandry, using better breeding methods to produce smaller, hardier herds. They still disliked farmers and disdained sheepmen, but cattlemen were clearly on the defensive, with a shrinking expanse of land. Although there would continue to be skirmishes in the "range wars" into the early part of the twentieth century, the Great Plains increasingly went under the plow.

Populating the Plains with homesteaders did not work quite the way the government had originally intended, but it worked well enough. The Homestead Act's promise of cheap 160-acre sections appealed to speculators as well as settlers, and some of the best land fell into the hands of men who acquired it only to sell it to subsequent settlers. Railroads, with hundreds of thousands of acres given them in government grants, also had an economic interest in getting people to live along their rights-of-way. Land agents representing speculators, railroad companies, and local governments engaged in a vigorous promotional campaign to attract settlers, promising good land and transportation, two of the basic requirements of successful farming.

Beginning in the 1870s, farm families responded by the hundreds of thousands. Following their hopes to the Great Plains, emigrants established farms in desolate regions that had deterred earlier overlanders. Many, in fact a majority, did not stay in one place long enough to put down permanent roots, but when they moved on to the next farm on the frontier, there was almost always someone willing to buy their land and take their place.

Some of the strongest settlements were whole communities tied together by a common ethnic identity. To Europeans fed up with or forced out of their native country, America had long looked like the land of opportunity, and in the last third of the nineteenth century, opportunity often looked brightest on the Plains. Local promoters, only too happy to reinforce that feeling, sent recruiters to eastern cities and even to Europe to entice potential settlers. New immigrant communities cropped up seemingly everywhere from Kansas to Minnesota and the Dakotas, populated by seemingly every sort of northern and eastern European—Scots, Swedes, Norwegians, Danes, Germans, Czechs, Poles, Russians, and others. Most of these communities persisted, and some even prospered.

Some, of course, did neither. One of the more remarkable and certainly exceptional of the newly formed immigrant communities in the West was an English settlement in Kansas named, perhaps predictably, Victoria. Founded in 1873 by Sir George Grant, a successful London silk merchant, Victoria was intended to be a haven not for the "huddled masses" but for the upper classes. Having purchased fifty thousand acres of open plains from the Kansas Pacific Railroad, Sir George recruited young people from some of

England's finest families to re-create the life of the landed gentry on the midwestern frontier. Not since the arrival of young gentlemen among the original settlers at Jamestown in 1607 had English immigrants come to the frontier with such aristocratic aspirations. They brought their finest furniture, tableware, and art treasures for their houses, and the best stock of English horses, cattle, and sheep for their fields. Apparently undaunted by any lack of resemblance between Kansas and the English countryside, the early colonists did what they could to make themselves feel at home, giving elegant garden parties, playing cricket, and holding formal fox hunts—using a coyote or cottontail rabbit as "fox."

Not surprisingly, Kansas soon got the best of them. Some of their native-born neighbors, who had no claim to high social breeding but who had a good eye for well-bred livestock, stole their very valuable animals. The inevitable environmental hazards of frontier farming—prairie fires, grasshopper infestations, and hard, dry soil—added to their discouragement. Regular infusions of family money from home helped them hold on for a few years, but by 1878 the sun had finally set on this American extension of the British Empire, and the era of Victoria, Kansas, came to an end.

In the adjacent county, but at the very opposite end of the social spectrum, there emerged a very different sort of ethnic community—the Nicodemus Colony, a settlement of former slaves. By the mid-1870s, Kansas was becoming the promised land for several thousand ex-slaves who sought to get out of the South. Even though the Civil War had brought an end to slavery, the end of Reconstruction in 1877 lifted the last official restraints on white racism in the old Confederacy, and life there became even more unbearable for blacks. Some looked to escape to Liberia, the African nation established earlier in the century for African-American emigrants, as a possible refuge, but Kansas was closer. The triumph of the anti-slavery forces in "Bleeding Kansas" in the 1850s and the continued commitment of Kansans during the Civil War—no other state had a higher casualty rate in fighting for the Union—made Kansas appear to be a hospitable home for freed blacks. As Nell Irvin Painter observes in her study of the Exodusters of the 1870s, "Kansas was no Canaan, but it was a far cry from Mississippi and Louisiana." Beginning as early as 1875 and reaching a peak in 1879, black emigration brought to Kansas upward of six thousand settlers who hoped to establish farms and finally be free.

They had only limited success. Nicodemus, the largest of the Exoduster communities, was located far out on the Plains—but not far enough, it turned out, to insulate its inhabitants from racism. Like other farmers, the people of Nicodemus experienced their share of conflict with cattlemen, complaining to the governor (to no avail) when cattle crushed their crops. But even their fellow farmers showed them little sympathy. White Kansans may have fought to put an end to slavery, but many of them did not want ex-slaves living (and voting) in the same county. Still, Nicodemus did reasonably well for a new town on the farming frontier, and it continued to grow slowly. Most other African-American emigrants remained in majority-white towns like Dodge City, Leavenworth, and Topeka. There they worked for what wages they could find— the men as farmhands and railroad workers, the women as wash- erwomen or housemaids. Some managed to save enough to buy their own homes, and others moved on to look for work elsewhere in Kansas or in Colorado, Nebraska, and, later, Oklahoma. Given the racial climate in the country at the time, Painter notes, any African-American effort at "seeking real freedom within America was destined to realize no more than a relative measure of success." Yet, despite the obvious obstacles and disappointments, the Exo- duster movement embodies the hopeful assumption that emigrants could find on the frontier, as Frederick Jackson Turner would later put it, "a gate of escape from the bondage of the past." No one needed it more than they.

In his 1893 address on "The Significance of the Frontier," Turner invited his readers to "stand at South Pass in the Rockies" and watch the procession of pioneers, all heading west in "successive waves" to bring the frontier experience to a finish. Had he directed his readers to look east as well as west, they would have seen even more movement. The transcontinental trek to the West Coast that began in the 1840s was only the most celebrated part of the emi- grant experience. During the second half of the nineteenth century, and especially after the Civil War, thousands traveled not just west but also north, south, and even east to settle in parts of the con- tinent that earlier overlanders had passed through or ignored altogether. Compared to the promised beauty and abundance of California and Oregon, the "Great American Desert" that stretched across the vast expanse in the middle of the continent had seemed a distant second choice for settlement. But, increasingly, as more people chose to seek new land in the West—and as their government encouraged them to do so—they began to establish a greater permanent presence in other regions west of the Mississippi. In the space of fifty years, the massive migration that began at mid-century had spread out over all parts of the West, creating a patchwork of frontier settlements across the western half of the continent.

The emigrants' experience added another important chapter not only to the history of frontier migrations but to the history of frontier warfare as well. Throughout the nineteenth century, Indian peoples had been on the move, too, sometimes backward in retreat, sometimes forward in attack, but almost always away from the lands where they lived. Since about half the remaining Indian population of North America now inhabited territories between the Mississippi and the Rockies, the continuing expansion of one nation led to the continuing dislocation of others. Increasingly surrounded by settlers, Indians had little room to move—and even less inclination. Thus it was with the post-Civil War wave of trans-Mississippi movement that Native Americans and Euro-Americans confronted each other in one of the most intense periods of intercultural conflict in American history.

SIX

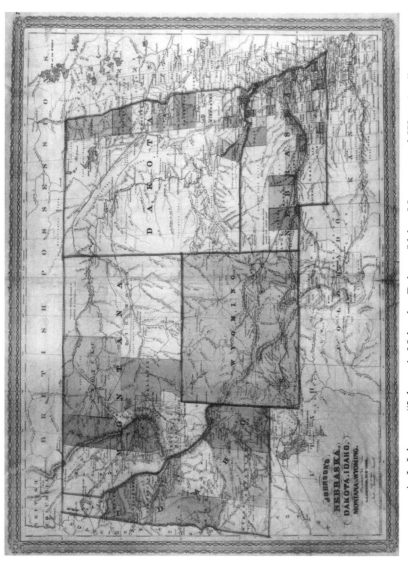

A. J. Johnson, "Johnson's Nebraska, Dakota, Idaho, Montana, and Wyoming," 1865. *Courtesy Special Collections Department, Robert W. Woodruff Library, Emory University*

Indians and
the Enclosing Frontier,
1860–90

J ust before noon on July 19, 1881, a band of almost two hundred Lakota Indians approached the gates of Fort Buford, a
United States Army outpost in the far northwest corner of Dakota
Territory, a little over fifty miles south of the Canadian border.
No one inside the fort had cause for concern, however: this was
clearly not a war party. Over three-fourths of the Indians were
women and children, most of them walking in a caravan of two-
wheeled carts that held their belongings. Most of the men were
walking, too; they had only fourteen scrawny ponies among them.
Riding one of those ponies, at the head of the procession, was one
of the most famous and feared Indian leaders of all—Sitting Bull,
a proud warrior who had spent most of his adult life fighting both
Indian and Euro-American foes. Now fifty years old, tired, sick,
and near-starving, he was finally coming in to surrender.

He could hardly comprehend what that would mean. The
following day, as he gave up his gun in the formal surrender ceremony, Sitting Bull told the assembled officers and onlookers that
he wanted it to be remembered that "I was the last man of my
tribe to surrender my rifle." And yet surrender it he did, handing
it to his young son, Crow Foot, who in turn passed it over to the
fort's commanding officer, Major David Brotherton. But in almost
the next breath Sitting Bull went on to say that he wanted to continue hunting and trading on both sides of the border between the
United States and Canada, where he had been living for the past

four years. Clearly, he could not yet accept the restraints of reservation life, with the limited mobility and near-sedentary life-style of farming in the white man's fashion. Two weeks later, he told a newspaper reporter that he considered himself essentially a free man: "When I came in I did not surrender. . . . I want no restraint. I will keep on the reservation, but want to go where I please." Still later, he told another reporter that the "life of white men is slavery. They are prisoners in towns or farms. The life my people want is a life of freedom." Unfortunately, Sitting Bull was now a prisoner, and not just of a farm but of the United States government. He would never again live a life of freedom as he once knew it.

Yet, even though Sitting Bull had lost his freedom, he still had his fame. Now that he was disarmed and apparently harmless, white people often pestered him for his autograph, and he usually obliged (although, like a modern-day sports star, he began to charge a fee). On occasion, his celebrity status allowed him to escape the reservation for a while, albeit under controlled conditions. In 1883, James McLaughlin, the superintendent of the Standing Rock Agency, where Sitting Bull had been sent to live, took Sitting Bull and several other Indian leaders on trips to major midwestern cities. Ever mindful of the possible public relations (and perhaps pecuniary gains) to be garnered from showing off his exotic though increasingly "civilized" charges, McLaughlin helped arrange Sitting Bull's appearances before urban audiences and autograph-seekers. He also hoped that by showing Sitting Bull and the others the supposed benefits of modern technology, he could convince them to accept their status as "agency" Indians and look forward to the future amalgamation of their people into white society. By 1884, McLaughlin could express satisfaction that Sitting Bull had been duly impressed with his exposure to the cities, and that his influence among other Indians at Standing Rock was now "being turned in the right direction."

In 1885, Sitting Bull reached perhaps the pinnacle of his publicity value when he was recruited by former army scout, buffalo hunter, and Indian fighter William F. Cody to join his popular touring show, Buffalo Bill's Wild West and Congress of Rough Riders of the World. An idealized, romanticized, and dramatized image of the West had long been a commodity of popular culture, and Buffalo Bill gave audiences what they wanted to see—including, now, a veritable Indian icon. As the show played major arenas both in Canada and in the United States, Sitting Bull became a prominent member of the troupe, riding in parades and performing tricks on his horse and giving live demonstrations and lectures about Indian life. If Sitting Bull resented having crossed the line into an alien culture to provide a near-caricature of his own, he did not say so openly. On the contrary, he seemed to like the attention and travel, and he certainly enjoyed the money he made. It was the Indian agent McLaughlin, not Sitting Bull, who brought the show business to an end. Too much independence and too much income exposed Sitting Bull to too many bad influences, McLaughlin argued, and in 1886 he declared that "for the good of the other Indians and the best interests of the Service I am forced to the conclusion that it would be unwise to have him go out this season." The ensuing confinement to Standing Rock disappointed not only Sitting Bull and Buffalo Bill, who had become good friends, but also thousands of people in the East who were willing to pay money to see this living legend of the West. After all, this was the man most people considered the mastermind of the massacre of George Armstrong Custer and the Seventh Cavalry not quite a decade before. Now apparently pacified, he had become a fixture in the popular memory of Euro-American culture.

But long before the famous battle above the Little Bighorn River (or the Greasy Grass, as Indians called it) on June 25, 1876, Sitting Bull had become a major figure in his own culture. Above all, he was a powerful military leader with more than thirty years of combat to his credit. He had made his initial first coup—a first blow struck against an enemy at close range—when he was fifteen, and he went on to add dozens more during his career as a warrior. Combining the physical courage of a fighter with the spiritual vision of a holy man, Sitting Bull became the most prominent leader among the Indian people of the Great Plains, not only his own Hunkpapas but the larger Lakota–Cheyenne confederacy as well. By the middle of the nineteenth century, the focus of conflict had shifted from their long-standing Indian enemies, like the Crows, to the fast-expanding population of the United States. Throughout the 1850s, 1860s, and 1870s, Sitting Bull took an almost absolute stand against the soldiers and settlers who moved into Indian territory. More to the point, he rejected the notion that the United States government, through either military or diplomatic means, could define what Indian territory was and, even worse, confine

Indian people to the restricted life of a reservation. His Hunkpapa people, like all the Indians of the Great Plains, had to remain free to follow the buffalo, because the buffalo was the source of their livelihood. Therefore, they fought anyone who threatened this way of life. Striking a coup against Custer was only one step in a much larger strategy.

But Custer's Last Stand was, in a sense, Sitting Bull's last stand as well. He would never win a significant victory against the soldiers again. The outcry that echoed across the United States at the Custer defeat—coming, as it did, in the summer of 1876, as the nation was in the midst of celebrating its centennial—pushed the military into a relentless campaign against Sitting Bull and his followers. Although the Indians would enjoy a brief respite by seeking safe haven in Canada, four years of military and diplomatic pressure by the United States forced them back across the border and into the restraints of the reservation. Sitting Bull would have his occasional forays into the outside world, but he would be a reservation Indian for the rest of his life—until, in December 1890, he was killed at the Standing Rock Agency.

In a sense, Sitting Bull defined the dilemma facing all Indian people, or certainly Indian leaders, in the nineteenth century. They could be resolute and resist the expansion of the United States and the expropriation of Indian lands, which they did—and nobody did it better than Sitting Bull. But, increasingly, the vast military and technological resources of the United States gave the government a staggering advantage over its Indian adversaries. By the second half of the nineteenth century, government policy was clear: the only alternative to extermination was the reservation. Choosing death before dishonor might be possible for individual warriors, but no leader could easily force that fate upon a whole people. Choosing survival meant accepting surrender, then. And yet, as Sitting Bull would find out after finally making that choice for his people, even surrender did not guarantee safety.

By the time Sitting Bull made his reluctant move onto the reservation, the United States had spent over half a century preparing a very narrow, one-way path for him and other Indians to follow. In the early part of the nineteenth century, Thomas Jefferson had envisioned making most of the Louisiana Purchase a Permanent Indian Frontier west of the Mississippi River; implicit in that plan, of course, was the assumption that some native peoples would have to move—or be moved—to that enclave, so that the citizens of the United States could inhabit all the lands to the east of the Mississippi without competition or conflict. It was not until the Indian Removal Act of 1830, however, that the government made clear its decision for dislocation, forcing thousands of Southeastern Indians along the Trail of Tears to a distant and very different new homeland in Indian Territory on the southern Plains. But almost immediately, the Permanent Indian Frontier proved to be anything but permanent. During the 1840s—as overland emigrants began to head for the Pacific coast and the United States carried on its conquest of the West in the war with Mexico—the notion of the Indian Frontier underwent a significant transformation. No longer would it be envisioned as a vast, unbroken region reaching across the middle of the continent; rather, it would be cut up into a patchwork of separate parcels set aside for particular Indian groups. The government would claim increasing expanses of land for its own purposes—trails, forts, townships, railroad routes—and extinguish Indian title by treaty or force.

The first major step in redefining the nation's Indian policy came in 1851, when the government invited Indians from all across the Plains to meet at Fort Laramie in Wyoming Territory. Upward of ten thousand Indians showed up—among them Sioux, Cheyennes, Arapahos, Crows, Shoshones, Assiniboins, Arikaras—to hear what the white men had to offer. What the government sought to promote, above all, was peace—peace between white people and Indian people, peace among Indian people themselves, who were at the time more habituated to fighting each other than to fighting the soldiers and settlers from the East. But in order to secure safe passage for these soldiers and settlers as they moved to the West, the government also proposed creating separate territories for each Indian tribe, theoretically isolating them from each other. To sweeten the offer, the government also promised to provide annuities of food and supplies to the Indians who ceded part of their land and accepted life within the assigned boundaries. Thus at Fort Laramie the United States established the basic elements of the reservation system that would develop over the rest of the century.

The plan was flawed from the outset. Many Indian leaders refused to accept the idea of living within arbitrary bounds, and some who did agree did not fully represent, much less control, all their people. Far greater were the problems created by the government officials charged with making the system operate, the Bureau of Indian Affairs. In inducing Indian people to live by the dictates of the treaty, they laid the foundation for future conflict.

In less than two decades after its creation in 1834, the Bureau of Indian Affairs had become a far-flung, federally funded, patronage-ridden, loosely supervised system that operated hundreds of miles away from Washington—in short, the sort of system that could easily foster incompetence and breed corruption. And it did. Superintendent and agent positions were ripe political plums that usually fell into the hands of the friends and family members of elected officials and political hacks who had some measure of leverage with the party in power. Although the official salary was fairly low, the opportunities for unofficial financial gain could be immense. The men who operated the agencies were local brokers with virtually unregulated access to government money and influence, and more than a few civil servants became true masters of manipulating the system. They had the authority to award contracts for goods and services that might or might not ever be delivered in full; whatever the case, agents were able to skim off personal benefits directly or to extract generous "considerations" from grateful contractors. They also had the power to grant cash payments to settlers who felt somehow aggrieved by Indian actions—the loss of livestock or other property, for instance—and many agents paid off with only the slightest investigation into the merits of the claim. Perhaps most important, they could grant trading licenses, which were essentially permits to profit at the public —and, above all, the Indians'—expense. Agency-approved traders had a near-monopoly on doing business with Indians on the reservation, and they used cheap alcohol and creative bookkeeping to keep their customers almost constantly in debt. Sarah Wakefield, the wife of the doctor on the Yellow Medicine Upper Agency in Minnesota, described the pressure put on the Dakota people who lived on the reservation:

> The Traders surround them, saying, you owe me so much for flour. Another says you owe me so much for sugar, &c. and the Indian gives it up, never knowing whether it is right or not. Many Indians pay before the [annuity] payment with furs, still they are caught up by these Traders, and very seldom a man passes way with his money. I saw a poor fellow one day swallow his money. I wondered he did not choke to death, but he said, "They will not have mine, for I do not owe them."

Not every Indian agent and trader was corrupt, of course, but there were enough unscrupulous operators to make it seem that almost everyone had access to the Indians' annuities but the Indians themselves. After watching the Dakotas take a financial fleecing from the system, Sarah Wakefield found herself "surprised that they would allow such cheating without retaliation." She soon found out that they would not.

The conflict and corruption inherent in the reservation system burst to the surface in Minnesota in 1862, with devastating results for hundreds of Indians and whites. For over a decade, government agents had been using the annuities at their disposal to favor some Indians at the expense of others. Even though the Dakota people had surrendered thousands of acres of their land, they had not completely surrendered their way of life. Only ten percent had taken the first steps toward assimilation into white culture—farming individual plots of land, building brick houses, going to a Christian church, sending their children to a mission school, and generally following the dictates of the reservation-system reformers. The remaining ninety percent of the Dakotas tried to hold on to their old ways as best they could. But even they, no longer able to ride and hunt as freely as they had in the past, had to rely increasingly on government annuities to survive. To encourage acceptance of reservation life, government agents distributed goods unequally: the farmer Indians received comparatively generous allotments of food and supplies, while the "blanket Indians" received just enough to keep them alive. This double standard created resentment between farmer Indians and "blanket Indians," but it created even greater hostility toward the government.

Moreover, the management of Indian affairs in Minnesota had created a morass of corruption that mostly benefited a handful of prominent political leaders. The first two governors elected after Minnesota became a state in 1858, Henry Hastings Sibley and Alexander Ramsey, had both been accused of self-aggrandizement during treaty negotiations with the Dakota Sioux in 1851, when the Indians ceded some 24 million acres of land in exchange for $1,410,000 in annuities. Both Sibley and Ramsey had become wealthy men with the help of Indian money, but the voters seemed not to hold that against them at election time. A few years later, in 1861, one of the state's senators, Henry Rice, managed to get a federal payment of $24,000 for his role in Indian removal. Not to be left out, the other Minnesota senator, Morton Wilkinson, successfully lobbied the Lincoln administration to make sure that his political cronies got control of the Indian agencies—and first cut at the annuities. In general, virtually everyone in the upper echelons of the state's political structure had been lining his pockets with Indian money, so much so that even government officials in Washington had to take notice.

A congressional investigator sent to Minnesota in 1861 found evidence of "voluminous and outrageous frauds upon the Indians" being perpetrated by the state's political elite, and he concluded that these men clearly knew what they were doing: "Had the most skillful thieves and rogues in the [world] been employed to set up a safe mode of swindling . . . no more perfect system could have been devised." His report died a quiet bureaucratic death, however. These men from Minnesota were all loyal Republicans, well-placed political operators who had helped deliver the state for Lincoln in the election of 1860, and the new administration had to be appreciative of their past services—and therefore tolerant of their past and present sins. Moreover, with the Civil War now raging, the Lincoln administration gave comparatively low priority to the problems of a few thousand agency Indians in Minnesota.

The Dakota people had their own political priorities, however, and they made them an unavoidable item on the administration's agenda as well—especially as it became clear that the growing requirements of the great war in the South were making it difficult for the government to deliver its goods in the North. From mid-June to mid-August 1862, while the main Union and Confederate forces were regrouping in Virginia between the battles of the Peninsula Campaign and the Second Battle of Bull Run, hungry Dakotas had begun gathering angrily at the Minnesota agencies, agitating to have the storehouses opened and the supplies distributed among the people for whom they were intended. The agent for the region, Thomas J. Galbraith, managed to avoid a crisis by passing out some (but not all) of the provisions the Indians wanted and then entering into negotiations concerning the rest. Unfortunately, an Indian trader named Andrew Myrick sneered that if the Indians wanted food they should "eat grass or their own dung." Once his comment made the rounds, most Indians gave up negotiating with white men and took another approach. On August 17, four young Dakota men, initially intending only to steal an egg or two, wound up killing five white people in a local farm family. The following day, a much larger band of Dakotas attacked the Redwood Lower Agency to seize food supplies, and then they moved out to expand the attack to other white settlements. Three days later, on August 21, Governor Ramsey anxiously telegraphed Washington to warn Secretary of War Edwin M. Stanton: "The Sioux Indians on our western border have risen, and are murdering men, women, and children." Minnesota, so far away from the bloodshed in Virginia, had now become a battlefield.

Additional anxious reports flowed out of Minnesota for the next two months. Initial estimates put the number of whites killed at more than five hundred, with fifty thousand made refugees. "The panic among the people has depopulated whole counties," Ramsey insisted. Fifty thousand was also the wildly inflated figure of the number of Indians in the uprising—not just Dakotas, but neighboring Ojibwas and Winnebagos as well. Some Minnesotans even saw a Confederate conspiracy in the crisis, asserting that southern agents had been working to stir up the Indians in the first place and now had opened up a western front with the help of their Indian allies.

All this came at a point when President Lincoln had little time to separate fact from fantasy. He had a very real Confederate threat on his hands just a few miles from Washington, where rebel forces defeated a Union army under General John C. Pope at the Second Battle of Bull Run on August 29–30. Lincoln had wanted to draft more than five thousand additional men from Minnesota for the larger war effort, but now he was faced with urgent requests that he instead send federal troops to Minnesota. He ordered a Minnesota regiment, which had been captured by the Confederates and then paroled on the promise that it would no longer fight against the South, back to Minnesota to join the fight against the Indians. Moreover, to take command of the military effort in Minnesota, Lincoln dispatched General Pope, the loser at Bull Run. No doubt, Pope understood that this posting was hardly a promotion, and he came to Minnesota intent on reclaiming his military reputation. To Henry Sibley (himself lately a loser in the state's political wars but now the senior officer in the Minnesota militia), Pope declared it "my purpose utterly to exterminate the Sioux. . . . They are to be treated as maniacs or wild beasts, and by no means as people with whom treaties or compromises can be made." To underscore the importance of his situation to Lincoln, Pope lay before the president a picture of horrid atrocity:

> Over 500 people have been murdered in Minnesota alone and 300 women and children now in captivity. The most horrible massacres have been committed; children nailed alive to trees and houses, women violated and then disembowelled—everything that horrible ingenuity could devise. It will require a large force and much time to prevent everybody leaving the country, such is the condition of things.

Like most military commanders in most wars, Pope could not resist requesting more men, but, in fact, a fairly small force did the job in a fairly short time. By November 1862, Sibley had forced most of the Indians into surrender or flight. He held some fifteen hundred captives, many of whom were put on trial before vengeance-minded military commissions; after a series of hasty and shoddy hearings, just over three hundred were condemned to hang. Pope applauded Sibley's quick actions and urged that he "not allow any false sympathy for the Indians to prevent you from acting with the utmost rigor."

Other observers of the Minnesota situation did show some sympathy, however, and the crisis brought a more benign approach to Indian relations into public focus. The most articulate and emphatic advocate was Episcopal Bishop Henry Benjamin Whipple, who became an outspoken supporter of the Dakota people and an equally outspoken critic of the corruption in the administration of Minnesota's Indian affairs. Even before the uprising broke out, Whipple had warned Lincoln that avaricious agents had created a crisis that could easily end in bloodshed, and if so, the stains would be on the hands of the whites. Now, with Indians about to be hanged by the hundreds, Whipple begged the president to restrain the Minnesotans from legalized murder. Looking to the longer term, Whipple insisted that the only solution to the Indian problem was a thorough reform of the reservation system.

But this seemingly sympathetic stance depended on a critical assumption: that reforming Indian reservations was only a necessary step to reforming Indians themselves. Like many other defenders of the Indian, Whipple drew upon a long-established notion of the "noble savage," the native whose natural virtues were essentially the same as those of "civilized" people:

> The North American Indians are the best of the heathen uncivilized races. They are not idolators. They believe in a Great Spirit. They have home affections. They have strong national pride and love of country. They are generally chaste, truthful, honest, generous and hospitable.

In Bishop Whipple's eyes, to be "the best of the heathen uncivilized races" meant that Indians had great potential, making them most likely to succeed someday in the white man's world. The long list of favorable traits he saw in Indians made it plausible that, given the right guidance and environment, Indians could become productive Christian citizens, just like white people. More to the point, there was the assumption that if Indians *could* live like whites, then they *should*. Even comparatively friendly allies like Whipple accepted the basic approach of the reservation system: they looked forward to a future when Indians would settle on individual family farms and give up their mobility and identity as members of tribal groups; for the time being, they hoped a properly run reservation system would give Indians a chance to start becoming Americanized—or, more properly, Euro-Americanized. The idea that Indians might be left alone to live on their own terms did not seem a viable prospect even to the most sympathetic reformers.

Faced with the conflicting policy options embodied by General Pope and Bishop Whipple, Lincoln tried to occupy the political middle ground. To appease Bishop Whipple and the others sympathetic with the Indians' plight, Lincoln promised to reform the Indian system in the future and, in the more immediate crisis, to review the records of the military commissions that had condemned so many Indians so quickly to death; in the end, Lincoln did reduce the number of executions from 303 to thirty-eight. But the political pressures of the ongoing war and the upcoming elections made Lincoln reluctant to alienate his allies in Minnesota by stopping the executions altogether; thus, on the day after Christmas 1862, the thirty-eight condemned Indians were hanged. Lincoln returned his attention to the Civil War, but never got around to reforming the Indian system. With Minnesota's military affairs left in the hands of Pope, Sibley, and the state militia, many other Indians died as well. Over sixty Indians fell victim to disease while they were in prison, even after the orders for execution had been overturned. The other captive Indians were moved out of Minnesota, several hundred miles to the west to a reservation on the upper Missouri River, where, once again, corrupt agents stole the supplies that could have reduced starvation and suffering. Then, over the course of the next few years, the Minnesota militia chased the remaining Dakotas out of the state, pursuing them as far west as the Yellowstone River—into the territory of their Lakota kinspeople and Sitting Bull. With Minnesota all but cleared of Indians, the state's officials opened the former reservations to white settlers.

The events in Minnesota were more than a mere sideshow to the Civil War. They reflected and, to some extent, reinforced the larger pattern of Indian policy that had begun to emerge in the decade before the Civil War and would continue to dominate the government's actions during the post-war era. In one sense, there would be no single Indian policy, at least not a well-crafted, coherent, and consistent formula for frontier planning. Rather, the government adopted what appeared at first to be a two-pronged approach. In the immediate aftermath of the Minnesota crisis, federal officials could hardly ignore Bishop Whipple and other well-meaning moderates who continued to clamor for reservation reform and a peaceful approach to Indian affairs; it certainly took no outright apologist for Indian rights to recognize that the government bore its share of responsibility for the corruption and conflict that had occurred. Accordingly, post-war Indian policy included establishing peace commissions, negotiating treaties, and placing reservations under the care of church people. Yet, at the same time, most policymakers realized that reservation reform alone would not encourage Indians to surrender their lands and submit to a settled life of government-enforced farming. For that, federal officials would still rely on the impressive military power at their disposal.

They had never completely interrupted the military campaigns against Indians, even during the Civil War. In the early 1860s, regular army and state militia forces had fought not only against the Dakotas in Minnesota but also against the Navajos and Apaches in New Mexico, the Shoshones in Utah, and the Cheyennes in Colorado. In the Indian Territory of the southern Plains, some parts of the Cherokees, Creeks, Choctaws, Chickasaws, and Seminoles had allied with the Confederates, and they, too, faced the Union Army in battle. The end of the Civil War in 1865 meant that the United States Army no longer had Confederates to worry about and could turn its full attention to Indians. In the immediate post-Civil War era, federal troops took the field throughout the West: in New Mexico and Arizona against the Apaches; in Oregon and Idaho against the Paiutes; in California against the Modocs; and, most doggedly, on the Great Plains against the Kiowas, Comanches, Arapahos, Cheyennes, and Sioux. Until 1898, the army would fight against no one but Indians. Moreover, some of the most prominent generals of the Union Army—above all, William Tecumseh Sherman and Philip Sheridan—would assume command of the forces on the western front, and they turned their Civil War tactics of total war against Indians who resisted reservation life. As General Sherman would explain in 1868, government policy toward Indians could be defined as a "double process of peace *within* their reservations and war *without*."

In that sense, the apparently separate approaches of reform and armed force converged: the government offered Indians a choice between war or peace—but peace only on conditions that whites considered benign confinement. More to the point, no matter what options seemingly competed in Indian affairs, one larger policy concern remained paramount—national expansion and integration. On that there would be no compromise or debate. Having fought a bloody civil war to reunify the eastern half of the nation, the United States government would do whatever it took throughout the rest of the century to complete its westward conquest of the continent.

One of the problems of making Indian policy in Washington

was the flow of conflicting information from the West. On one day, word would come of some attack or atrocity committed by Indians; on the next, the message might tell of equally outrageous behavior on the part of white settlers or soldiers. Anyone who compiled a record of all the massacres, murders, and mutilations could hardly argue that either side had a claim to clean hands; there was more than enough blood—and blame—to go around.

On the morning of November 29, 1864, for instance, a force of around seven hundred Colorado militiamen made an unprovoked surprise attack on some five hundred Cheyenne men, women, and children encamped at Sand Creek, in the southeastern corner of Colorado. The leader of the Cheyennes, Black Kettle, had brought his people there to talk peace with Colorado authorities after several months of fighting. But the leader of the Colorado soldiers, Colonel John M. Chivington, a former Methodist minister turned militia commander and would-be congressman, had no intention of allowing the Cheyennes a peaceful settlement. He, along with the territorial governor, John Evans, wanted to turn military glory into political gain, and the Cheyennes seemed the most available target. While many of Black Kettle's warriors were away on a hunting expedition, Chivington's mounted men swept through the sleeping camp and commenced an orgy of violence that lasted most of the morning. In the end, well over a hundred Cheyennes had been killed and many mutilated, the hair on their heads and genitals taken as trophies and later displayed back in Denver. Although the Sand Creek Massacre was gleefully hailed by the Colorado citizenry as an impressive triumph, many people in the East recoiled at the savagery of Chivington's merciless militiamen. The federal government ordered an official investigation, but since Chivington and his fellow militiamen were civilians in a territory that was not yet a state, there was nothing federal authorities could do to punish them.

Such legal technicalities did not carry any weight with Black Kettle and the surviving Cheyennes, and they took the awful news of the massacre to their Indian allies. The slaughter at Sand Creek set off a round of retaliatory Indian attacks against whites, especially on the overland route along the Platte River; here again, the violence enveloped all available victims—men, women, and children. The most stunning strike, however, came on December 21,

1866, against soldiers stationed at Fort Phil Kearny, a recently constructed stockade in the northern part of Wyoming Territory that
guarded part of the Bozeman Trail. The Bozeman Trail was the
main route for miners heading for the Montana goldfields, but it
cut right through the heart of buffalo country, thus disrupting Indians' access to their most valued natural resource. A Lakota leader,
Red Cloud, one of the head warriors, or "shirt wearers," among
the Oglala band, had vowed to attack all whites using the Bozeman
Trail, and for months he had carried out his promise with a combined force of Lakotas (Oglalas, Miniconjous, Sans Arcs, and some
of Sitting Bull's Hunkpapas), Cheyennes, and Arapahos. A group
of his allies led by the Miniconjou warrior High-Back-Bone harassed the fort until a column of eighty soldiers under Captain
William J. Fetterman went out to disperse them—and fell into an
ambush set by almost two thousand Indians. In short order, the
soldiers were all killed, and the Indians set about scalping and mu-
tilating their bodies. To Red Cloud and other Indians of the Plains,
the Battle of One Hundred Slain no doubt seemed just retribution
for the Sand Creek Massacre two years earlier. To the political and
military leaders of the United States, the battle had a different
name—the Fetterman Massacre—and a different meaning.

It had different meanings even among government officials. The
shock of the Sand Creek and Fetterman massacres led some federal
officials to conclude that the cycle of violence would continue out
of control unless the government acknowledged its previous errors
and adopted new policies to placate Indian peoples. Just a month
after the Fetterman defeat, Senator James R. Doolittle of Wisconsin issued a long-awaited report on Indian affairs. In the course of
his investigation, Doolittle had traveled west to sense the sentiment
of his fellow whites in frontier regions, and he had good cause for
dismay. In Colorado, many citizens still celebrated the massacre of
the Indians at Sand Creek; when Doolittle told a Denver audience
that the choice in Indian policy lay between reservations and extermination, he was overwhelmed by a loud outcry for extermination. Most people he encountered in the West also favored
putting Indian affairs back under the control of the War Department and generally pursuing a military solution to problems with
the Indians.

But, back in Washington, Doolittle issued a report that advocated the reservation alternative. Like virtually everyone else—military men, civilian officials, and reformers in and outside government—Doolittle agreed that the primary goal of reservations was to "civilize" Indians by turning them into settled farmers and converted Christians. Clearly, that was not a task for the army, he argued; Indian affairs should stay under the control of civilians in the Interior Department. Military men might take part in special boards of inspection to oversee the Indian system, but only with an eye to reforming the system, not to destroying the Indians.

But many people argued quite openly that destroying Indians was precisely the role of the military. Each report of Indian attacks resulted in a cold-blooded call for further retaliation in kind—and not necessarily against the Indians actually responsible for the incident. In the wake of the Fetterman disaster, General Sherman angrily insisted that the government "must act with vindictive earnestness against the Sioux, even to their extermination, men, women, and children." His colleague in the officer corps, General Sheridan, would gain lasting notoriety for his declaration that "the only good Indians I ever saw were dead."

Yet, despite the anger and swagger that accompanied such calls for government-sponsored genocide, many army officers realized that actual extermination was not a viable option, either militarily or morally. More often, officers in the field argued in favor of forcing Indians onto reservations, where they could be regulated and reformed—under military, not civilian, control. Like many reformers, officers familiar with the reservation system knew only too well the depths of greed and corruption to which politically appointed Indian agents had descended; they also knew that the army would have to deal with the consequences should corruption breed open conflict. But, unlike the reformers, army men did not generally advise gentle treatment of Indians; that approach would lead only to Indian disregard for reservation rules and disdain for mild-mannered administrators. Rather, they argued, as one western officer put it, that Indians "must be subjected and made to respect and fear the whites" because the "desperate and bitter" Indian "looks upon the rash white man as a sure victim, no less than he does a coward." To enforce this policy of firmness and fear, the army undertook a campaign, first, to have control of the reservation system returned to the War Department, which had originally overseen Indian affairs until the creation of the Department of the Interior in 1849; and second, to show Indians not yet on the reservation that the army would drive them there by force, if need be. The army never had enough political clout to achieve the first goal, but it had more than enough military power to pursue the second for years.

Whatever their disagreements on the details about who should direct the reservation system, both civilian and military officials generally agreed on one point: the greatest challenge facing them was the Great Plains. This vast expanse of land in the center of the continent provided the necessary connection between the East and the West, the missing link in completing the course of Manifest Destiny. For years, emigrants had crossed the Plains on their way west, and the army had established a string of forts along the overland trails to protect people passing through. But in the post-war era, as the extension of the railroads accelerated transcontinental travel and helped increase the two-way traffic in people and goods, government officials felt the need for a more permanent and pervasive presence on the Plains, a broader band of control that would create an open, Indian-free corridor across the land.

Although government officials did not know it, disease had already done much of the work for them. The Plains people had experienced a drastic decline in population in the middle of the century, when European diseases such as smallpox and cholera spread like plagues across the Plains. In the wake of the smallpox epidemic of 1837–40, for instance, some of the smaller tribes, especially those that tended to live comparatively sedentary lives in semi-permanent villages, became easy targets for the spread of deadly microbes, and their numbers fell by over fifty percent. Even some of the larger, nomadic groups suffered a population loss of over thirty percent. The outbreak of cholera in 1849–50 only added to the decline of the Indian population. By the 1860s, the Plains contained far fewer native people than had been there just a generation earlier, and the government's plan to clear a path through them had demography, if not destiny, on its side.

Still, securing a wide swath of territory would mean removing some of the fiercest and most effective fighters government troops would ever encounter—above all, the Sioux, the Cheyennes, and the Comanches. Even though their numbers had been depleted by disease, they remained the the most mobile and militarily powerful people in the middle of the North American continent. Dealing with them would require considerable diplomatic skill and, if that failed, physical force.

In 1867, the government set out to try the first approach. During the summer of that year, military and civilian policymakers reached a rough consensus on a plan they thought would provide something for everyone. According to a proposal put forward by the newly appointed Commissioner of Indian Affairs, Nathaniel G. Taylor, the government would create two large reservations on the central Plains—one south of Kansas, one north of Nebraska—for Indians alone. Only a small number of government officials would be allowed on the reservations, and the Indians would otherwise be insulated from contact with whites and, presumably, protected from outside interference. As long as they stayed on the reservation, Indians would be able to ride after buffalo and generally range almost as freely as they had before—although it was hoped that they would eventually put down roots and become settled farmers. The land between these two reservations—a band several hundred miles wide—would then become a safe zone of transit and settlement for whites. Even the bellicose General Sherman could support such a plan, although he wanted to make quite sure that any Indians who could not be coaxed or coerced out of the middle zone would be killed. In the end, Congress appointed a seven-man "peace commission," which included both Commissioner Taylor and General Sherman, to head west and begin treaty talks with the Indians of the Plains.

The result was, perhaps understandably, uneven. In October 1867, at their first major meeting at Medicine Lodge, Kansas, the commissioners had some initial success with five thousand Indians of the southern Plains—the Kiowas, Kiowa–Apaches, and Comanches of the west Texas–New Mexico region, and the Southern Cheyennes and Arapahos of the western Kansas–eastern Colorado region. After an appropriate period of giving gifts, feasts, and speeches, the government commissioners concluded agreements that called for the creation of two reservations, one for the Kiowas, Kiowa–Apaches, and Comanches, another for the Cheyennes and

Arapahos. (These were not altogether new reservations, but sections carved out of the existing reservations established in the 1830s and 1840s for the so-called Five Civilized Tribes of the South—the Cherokees, Creeks, Choctaws, Chickasaws, and Seminoles—the reluctant emigrants who had been forced to move beyond Mississippi as a result of the government's earlier Indian removal policies in the Jacksonian era. In the Civil War era, significant factions within these displaced tribes had given their support to the Confederacy, and this diplomatic gamble cost them dearly. The United States punished them now by forcing them to concede some of their land to accommodate new arrivals from the Plains.) According to the terms of the Medicine Lodge treaty, the Indians of the southern Plains would give up their claims to their traditional territories and live peaceably on the reservations, with the understanding that they would not be rigidly restricted to the reservation in hunting buffalo. They were also to be given annual allotments of clothing and other supplies, including arms and ammunition, for thirty years, during which time they would also receive instruction in farming and other ways of white society. The Indians' calculus of acquiescence required weighing short-term benefits against longer-term costs: the attractions of holding on to the buffalo hunt and getting their hands on government-supplied goods overshadowed the prospect of being turned into farmers— a future development that, with luck, might never happen anyway. Thus, most of the major leaders of the southern Plains people accepted the treaty.

Encouraged by their success at Medicine Lodge, the government commissioners drafted a similar agreement to take north, where they hoped to create a reservation for the Sioux and their Cheyenne and Arapaho allies in the southern part of the Dakota Territory. The northern Plains peoples were generally reluctant to engage in treaty talks, however, and for several months the proposed gathering at Fort Laramie (the site of the 1851 talks) attracted only a scattering of Sioux bands, none of whom held the key to peace on the Plains.

Most conspicuous in his absence was Red Cloud, the Oglala warrior leader who had become one of the most influential Indians in the region. In the wake of the victory over Fetterman's force in late 1866, Red Cloud had remained resolute in his determination to close down the Bozeman Trail and, above all, to make the government give up the string of forts that protected it; he had no intention of engaging in any discussion until the forts were abandoned. His refusal to engage in the Fort Laramie talks proved to be a powerful piece of diplomacy. Even though the commissioners made what they thought were the necessary concessions—they agreed not only to give up the forts but also to set aside Red Cloud's Powder River country as "unceded Indian territory," acknowledging the Indians' right to restrict entry—Red Cloud remained aloof. Even though almost two hundred Indian leaders eventually accepted the Fort Laramie agreements, Red Cloud still waited. Only in November 1868—after most of the government commissioners had already left Fort Laramie, after the government troops had actually evacuated the forts along the Bozeman Trail, and after Red Cloud's warriors had burned two of the forts to the ground—did Red Cloud finally come in and add his mark to the treaty. Having done so, he followed the path of peace for the rest of the century; although he remained a fervent advocate for his people (and therefore a frequent irritant to government officials), he eventually accepted reservation life and never went to war against white people again.

Red Cloud's apparent ability first to dictate and then to endure the terms of peace proved to be remarkable in the broader realm of nineteenth-century intercultural relations. No matter how hopeful or honorable treatymakers might be, negotiated agreements faced almost certain failure soon after they were signed. Perhaps especially on the Great Plains, given the increasingly incompatible interests of the region's semi-nomadic native inhabitants and the land-hungry newcomers, mutual accommodation and respect for equal rights required more good faith and forgiveness than most people on either side could muster, much less sustain. It was always much easier for cynics and skeptics to point to any number of treaty violations and incidents of violence as ample reason for rejecting the possibility of a lasting peace.

One of the main problems for the proponents of peace was that neither side could maintain a widespread and workable consensus, nor could either exercise effective control over its own people. Even the United States government, with the increasingly centralized authority and bureaucratic organization of an emerging nineteenth-century nation-state, could hardly guarantee acquiescence among all the disparate constituencies it represented. Political rivalries and institutional jealousies within the national government, not to mention the individual or regional interests of the various states, made any Indian policy seem to be impermanent, sometimes almost impossible. The dictates of the political process and the military chain of command might make dissenting voices in the higher reaches of government accept, albeit reluctantly, a particular policy decision, but there was little anyone could do to control people farther out in the field. On the local level, Indian agents, soldiers, and civilian settlers sometimes took actions that had much broader repercussions, threatening or offending Indians, further convincing them that the soothing words of white men meant nothing.

By the same token, Indian leaders often had even less control. The Indians of the Plains (or of other regions, for that matter) were not a monolithic people with a single political system, and making generalizations about their methods of government can be difficult, if not dangerous. The very diversity of Plains people provides the key to their political culture. Nowhere was there a centralized, hierarchically organized source of authority with a strong hand of command and control. A particular tribe might have a single individual who assumed the overall office of chief—Sitting Bull of the Hunkpapas, for instance—but no chief could create tribal unity on his own. The real source of authority, or certainly identity, lay at the level of the band, a smaller collectivity defined primarily by kinship. When the need arose, especially in time of war, leaders from various tribal bands might meet in council to devise a collective plan for confronting a common enemy, and sometimes several bands would join together for an extended period of time. But, for the most part, each band remained an independent entity, free to make its own internal decisions and take its own course of action. Within the band, moreover, decision-making relied upon consensus among a group of leaders, one of whom might have greater power than the others, but none of whom held ultimate authority. These men did not gain their positions by inheritance or popular election, as was the case with government leaders in Europe and the United States; they relied on personal qualities, especially prowess in fighting and hunting, to foster and enhance their individual influence among others. Still, influence did not automatically command authority: leaders could only try to persuade their people to make war or make peace. In either case, some of those people, particularly young warriors, could not always be persuaded, and they would refuse to support a particular policy or sometimes leave the band altogether. In general, the traditions of independence that had developed among the diverse and dispersed peoples of the Plains made good sense, especially for mobile hunters who followed the buffalo herds; they did not, however, encourage concerted action on an enduring basis.

In the end, the greater flaw in the treaty process was not the relative degree of division on either side, but the inherently negative implications of relegating people to reservations. No Indian leader, even one who had put his name to the Medicine Lodge or Fort Laramie treaties, could easily convince himself, much less his followers, that reservation life represented a superior alternative to the traditional ways of the Plains people. Rather, it was at best a necessary evil, perhaps a way of temporizing until conditions changed for the better.

By the late 1860s, conditions for the Indian peoples of the Plains were discouraging indeed. The presence of military troops was daunting enough, but equally disturbing was the increasing influx of other white people—farmers, miners, railroad workers—all of whom put pressure not only on the native population but on the buffalo population. As recently as the 1850s, buffalo numbered in the millions, and the great herds that roamed across the center of the continent provided important sources of sustenance, both material and spiritual, for Plains people. In addition to making food, clothing, shelter, weapons, tools, and toys out of the buffalo, Indians also incorporated the animal into their religious life; among the Kiowas, for instance, a white buffalo calf was sacrificed during the Sun Dance ceremony, and priests used various buffalo parts in other religious rituals. Indians knew that white people valued the buffalo as well; for years they had exchanged buffalo skins for guns and other goods with white traders. But they had no idea how destructive the demand for the buffalo would become. Unlike Indians, who used virtually every part of the animal, white hunters usually took only pelts, hides, and choice cuts of meat, especially the tongue, leaving the rest of the carcass to rot.

With the extension of the railroads, buffalo hunting reached dramatic levels on the Plains. Hunters hired by the railroad companies—one of whom was "Buffalo Bill" Cody, who would later become Sitting Bull's show-business employer—had a devastating effect on the herds, killing thousands of animals to feed work crews. Once the tracks were laid, trains would bring sport hunters out to bag buffalo trophies. Military officials condoned and even encouraged this hunting for fun and profit, knowing that the smaller the buffalo population, the greater the pressure on Indians to accept reservation life.

In the decade after 1867, the great herds of the Plains were virtually destroyed; a few thousand wandered where once there had been millions. Although no Indian leader could have predicted at the time of the treatymaking just how frightful the future would be, some clearly understood that they would need some additional way to supply their people's needs. Given the limited alternatives, the government's promise of provisions seemed to offer an acceptable strategy for survival.

But it was a strategy that many Indians simply could not accept. What might have seemed to some a necessary concession appeared to others to be nothing more than spineless capitulation. Sitting Bull would later accuse Red Cloud and other leaders who led their people into reservation life of being "rascals . . . [who] sold our country without the full consent of our people." They and their followers were foolish, he said, for becoming "slaves to a piece of fat bacon, some hard-tack, and a little sugar and coffee." He and his Hunkpapa people, along with thousands of other Indian people of the northern Plains, would remain defiantly free, determined to continue hunting and fighting as they always had for as long as they could. Other Indians who had moved onto reservations refused to stay there, especially young men who were more intent on proving themselves as warriors than as farmers.

In the summer of 1868, for instance, Cheyenne warriors in Kansas staged raids against villages of their old rivals, the Kaws and the Pawnees. Not wanting to facilitate further violence, the Superintendent of Indian Affairs, Thomas Murphy, delayed giving them the guns and ammunition they had been promised as part of their annuity under the Medicine Lodge treaty. Angry with this breach of the agreement, the warriors then turned their attacks against white settlers, creating terror across the prairies. As other Indian groups—Arapahos, Comanches, and Kiowas—joined in, widespread warfare came to the southern Plains.

The outbreak of violence gave Generals Sherman and Sheridan all the excuse they needed to mount a major military campaign against the Indians, and they went after them with all the destructive fury they had once used against the Confederates. Sherman told Sheridan that the soldiers should use any means necessary to subdue the Cheyennes, and even if moralists objected to the military's methods, he would not allow any "mere vague general charges of cruelty" to tie the hands of the troops.

> If it results in the utter annihilation of these Indians, it is but the result of what they have been warned again and again. . . . [T]hese Indians, the enemies of our race and of our civilization, shall not again be able to begin and carry out their barbarous warfare . . . [and] we will not accept their peace, or cease our efforts till all the past acts are both punished and avenged.

Clearly, the issue for Sherman was not reservation policy but racial policy, and he would accept no restraints in his pursuit of total war. Sheridan carried out the campaign, which owed much of its eventual success to one of his subordinates, a young and headstrong cavalry colonel, George Armstrong Custer, the commander of the Seventh Cavalry. The climactic battle of the Cheyenne campaign came on November 27, 1868, as Custer's troops swooped down at dawn on an encampment led by Black Kettle. Black Kettle had been appealing for peace, but his entreaties seemed not to matter —for the second time in four years. In 1864, when Black Kettle had tried to make peace with the officials of Colorado, all he got for his efforts was a similar daybreak raid on his camp at Sand Creek. Unlike most of his people, Black Kettle had escaped the Sand Creek Massacre, and now he was again trying to avoid violence in Kansas. But against his wishes, some of his warriors had been out on a raid of their own, and their trail led Custer back to Black Kettle's village. This time Black Kettle did not escape. As he and his wife tried to get away from attacking soldiers, they both took bullets in the back and fell dead into the waters of the Washita River. While the Battle of the Washita was not a massacre on the

scale of Sand Creek, it was still a major defeat for the Cheyennes:
the soldiers not only killed around a hundred men, women, and
children, but they also destroyed all the food, shelter, and horses
they could find, thus making life even more difficult for the surviving Cheyennes. For the next four months, Custer followed
whatever Cheyenne trails he could find, until he finally tracked
down a large Cheyenne settlement in the Texas panhandle and,
after tense negotiations, made them promise to go onto a reservation in Oklahoma. Although the Cheyennes dallied and tried to
delay their eventual surrender, most of them finally gave up and
came in by the fall of 1869.

Throughout the late 1860s and early 1870s, similar tensions and
transgressions on both sides undermined the peace that treatymakers thought they had achieved in 1867–68. Indians who stayed on
reservations often found that the government provisions promised
them failed to come on schedule or in sufficient quantity. Those
who strayed from the reservations to carry out raids found themselves subject to fierce retaliation from Sherman's army. From the
southern Plains to the desert Southwest to northern California,
independence-minded Indians faced a determined military force
that stalked them, fought them, and forced them onto reservations.
From 1869 to 1876, no matter how much President Ulysses S.
Grant, another great general of the Civil War era, talked about
promoting a peace policy toward Indians, it was his fellow generals,
Sherman and Sheridan, who made war the decisive factor in Indian
affairs.

It was on the northern Plains that the most significant struggle
was to take place. Throughout the spring and summer of 1876,
thousands of Indians—Northern Cheyennes and several bands of
Lakota Sioux, including Oglalas, Miniconjous, Sans Arcs, Black-
foots, and Sitting Bull's own Hunkpapas—had come to congregate
in the hilly hunting grounds north of the Wyoming border, in what
had traditionally been Crow territory. If they had any intentions
of making war, it would be against the Crows, who had long been
the enemies of the Cheyennes and Lakotas. But also converging
on the area from the south and east were two columns of United
States cavalry, who were coming to order the Indians to move onto
reservations or face punishment at the hands of the military. The
government no longer wanted them making life difficult for emi-

grants and miners. What the government did not know, however, was that the Indians numbered around seven thousand in all, with between one thousand and two thousand warriors, and that they could make life very difficult for any soldiers who tried to dislodge them.

Custer tried first, and he failed disastrously. Always as brash as he was brave, Custer led a column of over seven hundred mounted troopers—including a number of Indian scouts, mostly Rees and a few Crows, who had long been hostile to the Hunkpapa and other Sioux groups—against the Sioux–Cheyenne encampment, confident that he could scatter the Indians and claim a significant victory. Custer's actions in launching a mid-afternoon attack—especially his failure to reconnoiter effectively and his decision to split his force in two—have long been the subject of intense, sometimes tedious, debate about what might have happened had he done things differently. What did happen, however, is clear: Custer lost his life and the lives of about half of his combined force, including all the men who fought with him in the celebrated Last Stand on the bluffs above the Little Bighorn.

There has also been some debate about Sitting Bull's actions in the battle. He fired on the soldiers attacking the Indian camp, and he frequently appeared on the fringes of the fighting to shout encouragement to his warriors. For the most part, though, he stayed in the camp, providing protection for the women and children and conferring with other Indian leaders—which was precisely his duty as a middle-aged chief. In the many postmortem analyses of the action, Sitting Bull was occasionally portrayed as a military genius, but, if so, usually as a "savage" who had been necessarily assisted by Euro-American education—perhaps a stint at West Point, some said, or instruction at the hands of French Canadian Jesuit priests, who taught him the tactics of Napoleon. The simple truth that Sitting Bull was an effective fighter and leader was apparently too difficult to accept without such fanciful cultural qualifiers. Others, emphasizing his generally defensive stance in the battle, tried to turn him into a coward. General Philip Sheridan, the commanding officer in charge of all military operations in the West, questioned Sitting Bull's very existence, suggesting that the term "Sitting Bull" referred to all hostile Indians in general, not to a particular leader. Sheridan offered this observation from behind his desk in Chicago;

other officers out in the field knew only too well that Sitting Bull
was very real indeed, and certainly not a coward.

It was one of those field officers, Colonel Nelson A. Miles, who
took up Custer's cause with a vengeance, turning his dogged pursuit of Sitting Bull almost into a personal vendetta. Like Custer,
Miles was young and ambitious, a "boy general" of the Civil War
who had stayed in the army to make his mark. Carrying on the
campaign against Sitting Bull was just the thing to advance his
career. More than any other officer, Miles made it clear to Sitting
Bull that he and his troops were not summer soldiers; he kept his
men in the field throughout the winter of 1876–77, pursuing the
Hunkpapa and Oglala bands relentlessly, keeping men, women,
and children constantly on the run. Cold and hungry, the Lakota
Sioux struggled to stay one step ahead of the soldiers as they tried
to keep up with the buffalo herds.

While Miles pursued Sitting Bull relentlessly, other army units
kept the pressure on other Sioux and Cheyenne bands, wearing
down their strength and supplies and eventually forcing them into
submission. One by one, Sitting Bull's allies retreated north across
the border into Canada or surrendered to the army and made their
way onto reservations. Even Crazy Horse of the Oglalas eventually
gave up and went onto a reservation in Nebraska (where he would
soon be killed in a fracas in the guardhouse, stabbed by a soldier's
bayonet). Increasingly isolated and unceasingly on the run, yet still
determined never to set foot on a reservation in the United States,
Sitting Bull decided to go the other way. In early May 1877, less
than a year after the stunning victory over Custer, Sitting Bull led
a mere remnant of his original force into Canada. There, at least,
they would still be free.

For four years, Canada seemed a comfortable enough haven.
Whatever his earlier problems with the various officers and agents
of the "Great White Father" in Washington, Sitting Bull seemed
to get along well with the representatives of the British "Grand-
mother," Queen Victoria. He developed an especially strong respect for Major James M. Walsh of the North-West Mounted
Police, a firm but fair official who showed sympathy for Sitting
Bull and his people. Indeed, Sitting Bull's relationship with Walsh
gave him a diplomatic advantage that most Indian leaders had not
known since the early part of the century: the ability to play one

Euro-American power off against the other—at least for a while. Walsh understood the injuries inflicted on Indians by the United States, and he made sure that military men like Colonel Miles did not cross the border in pursuit of the Lakota people. On the other hand, he could not always keep the Lakotas from crossing the border as they followed the dwindling buffalo herds into northern Montana, which increased the tension not only between the Indians and the soldiers but between Canada and the United States. In time, Walsh's uneasy superiors transferred him to another post far away from Sitting Bull and sent a replacement who was much less inclined to take the Indians' side. From that point on, Sitting Bull felt pressure on both sides of the border to return to the United States. Thus in 1881, running out of food as well as options, Sitting Bull finally and reluctantly headed down the trail that would take him first to surrender at Fort Buford and then to the reservation at Standing Rock.

The 1880s, writes Robert M. Utley, were a time of "profound stress and profound change" for Indian peoples throughout the American West: "They had been truly conquered." In the decade after Custer's defeat, the United States Army pursued and subdued Indian groups throughout the West—the Nez Perce of Oregon, the Bannocks and Paiutes of Idaho, the Utes of Colorado, and the Apaches of New Mexico and Arizona. The ambitious and seemingly ubiquitous Colonel, then General, Nelson A. Miles personally accepted the surrender of the Nez Perce Chief Joseph and the Chiricahua Apache leader Geronimo. In almost all cases, the Indians were sent to reservations some distance from their homelands. Geronimo and the Chiricahuas were first imprisoned in an old Spanish fortress in Saint Augustine, Florida, then, after a series of moves, eventually wound up in Oklahoma. Most of the young Apache men were shipped off to the new Carlisle Indian School in Pennsylvania, where the reform-minded superintendent, Captain Richard Henry Pratt, practiced a form of cultural transformation by total immersion intended, he said, to "kill the Indian and save the man." (Pratt's words turned out to be truer than he had imagined: twenty-seven of the original 107 Apache youths who went to Carlisle in 1886 were dead by 1889.) The situation of the students at the Carlisle Indian School was just one manifestation of a much more widespread fate facing Indians in the late 1880s. "For the first time," Utley concludes, "the Great Father had corralled all Indians on reservations, could keep them there, and could indulge any social or penal experiment he wished without fear of another major outbreak."

But there was one other outbreak, this one initially religious in nature, not military. In Nevada, a young man named Wovoka, the son of a Paiute prophet (who had lived a while with a white family and had received a new name, Jack Wilson), had suddenly become something of a Messiah. Having lived in both Indian and Euro-American cultures, Wovoka had developed a new religion that blended elements of Christianity with traditional Paiute beliefs. He told of a new world where Indians of all generations could return to life and live in peace and plenty, where buffalo would be bountiful and there would be no white people. For people who had endured years of military defeat, removal to reservations, and reform-minded confinement, Wovoka's world was a vision of heaven indeed. To make it a reality, he said, all they had to do was live a peaceful life, doing good and not fighting among themselves—and practice a new rite called the Ghost Dance.

Word of Wovoka's new religion quickly spread from reservation to reservation across the West. Some Indian groups even sent delegations to Nevada to visit the holy man. Most came back convinced that he held the key to a new future.

The sudden interest in this cultural and religious revival came at a critical time for Indian people all over the West, when the restraints of reservation life had led to widespread division and demoralization. The officials who ran the reservations were constantly cutting into the Indians' autonomy, seeking to outlaw or undermine important aspects of their culture. They imposed controls on Indian spiritual leaders, giving Protestant missionaries an open opportunity to incorporate Christian practices into Indian religion. Reservation agents used the material resources at their disposal to reward some Indian leaders and deny others, thus creating—or increasing—divisions between those Indians who had accommodated to reservation life and those who still resisted. Agents also established Indian police forces on the reservation, supplanting the old forms of self-regulation within the bands. And everywhere reservation agents and missionaries sought to promote a settled life of farming and grazing. The closest some Indians came to the old days of the buffalo hunt was herding government-supplied cattle.

Then, on the eve of the Ghost Dance excitement, the government took one additional step that seemed designed to weaken native culture even further. For years, reform-minded opponents of the reservation system, both in and out of government, had hoped to promote an alternative way of life for Indians—not a return to the freedom of the past, but a different form of independence through fee-simple ownership of land. The notion of severalty—that is, breaking up the reservations into individual landholdings—had special appeal among reformers because it promised to engender individual initiative and eventual integration into white society: Indian homesteaders working their farms would become just like their Euro-American counterparts. In 1887, after several failed efforts at severalty legislation, the reformers succeeded in getting the Dawes General Allotment Act through Congress (named for its sponsor, Senator Henry L. Dawes of Massachusetts). The Dawes Act called for using reservation lands to create 160-acre family farms (or, where grazing was deemed a more suitable means of support, into holdings twice that size) and allowing Indian homesteaders to choose their plots. To protect Indians from land-hungry whites, the government would hold title to the land for twenty-five years—enough time, it was hoped, for Indians to learn how to function safely in a freewheeling land market— and then the land would become the Indian's private property. In the meantime, the rest of the reservation land would be opened to settlement by whites. The vision of Indians as independent American citizens, living like (and increasingly with) white people, struck reformers as an enlightened alternative to the exploitation they saw on the reservations.

Sometimes, though, well-meaning people can be the most dangerous. To many Indians, the Dawes Act seemed yet another unwelcome intrusion into their lives, an additional threat to their cultural traditions. Reservation life, restrictive though it was, still allowed Indians to maintain at least a measure of cohesion as a people. The division—and, equally important, the diminution—of their lands would only accelerate the destruction of their culture.

In general, Indians expressed no desire to be reformed any further by white people. If there was any reform to come to the reservation, it would be determined by Indian people themselves. And in the immediate context of dealing with the Dawes Act, Wovoka's Ghost Dance religion seemed just the kind of cultural revival they needed.

Once again, the experience of Sitting Bull and the Lakota Sioux provides a dramatic example of Indian response. By the late 1880s, Sitting Bull was living a comparatively peaceful life on the Standing Rock Agency, with two wives and five children in his immediate household and numerous extended kin in the surrounding area. He had little initial interest in the Ghost Dance, but even less enthusiasm for the new land law. As government commissioners sought to entice Indians into ceding their "surplus" lands, Sitting Bull was one of many Indian leaders who counseled his people to resist, or at least hold out for better terms. But eventually, as the commissioners cajoled some Indians and intimidated others, many of Sitting Bull's own people began to accept the government's conditions. Sitting Bull was left frustrated and furious. He saw that the commissioners, for all the promises they made, were not likely to provide for the welfare of his people.

Thus, as the Ghost Dance began to attract more attention at Standing Rock, Sitting Bull began to take a more sympathetic, or at least ambiguous, position toward the spiritual revival. If he did not embrace it fully, he still understood that a new movement of the Indian people, something that the white men could not quite fathom and certainly could not control, would be a means of challenging the power of the government officials on the reservation —especially Agent McLaughlin, the one man who exercised the most authority at Standing Rock, more than Sitting Bull himself.

McLaughlin understood this too, and he became increasingly uneasy as the Ghost Dance movement took on a more threatening tone. At other Sioux reservations in the region, the non-violent stance initially associated with Wovoka's preachings was giving way to open defiance of government authority, with more than a hint of violence. Some local leaders of the Ghost Dance were even assuring their people that wearing special ghost shirts would make them invulnerable to white men's bullets. Nervous reservation agents, worried that they were on the verge of losing control, be-

gan to call for military protection. McLaughlin, however, would
have none of that on his Standing Rock Agency if he could help
it; he would maintain his authority on his own terms. Knowing
that Sitting Bull was the key to keeping the Ghost Dance movement under control, he tried to convince the Indian leader that the
dance was only an example of emotional excess, an overwrought
manifestation of false religious feeling. When persuasion failed,
when Sitting Bull refused to denounce the dance, McLaughlin ordered him arrested.

Arresting Sitting Bull was a calculated risk. Knowing that sending soldiers to take Sitting Bull would be far too provocative,
McLaughlin assigned the task to the agency's Indian policemen.
Their commander, Bull Head, had once fought alongside Sitting
Bull and had been a hero among the Hunkpapa warriors; now he
was fully under the sway of the reservation agent. Early on the
morning of December 15, 1890, Bull Head and his men came to
Sitting Bull's cabin and roused him from bed, naked and barely
awake. Asking for enough time to get dressed, Sitting Bull agreed
to come along peaceably. But some of his supporters, attracted by
the commotion around Sitting Bull's cabin, surrounded the policemen as they were taking Sitting Bull away, angrily protesting the
arrest. Suddenly, someone shot Bull Head, Bull Head in turn shot
Sitting Bull, and gunfire broke the morning quiet. Within a few
minutes, when all was quiet again, a dozen Indians lay dead—policemen, Sitting Bull's supporters, and Sitting Bull himself. Bull
Head would die of his wounds a few days later; by that time, Sitting
Bull had been buried.

Two weeks later, another bloody event marked the tragic end of
the Ghost Dance movement among the Lakota Sioux. Big Foot, a
Miniconjou leader, was bringing over three hundred of his people
to the Pine Ridge Reservation when they were surrounded by
troopers of the Seventh Cavalry—Custer's old unit—who were
trying to round up Indians who had left the reservations. Neither
side planned violence, but the soldiers made it clear that they
intended to disarm the Indians. In the early morning hours of December 29, with nerves tense on both sides, a frightened Indian
fired his gun, and what might have been only a misunderstanding
turned into a massacre. Once the shooting started, it did not end
until over 150 Indians and twenty-five soldiers lay dead on the

freezing ground around the Wounded Knee Creek in southern South Dakota. Like Sitting Bull, the Indian victims of the Wounded Knee debacle were buried without ceremony. Also buried in those mass graves was the last vestige of significant resistance to the government's Indian policy in the nineteenth century.

There may be many reasons for calling 1890 a critical year in frontier history. The death of Sitting Bull, followed so soon after by the slaughter of Big Foot's followers at Wounded Knee, should certainly qualify for inclusion at the top of any historian's list. Frederick Jackson Turner, of course, chose a much quieter, much less violent event: the assessment by the Superintendent of the United States Census that "the unsettled area has been so broken into by isolated bodies of settlement that there can hardly be said to be a frontier line." Accordingly, the Superintendent declared that the discussion of the frontier "can not, therefore, any longer have a place in the census reports." Writing with a note of nostalgia and considerable concern, Turner saw in the Superintendent's pronouncement "the closing of a great historical movement." After explaining how great that movement had been in defining "the significance of the frontier," Turner closed his essay with another "closing":

> And now, four centuries from the discovery of America, at the end of a hundred years of life under the Constitution, the frontier has gone, and with its going has closed the first period of American history.

In fact, Turner could just as easily have argued that the North American frontier had never been more open to his fellow Euro-Americans. The historical markers he used in his final paragraph should be indication enough. For four centuries, since the arrival of Columbus and the onset of a European presence in the Americas, people of European origin had asserted increasing control over the North American continent—and the people who had lived there for millennia. Then, in the century or so that it had been an independent nation, the United States had continued and essentially completed that process. Indeed, during the nineteenth century, the United States became the single most powerful—and most powerfully single-minded—force on the North American frontier.

That was an important departure from the past. In the earlier era of European settlement and colonization, the patterns of contact between newcomers and natives were often complex, marked almost always by military conflict, but also by intercultural collaboration. Neither Native Americans nor Euro-Americans represented cultural monoliths: various groups within each category competed bitterly against each other and, in so doing, often cooperated with people of the other culture. Moreover, throughout the era of European colonization, the fluidity of frontier affairs—the competing claims for territory, the continuing realignments of alliances, the sometimes sudden and seemingly inconsistent shifts in strategies—made it appear that no one had the power or even the vision to determine a lasting outcome.

But during the nineteenth century, as the other major Euro-American competitors for the continent left the scene, the United States developed an overarching national agenda: to extend its authority across the continent. To achieve this goal, the government adopted a variety of distinct, sometimes seemingly contradictory strategies in dealing with the Indians who inhabited the interior. Soldiers and social reformers argued over appropriate policies for pacifying native people, and the government pursued two or more policies at once, making war or peace as best suited the situation and, like the earlier Euro-American imperial powers of previous centuries, playing one Indian group against the other in military or diplomatic or economic alliances. But in the end United States Indian policy pointed in only one direction: toward the reservation.

By 1890, the policy seemed to have worked. After centuries of disease, military defeat, and dislocation, the Indian population of North America was approaching its lowest point in recorded history, a fact Frederick Jackson Turner might likewise have noted in his analysis of the 1890 census. Moreover, thanks to the Dawes Act, even the size of Indian reservations was facing a decline. Indians realized that their reservations would soon be, to use the Census Superintendent's phrase, "so broken into" by aggressive settlers that they would no longer have a secure hold even on the last lands they had left. This opening of the Indians' frontier to white settlement was only another step in the enclosing of the Indian people.

Epilogue

I n July 1895—two years to the month after Frederick Jackson Turner delivered his paper on "The Significance of the Frontier"—Mark Twain left his home in the East and headed west. He crossed the continent to the Pacific coast of North America, but then kept going farther west, all the way across the Pacific to Australia and New Zealand. Twain was traveling to see the sights but also to deliver some lectures and, he hoped, to make some money. At the time of this trip, he had two major maladies in life: carbuncles and creditors. Although a lecture tour would irritate the former, it was the only way he could think of to soothe the latter.

As usual, Twain wrote almost as much as he talked. The account of his Australasian adventures, *Following the Equator* (1897), provides an entertaining travelogue intertwined with wry social commentary and, most important, perceptive reflections on the recent past. Twain was not a professional historian like Turner, of course, but a humorist. Yet humor, like history, is serious business, and if we look past the laugh lines we can see what Twain was trying to say to his nineteenth-century—and primarily American—audience. By taking them beyond the bounds of their country and offering his observations about another society, he encouraged, perhaps forced, his fellow Americans to look again at their own. Certainly for people who had reached the end of the century thinking that they had reached an honorable end to their conquest of the continent, some of the issues Twain addressed in Australasia must have suggested unmistakable, even uncomfortable, comparisons with the

American experience. Turner told Americans that the frontier had "closed," but Twain opened it up again.

Above all, he understood how national expansion worked, and how far it could go. Twain's first view of the Southern Hemisphere's great constellation, the Southern Cross, led him to reflect on the relationship between the stars in the heavens and the nation-states on earth. The Southern Cross did not look quite like a cross, he thought, but more like a coffin or, more happily, a kite. "Constellations have always been troublesome things to name," he noted. He went on to explain how the major constellation of the Northern Hemisphere, the Great Bear, had been unrecognizable "for thousands of years; and people complained about it all the time, and quite properly." But then, "as soon as it became the property of the United States, Congress changed it to the Big Dipper, and now everybody is satisfied." The same change awaited the Southern Cross.

> In a little while now—I cannot tell exactly how long it will be—the globe will belong to the English-speaking race; and of course the skies also. Then the constellations will be reorganized, and polished up, and re-named—the most of them "Victoria," I reckon, but this one will sail thereafter as the Southern kite, or go out of business.

Beneath the humorous reflections on the heavens lay two important points. First, as explorers and mapmakers had long known, naming was the first step in appropriation: to label some place "Victoria" was to stamp it as unmistakably British. But second, as Twain suggested, it was not the British alone. The United States, as an increasingly powerful part of the "English-speaking race," stood ready to play a role in taking control of the globe.

The heavens might remain beyond reach of the imperial powers, but not so the land—and, more important, the people on it. Twain's reference to the "English-speaking race" raised the most troubling issue in nineteenth-century expansion: the conceptualization—and consequences—of cultural encounters. To be sure, Twain's attitudes toward the indigenous people of his own country had been ambivalent at best. Earlier in his life, in 1861, when Twain made his first journey to the American West (which would later be recounted in *Roughing It*), he came into contact with a small band of Gosiute Indians, a desert-dwelling group he disparaged with disgust. The Gosiutes—or "Goshoots," as he called them—were "small, lean, 'scrawny' creatures; in complexion a dull black like the ordinary American negro; . . . a silent, sneaking, treacherous looking race . . . who produce nothing at all." The disagreeable example of the Goshoots caused Twain, a self-described "worshipper of the Red Man," to reconsider his admiration of the Indian in general:

> The revelations that came were disenchanting. It was curious to see how quickly the paint and tinsel fell away from him and left him treacherous, filthy, and repulsive—and how quickly the evidences accumulated that wherever one finds an Indian tribe he has only found Goshoots more or less modified by circumstances and surroundings—but Goshoots, after all.

Clearly, such a hostile, vituperative evaluation of one Native American group—and, more to the point, its extension to all others—was the near-epitome of anti-Indian sentiment in nineteenth-century America.

Yet almost thirty years later, in observing another group of indigenous people, the Maoris of New Zealand, Twain came close —or closer—to replacing outright racism with an understanding of other cultures; Twain's Maori encounter resulted in an important moment of cross-cultural clarity. By the time Twain arrived in New Zealand, the Maori had been involved in a long series of struggles against the British, who had declared their sovereignty over New Zealand in 1840. Through warfare, treaty, and occasional legal trickery, the British had gained control of millions of acres of Maori lands, leaving the Maoris much diminished in both property and population.

Twain seemed sympathetic to the Maoris' situation. On one level, he considered it a

> compliment to them that the British did not exterminate them, as they did the Australians and Tasmanians, but were content with subduing them, and showed no desire to go further. . . . [I]t has not been the custom of the world for conquerors to act in this large spirit toward the conquered.

This rendering of recent history would no doubt have astounded many Maori people: with "compliments" like this, who needed insults? But Twain made a more important point about the outcomes of history when he encountered "a couple of curious war-monuments" commemorating the recent conflict.

The first stood in tribute to the British soldiers who, as the inscription put it, "fell in defense of law and order against fanaticism and barbarism." Twain let the word "barbarism" go by without comment, but he recoiled at the use of "fanaticism." It was one thing—and a very proper thing, Twain said—"to praise these brave white men who fell in the Maori war—they deserve it." But it demeaned them, not to mention their Maori opponents, to refer to the Maori position as fanaticism. The Maori people who fought against the British "fought for their homes, they fought for their country." They were, Twain said, "Maori patriots."

This appreciation of patriotism led Twain to detest the other war memorial, a British-built monument in honor of around twenty Maori men who fought on the side of the British against other Maoris. Such a monument "invites to treachery, disloyalty, unpatriotism." There was only one way to rectify such a mistaken message, Twain concluded—"with dynamite."

Such incisive, even indignant, observations on patriotism and public symbolism in New Zealand may have stemmed from the clarity of an outsider's insight, but Twain no doubt had another point of reference as well. Although he made no specific mention of the recent history of the United States, the experience of the American peoples could not have been too far from his mind. They, too, had just fought a long series of land wars in the late nineteenth century, and by the 1890s the situation seemed resolved. As was the case in New Zealand, the European population had asserted its sovereignty over the land by making wars and treaties with the indigenous peoples. The native peoples had resisted forcefully, but not always with a united front: some had fought on the side of the whites, partly out of military or diplomatic necessity, but also partly in the interest of old conflicts against long-standing Indian enemies. By the 1890s, however, almost all of them had suffered the same fate of being relegated to reservations. The ultimate meaning of the American outcome depended, of course, on one's perspective. If people read Frederick Jackson Turner, they would find that a westward-moving "civilization" had triumphed over "savagery," and now the frontier was closed. But if they read Mark Twain they would find a broader, more ambiguous picture of the role of the "English-speaking race" and its relationship with the rest of the world's people—including the Native American inhabitants of the North American frontier. They, too, had fought for their homes, for their country, just as the Maoris had; they, too, could be called patriots.

Unfortunately, Twain's Pacific perspective on the American past remained underdeveloped and certainly underappreciated. Most people preferred the Turnerian telling of history; in the United States as in New Zealand, most of the monuments and popular memory celebrated the soldiers and settlers who had carried out the conquest.

From the 1890s on throughout much of the twentieth century, native peoples had little to celebrate in their ongoing relationship with the United States. Their reservations remained semi-autonomous enclaves enclosed within the geographical and political boundaries defined by the Bureau of Indian Affairs. But the comparative isolation of the reservations could not keep them free from the effects of the sometimes sudden shifts in the broader economic and political system of the United States.

The changing policies of the national government required frequent strategic adjustments and continuing struggle on the part of Indian peoples. In the five decades after the passage of the Dawes Act in 1887, for instance, the government's policy of promoting native assimilation through the individual allotment of reservation lands resulted in a huge loss of tribal territory; by the 1930s, non-Indians had purchased so much property that Indian holdings had fallen to about a third of what they had been in the 1880s. But in the 1930s, with the advent of the New Deal, a more sympathetic leadership in the Bureau of Indian Affairs attempted to reverse the administrative emphasis on individual ownership and restore tribal control of unallocated lands. Perhaps more important, a legal opinion issued by the Department of the Interior in 1934 argued that Indian tribes retained their internal sovereignty and rights of self-government in all areas except those specifically restricted by Congress. Then, in the wake of World War II, a more conservative federal government took an altogether different tack by trying to terminate treaty relations that originally gave Indians their special sovereign status as semi-independent nations within the United States. The goal was to end the reservation system and encourage Indians to move to the cities, where they could presumably be more easily assimilated into mainstream American life. Not incidentally, the urbanization of Indians would also allow outside interests easier exploitation of the land and resources on the reservations. Indian opposition and legal challenges to these policies led to yet another reversal in the 1960s and 1970s, when several critical decisions in United States courts reasserted Indian sovereignty and the right of Indian tribes to exercise greater control of the education of their children and the economic development of their lands.

Throughout this almost century-long series of shifts in government policy, Indian people have tried in a variety of ways to preserve their tribal identities and interests, even in the face of demoralizing political and economic prospects. While Indians, both on the reservations and in cities, have been plagued by numerous problems—unemployment, poverty, alcoholism, and sickness, to name only the most significant—there have also been a number of creative innovations, including reservation-based businesses and even colleges, which help ensure tribal survival and cultural continuity. Some of the Indian enterprises have been so striking and successful that they challenge our conception of the connection between past and present and raise intriguing issues for the future.

Nowhere is that more evident than in the case of the Pequot Indians, who have made a remarkable comeback in Connecticut. For over 350 years, the Mashantucket Pequots, a remnant of the powerful Pequot tribe that was defeated and declared dissolved by the English Puritans in the 1630s, lived on a small reservation in southeastern Connecticut; by the 1980s, the reservation's population had fallen to a handful of older people, and the future seemed quite doubtful, indeed. But thanks to the energy, economic savvy, and political skill of a few enterprising tribe members, the Mashantuckets managed to turn the unpromising prospects around by taking advantage of their special sovereign status and following a path pioneered by other Indian groups: they opened a gambling casino. Since its opening in 1992, the Foxwoods High Stakes Bingo and Casino (adjacent to Ledyard, Connecticut, not far from Hartford) has become the biggest gambling casino in the Western Hemisphere, complete with auxiliary facilities ranging from hotels to a sporting-events center, golf course, monorail, and virtual-reality theater. Within a year, Foxwoods had begun to bring in several hundred million dollars a year, and in addition to making a huge profit for the Pequots, the casino complex also pumped much-needed money and jobs into Connecticut's economy. Grateful state officials granted the Mashantuckets monopoly control of Connecticut's slot machines, thus increasing their opportunity for even greater profit. Suddenly, Indians had become agents of economic growth.

But the success of the Pequots caused some people considerable consternation. Donald Trump, the multimillionaire owner of the Taj Mahal casino in Atlantic City, New Jersey—which formerly could claim to be the hemisphere's biggest—complained that federal policies gave Indian entrepreneurs an unfair advantage in the gambling business, and he filed suit to protest the Pequot's special status. Closer to home in Connecticut, uneasy neighbors watched warily as the Pequots took further steps for territorial expansion. In August 1993, tribal leaders announced that the Mashantuckets planned to buy an additional eight thousand acres of land in the surrounding region, which would more than quintuple the size of the tribe's trust lands. Non-Indians in Ledyard and other neighboring towns quickly, if quietly, became worried, wondering what the Mashantucket moves would mean for future control of their communities. On the one hand, Mashantucket money certainly appeared attractive to local landowners who took advantage of escalating real estate prices and sold out to the Indians. At the same time, other people complained about the negative effects of overcrowding and overdevelopment, casting Indians in the role of greedy and aggressive newcomers: as Bruce Kirchner, a member of the Mashantucket tribe and a senior vice president of the casino, noted to a *New York Times* reporter, the rising anti-Indian sentiment made it seem "that we're not really American, we're foreigners."

The fate of Foxwoods and the surrounding Connecticut communities remains to be seen, of course, but the image of Indians as "foreigners"—as land-hungry invaders who threaten to damage the environment and disrupt a simple, stable way of life—certainly puts a new twist on an old story. Those Euro-American neighbors of the Mashantucket Pequots who have studied the early history of the region might well have had occasion to reflect on how it feels—and how it might have felt—to confront people who claim their own sovereignty and who have the economic resources to assert themselves from a position of strength. No doubt Mark Twain, who spent much of his later years in Hartford, where he died in 1910, would have relished the irony in this turn of events. The rest of us, especially those with an interest in the many facets of intercultural interaction in the American past, can perhaps find in the Pequots' apparent resurgence a useful long-term perspective for the future study of American frontiers. History may not repeat itself, but it does allow for some remarkable reversals. Nothing stays closed forever.

BIBLIOGRAPHICAL ESSAY

B ecause this book is intended to provide an interpretive synthesis of recent scholarship, I have chosen to discuss the
sources in a bibliographical essay rather than in standard academic
footnote form. The essay that follows, though, does not offer a
comprehensive treatment of all the books and articles relevant to
the history of the North American frontiers; that would be virtually
impossible and would produce an essay as long as the preceding
text. I have tried to cite important works in the field, especially
those that have provided the most useful evidence and insights for
this study. In the interest of avoiding repetition and overlap, I have
grouped the chapters in pairs that fit together topically and chro-
nologically, and I have cited each work only once, usually the first
time it figures in the narrative, except where a second citation
seemed necessary for the sake of coherence and clarity. The end
result, I hope, is an essay that not only tells where I am coming
from but, more important, helps direct the reader toward the many
paths of reading and research.

INTRODUCTION
An earlier version of the Introduction appeared as Gregory H.
Nobles, "Frederick Jackson Turner: Deposed King of the Wild
Frontier," in a special Turner centennial issue of the *Hayes
Historical Journal* 12 (1992–93), 7–19. (Unfortunately, it proved to
be the final issue of that publication; whatever one might say about

the frontier, the *Hayes Historical Journal* is now decidedly closed.) Although Frederick Jackson Turner is no longer the central figure in frontier historiography, it is still virtually impossible to understand the current state of the field without first taking note of Turner's place in the debate. The standard source for his essay on "The Significance of the Frontier in American History" is in *The Frontier in American History* (New York: Henry Holt, 1920), which also contains several of Turner's later essays on frontier and sectional history. A more recent source is John Mack Faragher, *Rereading Frederick Jackson Turner: The Significance of the Frontier in American History, and Other Essays* (New York: Henry Holt, 1994), which also offers a perceptive and generally positive analysis of Turner's place in the historical profession. For a brief and balanced biography of Turner, see James D. Bennett, *Frederick Jackson Turner* (Boston: Twayne Publishers, 1975).

Ray Allen Billington has been the most significant champion of Turner, and several of his works provide a supportive survey of Turner's career: *America's Frontier Heritage* (New York: Holt, Rinehart, and Winston, 1966); *The Genesis of the Frontier Thesis: A Study in Historical Creativity* (San Marino, Cal.: Huntington Library, 1971); and *Frederick Jackson Turner: Historian, Scholar, Teacher* (New York: Oxford University Press, 1973). Perhaps Billington's greatest tribute to Turner was the book he first published in collaboration with James Blaine Hedges, *Westward Expansion: A History of the American Frontier* (New York: Macmillan, 1949), which went through three additional editions (1960, 1967, 1974) and then a fifth edition in collaboration with Martin Ridge (1982). Although Billington rather grudgingly revised his book to accommodate the changing context of historical writing, his work remained essentially within the Turnerian mode. Similarly, the posthumously published book by Frederick Merk, *History of the Westward Movement* (New York: Alfred A. Knopf, 1978), reflected the Turnerian influence on the historian who had been Turner's colleague and successor in teaching the history of the American West at Harvard (where the course came to be called "Wagon Wheels" by irreverent undergraduates).

A more critical approach to the Turner thesis is provided by Richard Hofstadter, *The Progressive Historians: Turner, Beard, Parrington* (New York: Alfred A. Knopf, 1968) and Hofstadter and

Seymour Martin Lipset, eds., *Turner and the Sociology of the Frontier* (New York: Basic Books, 1968). A useful source for the state of the mid-century debate on the Turner thesis is George Rogers Taylor, ed., *The Turner Thesis Concerning the Role of the Frontier in American History: Problems in American Civilization* (Boston: D. C. Heath and Co., 1956). See also Ray Allen Billington, *The American Frontier Thesis: Attack and Defense* (Washington, D.C.: American Historical Association, 1971).

Turner's use of the term "frontier" came into question in several scholarly articles in the 1960s. John T. Juricek, in "American Usage of the Word 'Frontier' from Colonial Times to Frederick Jackson Turner," *Proceedings of the American Philosophical Society* 110 (1966), 10–34, noted that Turner used "frontier" in a way that it had not been used in the past by Americans; by imposing a late-nineteenth-century notion of the term on the past, Turner created a greater sense of unity and uniqueness in American history than was justified. A similar point was made by Jack D. Forbes in "Frontiers in American History," *Journal of the West* 1 (1962), 63–73; in a later article—"Frontiers in American History and the Role of the Frontier Historian," *Ethnohistory* 15 (1968), 203–35—Forbes offered an even more modern definition of frontier as an "intergroup contact situation," thus providing a useful alternative to Turner's notion of the frontier as a line "between civilization and savagery."

Beginning in the 1980s, the pages of the *Western Historical Quarterly* (hereafter *WHQ*) offered a regular reevaluation of Turner's perspective on frontier history. See, for instance, Donald K. Pickens, "Westward Expansion and the End of American Exceptionalism: Sumner, Turner, and Webb," *WHQ* 12 (1981), 409–18; Rodman W. Paul and Michael P. Malone, "Tradition and Challenge in Western Historiography," *WHQ* 16 (1985), 27–53; Donald Worster, "New West, True West: Interpreting the Region's History," *WHQ* 18 (1987), 141–56; William Cronon, "Revisiting the Vanishing Frontier: The Legacy of Frederick Jackson Turner," *WHQ* 18 (1987), 157–76; Martin Ridge, "Frederick Jackson Turner, Ray Allen Billington, and American Frontier History," *WHQ* 20 (1989), 5–20; Michael P. Malone, "Beyond the Last Frontier: Toward a New Approach to Western American History," *WHQ* 20 (1989), 409–27; and Allan C. Bogue, "The Significance

of the History of the American West: Postscripts and Prospects,"
WHQ 24 (1993), 45–68.

That period also saw the rise of the New Western Historians
and the publication of several books that have come to define the
field. The first and still most widely noted work is Patricia Nelson
Limerick, *The Legacy of Conquest: The Unbroken Past of the American West* (New York: W. W. Norton, 1987); Limerick's book so
quickly rose to prominence that it prompted its own set of essays
in the *Western Historical Quarterly*: Donald Worster, et al., *"The
Legacy of Conquest,* by Patricia Nelson Limerick: A Panel of Appraisal," *WHQ* 20 (1989), 303–22. Richard White's impressive text,
*"It's Your Misfortune and None of My Own": A New History of the
American West* (Norman: University of Oklahoma Press, 1991),
provides over four hundred pages of comprehensive analysis but
does not list Frederick Jackson Turner or the term "frontier" in
its index. Limerick and White have provided interesting interpre-
tive essays in James R. Grossman, ed., *The Frontier in American
Culture: An Exhibition at the Newberry Library, August 26, 1994–
January 7, 1995/Essays by Richard White and Patricia Nelson Limerick*
(Berkeley: University of California Press, 1994). Two other collections of essays by various scholars give a more complete introduc-
tion to the New Western History: Patricia Nelson Limerick,
Clyde A. Milner II, and Charles E. Rankin, eds., *Trails Toward a
New Western History* (Lawrence: University Press of Kansas, 1991);
and William Cronon, George Miles, and Jay Gitlin, eds., *Under an
Open Sky: Rethinking America's Western Past* (New York: W. W.
Norton, 1992). An excellent collection of essays that provides a
comprehensive historical overview is Clyde A. Milner, Carol A.
O'Connor, and Martha A. Sandweiss, eds., *The Oxford History of
the American West* (New York: Oxford University Press, 1994).

The sharp critiques of Turner offered by some of the New
Western Historians and other revisionists have led to a recent post-
revisionist view of Turner. See, for instance, Faragher's *Rereading
Frederick Jackson Turner,* cited above, and "The Frontier Trail: Re-
thinking Turner and Reimagining the American West," *American
Historical Review* 98 (1993), 106–17. Gerald D. Nash, *Creating the
American West: Historical Interpretations, 1890–1990* (Albuquerque:
University of New Mexico Press, 1991) chronicles the controver-
sies surrounding Turner's work throughout the century but still

offers a very evenhanded appraisal of Turner and his critics. Similarly, Wilbur Jacobs, *On Turner's Trail: 100 Years of Writing Western History* (Lawrence: University Press of Kansas, 1994) acknowledges the important contributions of Limerick, White, and others who focus on the West as a region, but he is still able to say that "Western history told as a Turnerian story of the whole nation in movement has, for me, more interest and significance" (p. 210).

Finally, a fictionalized Frederick Jackson Turner plays a prominent role in a recent novel by an Australian writer, Rod Jones, *Billy Sunday* (Sydney, Australia: Picador, by Pan Macmillan Australia, 1995). The portrayal of Turner is probably not what his friends and followers would like, but since professional historians are almost never considered interesting enough to figure as central characters in modern fiction, Turner's significance in the story is especially worth noting.

CHAPTERS ONE AND TWO

An early narrative of the war against the Pequots told from the Puritan perspective is that of the English officer in charge of the attack on the Pequot encampment in 1637, John Mason, *A Brief History of the Pequot War* (Boston: 1736; Readex microprint, 1966). Among recent secondary sources, the most detailed account of the context and events of the war—and one certainly not told from the Puritan perspective—is Francis Jennings, *The Invasion of America: Indians, Colonialism, and the Cant of Conquest* (Chapel Hill: University of North Carolina Press for the Institute of Early American History and Culture, 1975). Ian K. Steele offers a brief treatment of the war in *Warpaths: Invasions of North America* (New York: Oxford University Press, 1994), a book that, as the title suggests, owes a debt to Jennings's interpretation. Neal Salisbury, *Manitou and Providence: Indians, Europeans, and the Making of New England, 1500–1643* (New York: Oxford University Press, 1982) provides another excellent discussion of the context of the war. For a useful introduction to the native population of southern New England before the arrival of Europeans, readers should see the first two essays in Laurence M. Hauptman and James D. Wherry, eds., *The Pequots in Southern New England: The Fall and Rise of an American Indian Nation* (Norman: University of Oklahoma Press, 1990):

Dena F. Dincauze, "A Capsule History of Southern New England" and William A. Starna, "The Pequots in the Early Seventeenth Century." Two other essays in that volume—Laurence M. Hauptman, "The Pequot War and Its Legacies" and Neal Salisbury, "Indians and Colonists in Southern New England after the Pequot War"—discuss the subsequent history of the Pequots as they reestablished their group identity in the seventeenth century.

The history of native peoples in North America begins long before the Pequots encountered the Puritans, of course, and there are several important works that offer a broad historical perspective. *The Handbook of North American Indians*, under the general editorship of William G. Sturtevant (Washington, D.C.: Smithsonian Institution, 1978–   ), is projected eventually to number twenty volumes and provide a comprehensive overview of Native American life. Single-volume surveys include Alvin M. Josephy, Jr., *The Indian Heritage of America* (New York: Alfred A. Knopf, 1968); Wilcomb E. Washburn, *The Indian in America* (New York: Harper and Row, 1975); Francis Jennings, *The Founders of America* (New York: W. W. Norton, 1993); and Bruce G. Trigger and Wilcomb E. Washburn, eds., *The Cambridge History of the Native Peoples of the New World, vol. 3: North America* (New York: Cambridge University Press, 1993). Specific studies of the pre-contact period are Stuart J. Feidel, *Prehistory of the Americas* (New York: Cambridge University Press, 1987); Alvin M. Josephy and Frederick E. Hoxie, eds., *America in 1492: The World of the Indian Peoples Before the Arrival of Columbus* (New York: Alfred A. Knopf, 1992); Kendrick Frazier, *People of Chaco: A Canyon and Its Culture* (New York: W. W. Norton, 1986); and Lynda Norene Shaffer, *Native Americans Before 1492: The Moundbuilding Centers of the Eastern Woodlands* (Armonk, N.Y.: M. E. Sharpe, 1992).

After 1492, the most dramatic, or certainly the most immediate, effect of the European–Indian encounter was the devastating spread of European diseases among Indian peoples. The pathbreaking work in this field was Alfred W. Crosby, *The Columbian Exchange: Biological and Cultural Consequences of 1492* (Westport, Conn.: Greenwood Press, 1972); "Virgin Soil Epidemics as a Factor in Aboriginal Depopulation in America," *William and Mary Quarterly* (hereafter *WMQ*) 3rd ser., 33 (1976), 289–99; and *Ecological Imperialism: The Biological Expansion of Europe, 900–1900*

(New York: Cambridge University Press, 1986). For more recent works that contribute to our understanding of the magnitude of native depopulation, see William A. Starna, "The Biological Encounter: Disease and the Ideological Domain," *American Indian Quarterly* (hereafter *AIQ*) 16 (1992), 511–19; and Clark Spencer Larsen and George R. Milner, eds., *In the Wake of Contact: Biological Responses to Conquest* (New York: Wiley-Liss, 1994).

Understanding the implications of the encounter from the Indian perspective has been facilitated by the publication of several documentary sources that record the words of native speakers: Peter Nabokov, ed., *Native American Testimony: A Chronicle of Indian–White Relations from Prophecy to the Present, 1492–1992* (New York: Viking, 1991); Colin G. Calloway, ed., *The World Turned Upside Down: Indian Voices from Early America* (Boston and New York: Bedford Books of St. Martin's Press, 1994); and Lee Miller, ed., *From the Heart: Voices of the American Indian* (New York: Alfred A. Knopf, 1995). James Axtell, ed., *The Indian Peoples of Eastern America: A Documentary History of the Sexes* (New York: Oxford University Press, 1981) also contains documents that record Indian voices.

Of the many books that describe the early contacts and contrasts among Indians and Europeans, several deserve special notice. One of the first books to provide a truly multicultural perspective on early American history was Gary B. Nash, *Red, White, and Black: The Peoples of Early America* (Englewood Cliffs, N.J.: Prentice Hall, 1974). Nash and David G. Sweet, eds., *Struggle and Survival in Colonial America* (Berkeley: University of California Press, 1981), have also provided individual portraits of native peoples in North, Central, and South America. The Spanish approach to colonization is described in Charles Gibson, *Spain in America* (New York: Harper and Row, 1966), and the sixteenth-century Catholic debate about Indians is detailed in Lewis Hanke, *All Mankind Is One: A Study of the Disputation between Bartolomé de Las Casas and Juan Ginés de Sepúlveda in 1550 on the Intellectual and Religious Capacity of the American Indians* (De Kalb: Northern Illinois University Press, 1974). More recently, three excellent books have added significantly to the history of native peoples during the early Spanish colonization: Ramón Gutiérrez, *When Jesus Came, the Corn Mothers Went Away: Marriage, Sexuality, and Power in New Mexico, 1500–1846* (Stanford, Cal.: Stanford University Press, 1991); David J.

Weber, *The Spanish Frontier in North America* (New Haven: Yale University Press, 1992); and Charles Hudson and Carmen Chaves Tesser, eds., *The Forgotten Centuries: Indians and Europeans in the American South, 1521–1704* (Athens: University of Georgia Press, 1994).

Focusing on the northeastern part of North America, James Axtell's books have made a major contribution to our understanding of intercultural encounters in the French and English colonies: *The European and the Indian: Essays in the Ethnohistory of Colonial North America* (New York: Oxford University Press, 1981); *The Invasion Within: The Contest of Cultures in Colonial North America* (New York: Oxford University Press, 1985); *After Columbus: Essays in the Ethnohistory of Colonial North America* (New York: Oxford University Press, 1988); and *Beyond 1492: Encounters in Colonial North America* (New York: Oxford University Press, 1992). Karen Ordahl Kupperman, *Settling with the Indians: The Meeting of English and Indian Cultures in America, 1580–1640* (Totowa, N.J.: Rowman and Littlefield, 1980) provides an analysis of English attitudes. Neal Salisbury, in "Red Puritans: The 'Praying Indians' of Massachusetts Bay and John Eliot," *WMQ* 3rd ser., 31 (1974), 27–54, discusses the English effort to convert Indians to Christianity and, in the process, to English patterns of life, but in "Religious Encounters in a Colonial Context: New England and New France in the Seventeenth Century," *AIQ* 16 (1992), 501–9, he warns against drawing stereotypical distinctions between the religious approaches of the English Puritans and the French Jesuits.

Trade and other forms of exchange play an important part in the study of cultural contact. Calvin Martin, *Keepers of the Game: Indian–Animal Relationships in the Fur Trade* (Berkeley: University of California Press, 1978) explores the spiritual implications of Indians' increasing involvement in commercial relationships with Europeans. An outstanding study of the environmental and cultural consequences of the Indian–European encounter in New England is William Cronon, *Changes in the Land: Indians, Colonists, and the Ecology of New England* (New York: Hill and Wang, 1983), which pays special attention to differing forms of land use and agriculture as well as the fur trade. Timothy Silver, *A New Face on the Countryside: Indians, Colonists, and Slaves in South Atlantic Forests, 1500–1800* (New York: Cambridge University Press, 1990) offers a similar analysis for the Southeast. James Merrell, *The Indians' New World: Catawbas and Their Neighbors from European Contact through the Era of Removal* (Chapel Hill: University of North Carolina Press for the Institute of Early American History and Culture, 1989) discusses, among other things, the Indians' notions of trade, as do Christopher L. Miller and George R. Hammell, "A New Perspective on Indian–White Contact: Cultural Symbols and Colonial Trade," *Journal of American History* (hereafter *JAH*) 73 (1986), 311–28. The importance of the introduction of firearms among Indians is highlighted in Patrick M. Malone, "Changing Military Technology Among the Indians of Southern New England, 1600–1677," *AIQ* 25 (1973), 48–63, and, more fully, in *The Skulking Way of War: Technology and Tactics among the New England Indians* (Lanham, Md.: Madison Books, 1991), in which Malone shows how Europeans had to adapt their habits of combat to deal with Indians who had acquired guns. Thomas Frank Schilz and Donald E. Worcester make a similar point in "The Spread of Firearms among the Indian Tribes on the Northern Frontier of New Spain," *AIQ* 11 (1987), 1–10.

The issues of trade and warfare point to the complex diplomatic relationships that developed among Indian and European powers in the seventeenth and eighteenth centuries. The early maps and other a priori plans of the European imperial powers, including Sir Robert Mountgomery's designs for the Margravate of Azilia, are discussed in Gregory H. Nobles, "Straight Lines and Stability: Mapping the Political Order of the Anglo-American Frontier," *JAH* 80 (1993), 9–35. Maps as representations of political authority are discussed in J. B. Harley, "Deconstructing the Map," *Cartographica* 28 (1989), 1–20. Robert S. Weddle, *The French Thorn: Rival Explorers in the Spanish Sea, 1682–1762* (College Station: Texas A&M University Press, 1991) also deals with cartographic competition among the European imperial powers. For a very interesting comparison of Indian maps, see Gregory A. Waselkov, "Indian Maps of the Colonial Southeast" in Peter H. Wood, Gregory A. Waselkov, and M. Thomas Hatley, eds., *Powhatan's Mantle: Indians in the Colonial Southeast* (Lincoln: University of Nebraska Press, 1989).

A comprehensive resource on the imperial wars in North America is Alan Gallay, ed., *Colonial Wars of North America, 1512–1763:*

An Encyclopedia (New York: Garland Publishing, 1996). For an account of Queen Anne's War in the South, see Verner W. Crane, *The Southern Frontier, 1620–1732* (Ann Arbor: University of Michigan Press, 1929); and W. Stitt Robinson, *The Southern Colonial Frontier, 1607–1763* (Albuquerque: University of New Mexico Press, 1979). David J. Weber, *The Spanish Frontier in North America*, cited above, is also especially useful for an analysis of the internal tensions in the Spanish missions. The northern sphere of the war is discussed in Douglas Edward Leach, *The Northern Colonial Frontier, 1607–1763* (New York: Holt, Rinehart, and Winston, 1966). The best modern accounts of the attack on Deerfield are Richard Melvoin, *New England Outpost: War and Society in Colonial Deerfield* (New York: W. W. Norton, 1989); John Demos, *The Unredeemed Captive: A Family Story from Early America* (New York: Alfred A. Knopf, 1994); and Evan Haefeli and Kevin Sweeney, "Rewriting *The Redeemed Captive*: New Perspectives on the 1704 Attack on Deerfield," *WMQ* 3rd ser., 52 (1995), 3–47.

The history of Iroquois war and diplomacy in the context of the imperial struggles has become an especially engaging topic in recent years. The work of Daniel Richter represents an impressive contribution to the field: see, above all, *The Ordeal of the Longhouse: The Peoples of the Iroquois League in the Era of European Colonization* (Chapel Hill: University of North Carolina Press for the Institute of Early American History and Culture, 1992). Richter's earlier works include "War and Culture: The Iroquois Experience," *WMQ* 3rd ser., 40 (1983), 528–59; "Cultural Brokers and Intercultural Politics: New York–Iroquois Relations, 1664–1701," *JAH* 75 (1988), 40–67; and, with James H. Merrell, eds., *Beyond the Covenant Chain: The Iroquois and Their Neighbors in Indian North America, 1600–1800* (Syracuse, N.Y.: Syracuse University Press, 1987). Two essays in that volume—Richard L. Haan, "Covenant and Consensus: Iroquois and English, 1676–1760" and Michael N. McConnell, "Peoples 'In Between': The Iroquois and the Ohio Indians, 1720–1768"—are especially useful in analyzing the appearance and reality of Iroquois "imperial" power. Other important studies are Matthew Dennis, *Cultivating a Landscape of Peace: Iroquois–European Encounters in Seventeenth-Century America* (Ithaca, N.Y.: Cornell University Press, 1993); Anthony F.C. Wallace, "Origins of Iroquois Neutrality: The Grand Settlement of 1701,"

Pennsylvania History 24 (1957), 223–35; Richard Haan, "The Problem of Iroquois Neutrality: Suggestions for Revision," *Ethnohistory* 27 (1980), 317–30; Richard Aquila, "Down the Warrior's Path: The Causes of the Southern Wars of the Iroquois," *AIQ* 4 (1978), 211–21, and *The Iroquois Restoration: Iroquois Diplomacy on the Colonial Frontier, 1701–1754* (Detroit: Wayne State University Press, 1983); Francis Jennings, *The Ambiguous Iroquois Empire: The Covenant Chain of Indian Tribes and English Colonies from Its Beginning to the Lancaster Treaty of 1744* (New York: W. W. Norton, 1984); and Barbara Graymont, *The Iroquois in the American Revolution* (Syracuse, N.Y.: Syracuse University Press, 1972); and Anthony F.C. Wallace, *The Death and Rebirth of the Seneca* (New York: Alfred A. Knopf, 1970).

Other valuable works on Indians in the eighteenth-century imperial struggles are Francis Jennings, *Empire of Fortune: Crowns, Colonies, and Tribes in the Seven Years War in America* (New York: W. W. Norton, 1988), and "The Indians' Revolution," in Alfred F. Young, ed., *The American Revolution: Explorations in the History of American Radicalism* (De Kalb: Northern Illinois University Press, 1976); Richard White, *The Middle Ground: Indians, Empires, and Republics in the Great Lakes Region, 1650–1815* (New York: Cambridge University Press, 1991); Michael N. McConnell, *A Country Between: The Upper Ohio Valley and Its Peoples, 1724–1774* (Lincoln: University of Nebraska Press, 1992); Daniel J. Usner, Jr., *Indians, Settlers, & Slaves in a Frontier Exchange Economy: The Lower Mississippi Before 1783* (Chapel Hill: University of North Carolina Press for the Institute of Early American History and Culture, 1992); Colin G. Calloway, *The Western Abenakis of Vermont, 1600–1800: War, Migration, and the Survival of an Indian People* (Norman: University of Oklahoma Press, 1990); and Jack M. Sosin, *The Revolutionary Frontier, 1763–1783* (New York: Holt, Rinehart, and Winston, 1967).

The post-Revolutionary planning for the Old Northwest receives its best treatment in Peter S. Onuf, "Liberty, Development and Union: Visions of the West in the 1780s," *WMQ* 3rd ser., 43 (1986), 179–213, and *Statehood and Union: A History of the Northwest Ordinance* (Bloomington: Indiana University Press, 1987). Andrew Cayton, *The Frontier Republic: Ideology and Politics in the Ohio Country, 1780–1825* (Kent, Ohio: Kent State University Press, 1986) is also an outstanding study of the post-war situation in the Old Northwest.

CHAPTERS THREE AND FOUR

The story of frontier unrest in the Washington administration is well told in Thomas P. Slaughter, *The Whiskey Rebellion: Frontier Epilogue to the American Revolution* (New York: Oxford University Press, 1986). The concurrent conflict with Indians is discussed in Wiley Sword, *President Washington's Indian War: The Struggle for the Old Northwest, 1790–1795* (Norman: University of Oklahoma Press, 1985). More general studies of Washington's problems as president are John Alexander Carroll and Mary Wells Ashworth, *George Washington: First in Peace* (New York: Charles Scribner's Sons, 1957), which is the last of the seven-volume biography of George Washington begun by Douglas Southall Freeman; and James Thomas Flexner, *George Washington: Anguish and Farewell (1793–1799)* (Boston: Little, Brown, 1969).

The earlier instances of backcountry protest in North Carolina are covered in A. Roger Ekirch, *"Poor Carolina": Society and Politics in Colonial North Carolina, 1729–1776* (Chapel Hill: University of North Carolina Press, 1981), "The North Carolina Regulators on Liberty and Corruption, 1766–1771," *Perspectives in American History* 11 (1977–78), 199–256; Marvin L. Michael Kay, "The North Carolina Regulation, 1766–1776: A Class Conflict," in Alfred F. Young, ed., *The American Revolution: Explorations in the History of American Radicalism* (De Kalb: Northern Illinois University Press, 1976); and James P. Whittenburg, "Planters, Merchants, and Lawyers: Social Change and the Origins of the North Carolina Regulation," *WMQ* 3rd ser., 34 (1977), 215–38. The best recent works on the Regulator movement in Massachusetts are David P. Szatmary, *Shays Rebellion: The Making of an Agrarian Insurrection* (Amherst: University of Massachusetts Press, 1980) and Robert A. Gross, ed., *In Debt to Shays: The Bicentennial of an Agrarian Rebellion* (Charlottesville: University Press of Virginia, 1994). For a useful comparative perspective, see Richard Maxwell Brown, "Back Country Rebellions and the Homestead Ethic in America," in Richard Maxwell Brown and Don E. Fehrenbacher, eds., *Tradition, Conflict, and Modernization: Perspectives on the American Revolution* (New York: Academic Press, 1977). The continuing British presence in the post-war era is discussed in Colin G. Calloway, *Crown and Calumet: British–Indian Relations, 1783–1815* (Norman: University of Oklahoma Press, 1987) and Michael A. Bellesiles, *Revolutionary Outlaws: Ethan Allen and the Struggle for Independence on the Early American Frontier* (Charlottesville: University Press of Virginia, 1993).

Colorful but also critical characterizations of eighteenth-century frontier folk can be found in William K. Boyd, ed., *William Byrd's History of the Dividing Line Betwixt Virginia and Carolina* (Gloucester, Mass.: Peter Smith, 1984) and Richard J. Hooker, ed., *The Carolina Backcountry on the Eve of the Revolution: The Journal and Other Writings of Charles Woodmason, Anglican Itinerant* (Chapel Hill: University of North Carolina Press for the Institute of Early American History and Culture, 1953). A brief, readable biography of Hector St. John de Crèvecoeur is Thomas Philbrick, *St. John de Crèvecoeur* (New York: Twayne Publishers, 1970), which provides background for Crèvecoeur's *Letters from an American Farmer and Sketches of Eighteenth-Century America* (New York: Penguin Books, 1963).

The social and political history of white frontier settlers in the Early Republic has received considerable attention in recent years. Gregory H. Nobles, "Breaking into the Backcountry: New Approaches to the Early American Frontier, 1750–1800," *WMQ* 3rd ser., 46 (1989), 641–70, offers an overview of the scholarly literature, as does Albert H. Tillson, "The Southern Backcountry: A Survey of Recent Research," *The Virginia Magazine of History and Biography* 98 (1990), 387–422. Detailed studies include, in addition to the works by Cayton, Ekirch, and Bellesiles already cited, Terry G. Jordan and Matti Kaups, *The American Backwoods Frontier: An Ethnic and Ecological Interpretation* (Baltimore: Johns Hopkins University Press, 1989); Alan Taylor, *Liberty Men and Great Proprietors: The Revolutionary Settlement on the Maine Frontier* (Chapel Hill: University of North Carolina Press for the Institute of Early American History and Culture, 1990) and *William Cooper's Town: Power and Persuasion on the Frontier of the Early American Republic* (New York: Alfred A. Knopf, 1995); Laurel Thatcher Ulrich, *A Midwife's Tale: The Life of Martha Ballard, Based on Her Diary 1785–1812* (New York: Vintage Books, 1990); John Mack Faragher, *Daniel Boone: The Life and Legend of an American Pioneer* (New York:

Henry Holt, 1992); Richard R. Beeman, *The Evolution of the Southern Backcountry: A Case Study of Lunenburg County, Virginia, 1746–1832* (Philadelphia: University of Pennsylvania Press, 1984); Rachel N. Klein, *Unification of a Slave State: The Lives of the Planters in the South Carolina Backcountry, 1760–1808* (Chapel Hill: University of North Carolina Press for the Institute of Early American History and Culture, 1990); and Alan Gallay, *The Formation of a Planter Elite: Jonathan Bryan and the Southern Colonial Frontier* (Athens: University of Georgia Press, 1989). For additional studies of the contrasts—and, to some extent, convergence—between the ideals and behavior of settlers and wealthier landowners, see also Elliot J. Gorn, " 'Gouge and Bite, Pull Hair and Scratch': The Social Significance of Fighting in the Southern Backcountry," *American Historical Review* 90 (1985), 18–43; and Stephen Aron, "Pioneers and Profiteers: Land Speculation and the Homestead Ethic in Frontier Kentucky," *WHQ* 23 (1992), 179–98.

The impetus to expansion and exploration provided by Thomas Jefferson as president is a familiar and fascinating part of frontier history, and the many biographies of Jefferson offer numerous opportunities for its retelling: Merrill D. Peterson, *Thomas Jefferson and the New Nation: A Biography* (New York: Oxford University Press, 1970); Dumas Malone, *Jefferson the President: First Term, 1801–1805* (Boston: Little, Brown, 1970); Noble E. Cunningham, *In Pursuit of Reason: The Life of Thomas Jefferson* (Baton Rouge: Louisiana State University Press, 1987); and Willard Sterne Randall, *Thomas Jefferson: A Life* (New York: Henry Holt, 1993). The Louisiana Purchase is covered in great detail in Alexander De Conde, *This Affair of Louisiana* (Baton Rouge: Louisiana State University Press, 1976), and Drew McCoy, *The Elusive Republic: Political Economy in Jeffersonian America* (Chapel Hill: University of North Carolina Press for the Institute of Early American History and Culture, 1980) offers a perceptive explanation of its political significance. Until recently, James P. Ronda, *Lewis and Clark Among the Indians* (Lincoln: University of Nebraska Press, 1984) and David Lavender, *The Way to the Western Sea: Lewis and Clark Across the Continent* (New York: Harper and Row, 1988) were the standard studies of the expedition, but Stephen E. Ambrose's *Undaunted Courage: Meriwether Lewis, Thomas Jefferson, and the Opening of the American West* (New York: Simon and Schuster, 1996) provides another powerful narrative. Works that put the Lewis and Clark expedition in a broader context of state-sponsored exploration are William H. Goetzmann, *Army Exploration in the American West, 1803–1863* (New Haven: Yale University Press, 1959) and Richard A. Van Orman, *The Explorers: Nineteenth-Century Expeditions in Africa and the American West* (Albuquerque: University of New Mexico Press, 1984).

The study of the development of federal Indian policy begins with the background provided by Robert F. Berkhofer, Jr., *The White Man's Indian: Image of the American Indian from Columbus to the Present* (New York: Vintage Books, 1979) and Bernard W. Sheehan, *Seeds of Extinction: Jeffersonian Philanthropy and the American Indian* (Chapel Hill: University of North Carolina Press for the Institute of Early American History and Culture, 1973). The most comprehensive treatment of federal Indian policy is Francis Paul Prucha, *The Great Father: The United States Government and the American Indians*, 2 vols. (Lincoln: University of Nebraska Press, 1984). Reginald Horsman has also made a major contribution to the field with a series of books, including *Expansion and American Indian Policy, 1783–1812* (East Lansing: Michigan State University Press, 1967); *The Origins of Indian Removal, 1815–1824* (East Lansing: Michigan State University Press, 1970); *The Frontier in the Formative Years, 1783–1815* (New York: Holt, Rinehart and Winston, 1970); and *Race and Manifest Destiny: The Origins of American Racial Anglo-Saxonism* (Cambridge, Mass.: Harvard University Press, 1981). Cherokee responses to United States expansionist policies in the early nineteenth century are detailed in Theda Perdue, *Slavery and the Evolution of Cherokee Society, 1540–1866* (Knoxville: University of Tennessee Press, 1979); Mary Young, "The Cherokee Nation: Mirror of the Republic," *American Quarterly* 33 (1981), 502–24; William G. McLoughlin, "Experiment in Cherokee Citizenship, 1817–1829," *American Quarterly* 33 (1981), 3–25; *Cherokees and Missionaries, 1789–1839* (New Haven: Yale University Press, 1984); and *Cherokee Renascence in the New Republic* (Princeton: Princeton University Press, 1987). For the more militant stance of the Shawnees and other peoples, see Gregory Evans Dowd, *A Spirited Resistance: The North American Indian Struggle for Unity, 1745–1815* (Baltimore: Johns Hopkins University Press, 1992); R. David Edmunds, "Tecumseh, the Shawnee Prophet, and American History: A Reassessment," *WHQ* 14 (1983), 261–76, and *Tecumseh and the Quest for Indian Leadership* (Boston: Little, Brown, 1984); and Bil Gilbert, *God Gave Us This Country: Tekamthi and the First American Civil War* (New York: Atheneum, 1989). The role of Andrew Jackson as Indian fighter and promoter of Indian removal is discussed in the classic biography by John William Ward, *Andrew Jackson—Symbol for an Age* (New York: Oxford University Press, 1953) and, in more detail, in Michael Paul Rogin, *Fathers and Children: Andrew Jackson and the Subjugation of the American Indian* (New York: Alfred A. Knopf, 1975). The effects of removal on the native peoples of the Southeast are described in Anthony F.C. Wallace, *The Long, Bitter Trail: Andrew Jackson and the Indians* (New York: Hill and Wang, 1993); Michael D. Green, *The Politics of Indian Removal: Creek Government and Society in Crisis* (Lincoln: University of Nebraska Press, 1982); John R. Finger, "The Abortive Second Cherokee Removal, 1841–1844," *Journal of Southern History* 47 (1981), 207–26, and *The Eastern Band of Cherokees, 1819–1900* (Knoxville: University of Tennessee Press, 1984); and Theda Perdue, "Cherokee Women and the Trail of Tears," *Journal of Women's History* 1 (1989–90), 14–30.

The movement of people from the United States into Texas inevitably leads historians to the conflict at the Alamo, in which myth and history have been intertwined almost from the beginning. The story of Joe, the African-American survivor of the Alamo battle, is briefly told in David Drake, "Joe, Alamo Hero," *Negro History Bulletin* 44 (1981), n.p., and it also figures in the posthumously published diary of William F. Gray, *From Virginia to Texas, 1835* (Houston: Fletcher Young, 1985 [reprint of 1909 edition]). The parallel story of Susannah Dickinson can be found in C. Richard King, *Susannah Dickinson, Messenger of the Alamo* (Austin: Shoal Creek Publishers, 1976). Amelia Williams, "A Critical Study of the Siege of the Alamo and of the Personnel of Its Defenders," *Southwestern Historical Quarterly* 37 (1933–34), 1–312, provides additional documentation about Joe and Mrs. Dickinson. The note about Susannah Dickinson's attending the 1878 play about Davy Crockett comes from Susan Prendergast Schoelwer, *Alamo Images: Changing Perceptions of a Texas Experience* (Dallas: DeGolyer Library and Southern Methodist University Press, 1985), which is also an excellent introduction to the imagery and mythology of the battle.

On a similar note, see Don Graham, "Remembering the Alamo: The Story of the Texas Revolution in Popular Culture," *Southwestern Historical Quarterly* 89 (1985), 35–66.

An excellent bibliographical essay on the broader context of the conflict is Paul D. Lack, "In the Long Shadow of Eugene C. Barber: The Revolution and the Republic," in Walter L. Buenger and Robert A. Calvert, eds., *Texas Through Time: Evolving Interpretations* (College Station: Texas A&M University Press, 1991). An early analysis from the Mexican perspective is Carlos E. Castaneda, *The Mexican Side of the Texas Revolution* (Dallas: P. L. Turner, 1928), which has now been surpassed by David J. Weber's excellent *The Mexican Frontier, 1821–1846: The American Southwest Under Mexico* (Albuquerque: University of New Mexico Press, 1982). Also useful are Arnoldo de Leon, *The Tejano Community, 1836–1900* (Albuquerque: University of New Mexico Press, 1982); Paul D. Lack, "Slavery and the Texas Revolution," *Southwestern Historical Quarterly* 89 (1985), 181–202; and Nettie Lee Benson, "Texas as Viewed from Mexico, 1820–1834," *Southwestern Historical Quarterly* 90 (1987), 219–91. William R. Hogan, *The Texas Republic: A Social and Economic History* (Norman: University of Oklahoma Press, 1976) provides a good picture of the post-Alamo period.

The artistic image of the frontier and its native inhabitants has been the subject of several recent works, perhaps none more important or impressive than William H. Truettner and Nancy K. Anderson, *The West as America: Reinterpreting Images of the American Frontier, 1820–1920* (Washington, D.C.: Smithsonian Institution Press for the National Museum of American Art, 1991). Truettner's *The Natural Man Observed: A Study of Catlin's Indian Gallery* (Washington, D.C.: Smithsonian Institution Press, 1979) provides an exploration of George Catlin's "primitive ideal," and Marjorie Catlin Roehm, *The Letters of George Catlin and His Family* (Berkeley and Los Angeles: University of California Press, 1966) is a good source for Catlin's own observations. Readers should also consult Patricia Limerick's *The Legacy of Conquest*, cited above, for a brief but much less sympathetic discussion of the implications of Catlin's apparent infatuation with the "primitive" Indian. Two recent studies of George Caleb Bingham are E. Maurice Bloch, *The Paintings of George Caleb Bingham: A Catalogue Raisonné* (Columbia: University of Missouri Press, 1986) and Nancy Rash, *The Paintings and Politics of George Caleb Bingham* (New Haven: Yale University Press, 1991).

The classic work on the frontier in literature is Henry Nash Smith, *Virgin Land: The American West as Symbol and Myth* (Cambridge, Mass.: Harvard University Press, 1950), but the major work in the field is now the trilogy by Richard Slotkin: *Regeneration through Violence: The Mythology of the American Frontier, 1600–1860* (Middletown, Conn., Wesleyan University Press, 1973); *The Fatal Environment: The Myth of the Frontier in the Age of Industrialization, 1800–1860* (New York: Atheneum, 1985); and *Gunfighter Nation: The Myth of the Frontier in Twentieth-Century America* (New York: Atheneum, 1992), the first two of which concern the period under discussion here. The popularity of captivity narratives as a literary genre is discussed in June Namias, *White Captives: Gender and Ethnicity on the American Frontier* (Chapel Hill: University of North Carolina Press, 1993), and John Mack Faragher's *Daniel Boone*, cited above, discusses the popularity of Filson's *Kentucke*. Of the many books and articles on James Fenimore Cooper, D. H. Lawrence's *Studies in Classic American Literature* (New York: Viking Press, 1964 [1923]) is still one of the best brief introductions to the implications of his work. Alan Taylor's *William Cooper's Town*, cited above, does an excellent job of locating Cooper's fiction in the New York frontier. Separating fiction from fact in Davy Crockett's frontier history has been the task of James Atkins Shackford, *David Crockett: The Man and the Legend* (Chapel Hill: University of North Carolina Press, 1956, 1986); Dan Kilgore, *How Did Davy Die?* (College Station: Texas A&M University Press, 1978); Michael A. Lofaro, ed., *Davy Crockett: The Man, the Legend, the Legacy, 1786–1986* (Knoxville: University of Tennessee Press, 1985); Michael A. Lofaro and Joe Cummings, eds., *Crockett at Two Hundred: New Perspectives on the Man and the Myth* (Knoxville: University of Tennessee Press, 1989); Mark Derr, *The Frontiersman: The Real Life and Many Legends of Davy Crockett* (New York: William Morrow and Co., 1993). No one should overlook the allegedly autobiographical works that appeared under Crockett's name in the nineteenth century: *A Narrative of the Life of David Crockett of the State of Tennessee, by David Crockett: a Facsimile Edition with Annotations and Introduction by James A. Shackford and Stanley J. Folmsbee* (Knoxville: University of Tennessee Press, 1973); *Sketches and Eccentric-*

ities of Col. David Crockett of West Tennessee (New York: J. and J. Harper, 1833; reprint, New York: Arno Press, 1974); *An Account of Col. Crockett's Tour to the North and Down East* (n.p., 1835); and *Col. Crockett's Exploits and Adventures in Texas* (n.p., 1836).

The analysis of policies of the United States government in Texas and elsewhere in the mid-nineteenth century West begins with Frederick Merk's classic *Manifest Destiny and Mission in American History: A Reinterpretation* (New York: Alfred A. Knopf, 1963) and *Slavery and the Annexation of Texas* (New York: Alfred A. Knopf, 1972). Other important works on the ideology of expansion are Norman A. Graebner, *Empire on the Pacific: A Study in American Continental Expansion* (New York: Ronald Press, 1955); Thomas R. Hietala, *Manifest Design: Anxious Aggrandizement in Late Jacksonian America* (Ithaca, N.Y.: Cornell University Press, 1985); and Reginald Horsman, *Race and Manifest Destiny*, cited above. The causes and conduct of the war with Mexico are discussed in Otis Singletary, *The Mexican War* (Chicago: University of Chicago Press, 1960); Charles G. Sellers, *James K. Polk: Continentalist, 1843–1846* (Princeton: Princeton University Press, 1966); Glenn W. Price, *Origins of the War with Mexico: The Polk–Stockton Intrigue* (Austin: University of Texas Press, 1967); and David M. Pletcher, *The Diplomacy of Annexation: Texas, Oregon, and the Mexican War* (Columbia: University of Missouri Press, 1972). For greater emphasis on the military perspective, see K. Jack Bauer, *The Mexican War, 1846–1848* (New York: Macmillan, 1974). The impact of the war on American thought is analyzed in John H. Schroeder, *Mr. Polk's War: American Opposition and Dissent, 1846–1848* (Madison: University of Wisconsin Press, 1971) and Robert W. Johannsen, *To the Halls of the Montezumas: The Mexican War in the American Imagination* (New York: Oxford University Press, 1985).

The post-war politics of slavery in the West receive excellent treatment in David M. Potter, *The Impending Crisis, 1848–1861* (New York: Harper and Row, 1976) and Michael F. Holt, *The Political Crisis of the 1850s* (New York: Wiley, 1978). Eric Foner, *Free Soil, Free Labor, Free Men: The Ideology of the Republican Party before the Civil War* (New York: Oxford University Press, 1970) provides an excellent analysis of the ideas and appeal of the party of Lincoln. The violent events in Kansas are told in James A. Rawley, *Race and Politics: "Bleeding Kansas" and the Coming of the Civil*

War (Philadelphia: Lippincott, 1969) and Stephen B. Oates, *To Purge the Land with Blood: A Biography of John Brown* (Amherst: University of Massachusetts Press, 1970).

CHAPTERS FIVE AND SIX

The story of Jane Gould comes from an extract of her diary in Lillian Schlissel, ed., *Women's Diaries of the Westward Journey* (New York: Schocken Books, 1982). By far the best general study of the emigrant experience is John D. Unruh, Jr., *The Plains Across: The Overland Emigrants and the Trans-Mississippi West, 1840–60* (Urbana: University of Illinois Press, 1979). See also David Rich Lewis, "Argonauts and the Overland Trail Experience: Method and Theory," *WHQ* 16 (1985), 285–305. No one should miss the classic contemporary accounts of western travel in Francis Parkman, Jr., *The Oregon Trail* (New York and London: Penguin Books, 1982; originally published in 1849); and Mark Twain, *Roughing It* (New York and London: Penguin Books, 1981; originally published in 1872). For studies that focus on the experience of women on the trail, see Julie Roy Jeffrey, *Frontier Women: The Trans-Mississippi West, 1840–1880* (New York: Hill and Wang, 1979); Johnny Faragher and Christine Stansell, "Women and Their Families on the Overland Trail, 1842–67," *Feminist Studies* 2–3 (1975), 150–66; and John Mack Faragher, *Women and Men on the Overland Trail* (New Haven: Yale University Press, 1979). Faragher has also written of the midwestern context from which many emigrants like the Goulds came, in *Sugar Creek: Life on the Illinois Prairie* (New Haven: Yale University Press, 1986), and his "History from the Inside Out: Writing the History of Women in Rural America," *American Quarterly* 33 (1981), 537–57, provides valuable insights into the study of women in the West. The work of Glenda Riley has made a major contribution to the history of women on the frontier: see *Frontierswoman: The Iowa Experience* (Ames: Iowa State University Press, 1981); *Women and Indians on the Frontier, 1825–1915* (Albuquerque: University of New Mexico Press, 1984); "The Specter of a Savage: Rumors and Alarmism on the Overland Trail," *WHQ* 15 (1984), 427–44; and *The Female Frontier: A Comparative View of Women on the Prairie and the Plains* (Lawrence: University Press of Kansas, 1988). Other valuable works are Nancy Wilson Ross, *Westward the Women* (Berkeley: North Point Press, 1944;

reprinted 1985); Sandra L. Myres, *Westering Women and the Frontier Experience* (Albuquerque: University of New Mexico Press, 1982); Susan Armitage, "Women and Men in Western History: A Stereoptical Vision," *WHQ* 19 (1988), 381–95; Susan Armitage and Elizabeth Jameson, eds., *The Women's West* (Norman: University of Oklahoma Press, 1987); Lillian Schlissel, Vicki L. Ruiz, and Janice Monk, eds., *Western Women: Their Lands, Their Lives* (Albuquerque: University of New Mexico Press, 1988); Lillian Schlissel, Byrd Gibbens, and Elizabeth Hampsten, eds., *Far From Home: Families of the Westward Journey* (New York: Schocken Books, 1989); Christiane Fischer, ed., *Let Them Speak for Themselves: Women in the American West, 1849–1900* (Hamden, Conn.: Archon Books, 1977, 1990); and Frances M. A. Roe, *Army Letters from an Officer's Wife, 1877–1888* (Lincoln: University of Nebraska Press, 1981).

Among the emerging communities at the end of the trail, the Mormon settlement at Salt Lake has received perhaps the most scholarly attention. See, for instance, Thomas G. Alexander and James B. Allen, *Mormons and Gentiles: A History of Salt Lake City* (Boulder: Pruett Publishing Co., 1984); Eugene F. Campbell, *Establishing Zion* (Salt Lake City: Signature Books, 1988); Jan Shipps, *Mormonism: The Story of a New Religious Tradition* (Urbana: University of Illinois Press, 1985); and Lawrence Foster, *Religion and Sexuality: Three American Communal Experiments of the Nineteenth Century* (New York: Oxford University Press, 1981). Salt Lake City also figures along with San Francisco and Denver in Gunther Barth, *Instant Cities: Urbanization and the Rise of San Francisco and Denver* (New York: Oxford University Press, 1975), and the early history of San Francisco is covered well in Robert W. Lotchin, *San Francisco, 1846–1856: From Hamlet to City* (Lincoln: University of Nebraska Press, 1979). See also Lawrence H. Larsen, *The Urban West at the End of the Frontier* (Lawrence: University Press of Kansas, 1978). A good overview of the economic emergence of the West is William G. Robbins, *Colony and Empire: The Capitalist Transformation of the American West* (Lawrence: University Press of Kansas, 1994). Life in the mining camps gets its best treatment in Rodman W. Paul, *Mining Frontiers of the Far West, 1848–1880* (New York: Holt, Rinehart, and Winston, 1963), and Duane A. Smith, *Rocky Mountain Mining Camps: The Urban Frontier* (Bloomington: Indiana University Press, 1967). Smith's *Rocky Mountain West: Colorado, Wyoming, and Montana, 1859–1915* (Albuquerque: University of New Mexico Press, 1992) offers a more general treatment of the mining region. For details of the texture of life in mining regions, see also David J. Weber, ed., *Fortunes for the Few: Letters of a Forty-Niner* (San Diego: San Diego Historical Society, 1977); David A. Johnson, "Vigilance and the Law: The Moral Authority of Popular Justice in the Far West," *American Quarterly* 33 (1981), 558–86; Gunther Peck, "Manly Gambles: The Politics of Risk on the Comstock Lode, 1860–1880," *Journal of Social History* 26 (1993), 701–23; and Ann Butler, *Daughters of Joy, Sisters of Mercy: Prostitutes in the American West, 1865–1890* (Urbana: University of Illinois Press, 1985).

In the Midwest, cattle towns have been the subject of several useful studies, and two of the best are Robert R. Dykstra, *The Cattle Towns: A Social History of the Kansas Cattle Trading Centers, Abilene, Ellsworth, Wichita, Dodge City, and Caldwell, 1867–85* (New York: Atheneum, 1976); and C. Robert Haywood, *Victorian West: Class and Culture in Kansas Cattle Towns* (Lawrence: University Press of Kansas, 1991). A compelling portrait of rural women in that region, told largely through their own words, is Joanna L. Stratton, *Pioneer Women: Voices from the Kansas Frontier* (New York: Simon and Schuster, 1981). For other works on women in the Midwest, see Anne B. Webb, "Minnesota Women Homesteaders: 1863–1889," *Journal of Social History* 23 (1989), 115–36; and Sherry L. Smith, "Single Women Homesteaders: The Perplexing Case of Elinore Pruitt Stewart," *WHQ* 22 (1991), 163–83. Dean L. May, *Three Frontiers: Family, Land, and Society in the American West, 1860–1900* (New York: Cambridge University Press, 1994) discusses the importance of the settlers' cultural differences on the development of frontier farming communities. One of the best studies of frontier immigrant families is Jon Gjerde, *From Peasants to Farmers: The Migration from Balestrand, Norway, to the Upper Middle West* (New York: Cambridge University Press, 1985); see also Kathleen Neils Conzen, "Peasant Pioneers: Generational Succession Among German Farmers in Frontier Minnesota," in Stephen Hahn and Jonathan Prude, eds., *The Countryside in the Age of Capitalist Transformation* (Chapel Hill: University of North Carolina Press, 1985). Nell Irvin Painter's *Exodusters: Black Migration to Kansas after Re-*

construction (New York: W. W. Norton, 1976) is an excellent study of an otherwise little-known chapter of frontier history.

The history of the Indians' West in the second half of the nineteenth century has been treated by many writers, none more prolific and evenhanded than Robert Utley, whose work is reflected throughout Chapter 6. His biography of Sitting Bull, *The Lance and the Shield: The Life and Times of Sitting Bull* (New York: Ballantine Books, 1993) is a very detailed but quite readable account of the Hunkpapa leader's life. Utley's *The Indian Frontier of the American West 1846–1890* (Albuquerque: University of New Mexico Press, 1984); *Frontier Regulars: The United States Army and the Indian, 1866–1891* (New York: Macmillan, 1973); and Robert M. Utley and Wilcomb E. Washburn, *Indian Wars* (New York: American Heritage Books, 1985) are indispensable overviews of the wars in the West.

The details of the government's Indian policies are best discussed in Francis Paul Prucha, *The Great Father*, cited above, but see also Robert A. Trennert, *Alternative to Extinction: Federal Indian Policy and the Beginning of the Reservation System, 1846–51* (Philadelphia: Temple University Press, 1975) and Wilcomb E. Washburn, *The Assault on Indian Tribalism: The General Allotment Law (Dawes Act) of 1887* (Philadelphia: Lippincott, 1975). Sherry L. Smith, *The View from Officers' Row: Army Perceptions of Western Indians* (Tucson: University of Arizona Press, 1990) suggests that military men had more than the stereotypical point of view.

In addition to Utley's work, there are several valuable studies of the Sioux experience in the nineteenth century. Richard White, "The Winning of the West: The Expansion of the Western Sioux in the 18th and 19th Centuries," *JAH* 65 (1978), 319–43, describes the Sioux ascendancy in the time before the wars with the United States. The background of the Minnesota conflict that began in 1862 has its best treatment in David A. Nichols, *Lincoln and the Indians: Civil War Policy and Politics* (Columbia: University of Missouri Press, 1978). Kenneth Carley, *The Sioux Uprising of 1862* (St. Paul: Minnesota Historical Society, 1976) and Duane Schultz, *Over the Earth I Come: The Great Sioux Uprising of 1862* (New York: St. Martin's Press, 1992) provide good narratives of the events. For first-person accounts, see Gary Clayton Anderson and Alan R. Woolworth, eds., *Through Dakota Eyes: Narrative Accounts of the*

Minnesota Indian War of 1862 (St. Paul: Minnesota Historical Society, 1988) and Sarah F. Wakefield, *Six Weeks in the Sioux Tepees* (Fairfield, Washington: Ye Galleon Press, 1985; reprint of 1864 edition); Sarah Wakefield's story is also covered in June Namias, *White Captives*, cited above. The more famous Sioux struggle of the following decade, including the battle at Little Bighorn, is described in *The Great Sioux War, 1876–77: The Best from Montana The Magazine of Western History* (Lincoln: University of Nebraska Press, 1991). Precursors to Utley's biography of Sitting Bull are Alexander B. Adams, *Sitting Bull: An Epic of the Plains* (New York: G. P. Putnam's Sons, 1973) and Grant MacEwan, *Sitting Bull: The Years in Canada* (Edmonton, Ont.: Hurtig Publishers, 1973). Studies of other native groups include Mari Sandoz, *Cheyenne Autumn* (New York: McGraw-Hill, 1953); Alvin M. Josephy, Jr., *The Nez Perce Indians and the Opening of the Northwest* (New Haven: Yale University Press, 1965); William G. McLoughlin, *After the Trail of Tears: The Cherokees' Struggle for Sovereignty, 1839–1880* (Chapel Hill: University of North Carolina Press, 1993); and Richard J. Perry, *Apache Reservations: Indigenous Peoples and the American State* (Austin: University of Texas Press, 1993). Colin G. Calloway, ed., *Our Hearts Fell to the Ground: Plains Indian Views of How the West Was Lost* (Boston: Bedford Books of St. Martin's Press, 1996) offers the Indians' outlook on the end of the wars in the West.

INDEX